FAIR AND FOUL

FAIR AND FOUL

Beyond the Myths and Paradoxes of Sport

Fourth Edition

D. Stanley Eitzen

ROWMAN & LITTLEFIELD PUBLISHERS, INC.
Lanham • Boulder • New York • Toronto • Plymouth, UK

ROWMAN & LITTLEFIELD PUBLISHERS, INC.

Published in the United States of America
by Rowman & Littlefield Publishers, Inc.
A wholly owned subsidiary of
The Rowman & Littlefield Publishing Group, Inc.
4501 Forbes Boulevard, Suite 200, Lanham, Maryland 20706
www.rowmanlittlefield.com

Estover Road
Plymouth PL6 7PY
United Kingdom

British Library Cataloguing in Publication Information Available

Library of Congress Cataloging-in-Publication Data

Eitzen, D. Stanley.
   Fair and foul : beyond the myths and paradoxes of sport / D. Stanley Eitzen.
— 4th ed.
       p. cm.
   Includes bibliographical references and index.
   ISBN 978-0-7425-6177-9 (cloth : alk. paper) — ISBN 978-0-7425-6178-6
(pbk. : alk. paper) — ISBN 978-0-7425-6470-1 (electronic)
   1. Sports—Sociological aspects. 2. Sports—Psychological aspects. 3. Sports—
Social aspects—United States. I. Title. II. Title: Beyond the myths and
paradoxes of sport.
   GV706.5.E567 2009
   796—dc22   2008047982

Printed in the United States of America

∞ ™ The paper used in this publication meets the minimum requirements of
American National Standard for Information Sciences—Permanence of Paper
for Printed Library Materials, ANSI/NISO Z39.48-1992.

CONTENTS

ACKNOWLEDGMENTS

My sociological approach to sport and other social arenas results in large measure from the contributions of a number of friends, colleagues, and collaborators over a career. They have questioned me, cajoled me, challenged me, helped me, taught me, enlightened me, and inspired me. They are (in alphabetical order) Maxine Baca Zinn, Pete Birkhofer, Jay Coakley, Jo Anne Drahota, William Flint, James Frey, Janis Johnston, Kenneth C. W. Kammeyer, Marston McCluggage, Michael Messner, Stephen Pratt, Dean Purdy, Julie Rauli, George Ritzer, George Sage, John Schneider, Kelly Eitzen Smith, Eldon Snyder, Elmer Spreitzer, Kathryn Talley, Doug Timmer, Prabha Unnithan, and Norman Yetman.

Especially important to this project were the reviewers of the first edition, Mike Littwin, sportswriter for the *Denver Rocky Mountain News*, and sports scholars/sociologists/friends Michael Messner and George Sage. Thanks also to the anonymous reviewers of the second and third editions.

AP/Wide World

●

THE DUALITY OF SPORT

Human beings seek ekstasis, *a "stepping outside" of their normal, mundane experience. If they no longer find ecstasy in a synagogue, church, or mosque, they look for it in dance, music, sport, sex or drugs.*

—Karen Armstrong, historian of religions

Sport is a window on a changing society.

—David Halberstam, author

For some people, baseball is like a religion. It has all the elements: a creation story, falls from grace, redemption, prophets, heretics, icons, rituals, temples, worship, sacrifice, miracles, saviors and sinners—lots of sinners.

—John Longhurst, *Winnipeg (Manitoba) Free Press*

[Concerning the drug scandal in baseball] *Trying to find nobility in either the baseball owners or the players is a bit like feeling around for a quarter on the floor of a dark movie theatre. The reward is not worth the search.*

—Bernie Lincicome, *Rocky Mountain News*

[Referring to Tiger Woods] *It is riveting to watch the greatest there's ever been at the height of his powers. In a sports world awash in scandal and disillusionment, Woods's unrelenting brilliance is one of the few things we can count on.*

—Alan Shipnuck, *Sports Illustrated*

PRELUDE 1

Have you attended a high school sports banquet honoring the school's athletes? The guest speaker, typically a college coach, gives his message. With examples, humor, and sincerity, the speaker extols the many virtues of sports participation. And there are many character traits that sports require, such as perseverance, dedication, teamwork, and other achievement-oriented characteristics. But, as we will see, sports participation can also encourage selfishness, envy, conceit, hostility, and bad temper.

Similarly, there are many athletes engaged in generous activities toward others. Some examples:

- *A Cleveland Browns receiver pledged $1 million in 2007 to Cleveland's public schools for 100 scholarships for children who might not otherwise be able to attend college. He also created a $500,000 endowment at the University of Michigan.[1]*
- *NASCAR driver Kyle Petty and his wife donate $100,000 a year to a retreat for children with chronic conditions or serious illnesses in North Carolina.[2]*
- *Eight football players at Division III Wooster (Ohio) College spend at least eight hours each month working with Every Woman's House, a shelter for abused women and their children.[3]*
- *Avery Johnson, former coach of the Dallas Mavericks, is a native of New Orleans. Following Hurricane Katrina, Johnson and his wife used their home in Houston as a halfway house for victims of that devastating event. They also put displaced people up in hotels and vacant apartments around Houston.[4]*
- *Legendary Penn State coach Joe Paterno, his wife, and their five children donated $3.5 million to help endow faculty positions and*

scholarships, as well as support the university libraries and construct two new buildings.[5]

- *Tennis great Billie Jean King established the Women's Sports Foundation in 1974. Joined later by Donna Lopiano and others, the Women's Sports Foundation is the leading advocate for equity in girls' and women's sports.*

These generous actions are multiplied many times over in the sports world. As sportswriter Mike Sandrolini has said, "We must keep in mind that the overwhelming majority of athletes, pro or otherwise, are good, kind, charitable people who strive to play by the rules."[6] *But what are we to make of the dark side of athletes' behavior? Let's just examine the major sports scandals for one year—2007:*[7]

- *In the biggest steroids bust in U.S. history, the U.S. Drug Enforcement Administration caught 124 individuals, and found 56 steroid labs and more than 11 million dosage units.*
- *American cyclist Floyd Landis was stripped of his 2006 victory in the prestigious Tour de France for testing positive for doping. Danish cyclist Michael Rasmussen was leading the 2007 Tour de France when he was expelled from the race for failing a drug test.*
- *Barry Bonds broke the all-time career home run record, but he cannot shake the suspicion that he has used anabolic steroids to juice up his game. He was indicted on perjury charges.*
- *The Mitchell Report on steroids in baseball, after a 20-month investigation, named 96 players and called for a vast reformation of what is being called "the steroid era in Major League Baseball."*
- *Track great Marion Jones was formally stripped of her five Olympic medals from the 2000 Sydney Olympics for admitted drug use. Her relay teammates also lost their medals, although they were never accused of taking performance-enhancing drugs.*
- *NBA referee Tim Donaghy pleaded guilty to conspiracy to commit wire fraud and conspiracy to transmit gambling information across state lines, as well as admitting that he took cash payoffs and bet on games he officiated.*
- *Five NASCAR racing teams were penalized for breaking rules to unfairly increase the speed of their automobiles by changing their*

aerodynamics. Formula One levied a $100 million fine for a similar offense by team McLaren.

- NFL star quarterback Michael Vick pleaded guilty to running an illegal dog fighting operation resulting in a 23-month sentence in a federal prison.
- Indiana basketball coach Kelvin Sampson, found guilty of making illegal calls to recruits at his previous position as head coach of Oklahoma, was fired for the same offense at Indiana.
- Two dozen players were suspended for the Music City Bowl by Florida State for academic cheating.
- Coach Rush Propst of Hoover High School, winner of five Alabama state championships in eight years, resigned amid charges of using an ineligible player and giving football players preferential academic treatment, including changing players' grades without their teachers' knowledge.
- Coach Bill Belichick of the New England Patriots was fined $500,000 for videotaping opponents' signals.
- The University of Arkansas was stripped of its 2004 and 2005 men's outdoor track and field national championships for recruiting violations.

These scandals are but a sample of the dark side of sports.

But just as we are ready to condemn sports and vow to never watch SportsCenter on ESPN, an act of selflessness, of sportsmanship, restores one's faith in sport. Consider this crown jewel: In the spring of 2008 Sara Tucholsky of Western Oregon University hit a home run in a softball game against Central Washington University, but she missed first base. When she started back to tag it she collapsed with a serious knee injury. She crawled back to first but could do no more. Her options were limited. If her teammates helped her she would be called out. If a pinch-runner substituted for her, the home run would be counted only as a single. What happened was astounding. When the umpire said there was no rule against it, two of her opponents—Liz Wallace and Mallory Holtman—carried her around the bases, lowering her gently at each base so that she could touch it, thus allowing the three-run homer to count, contributing to their own team's elimination from the playoffs.[8] Wow!

What are we to make of this contradiction of sport and its actors having elements of the good and the bad—of being fair and foul? That is what this book is about.

PRELUDE II

Ah, the Super Bowl, the quintessential sports event in the United States. The media attention for this event is unparalleled in sports, with a record 4,786 media credentials issued for 2008. Football, the most telegenic of all team sports, is the most watched American television event (sport and nonsport), as one billion fans in 2008 watched in 234 nations and territories worldwide. More Americans watched the game (140 million) than the 131 million who voted in the 2008 presidential election.

Super Bowl Sunday is unique—a shared, nationwide social event organized around a single stage at a single time.[9] It is an unofficial national holiday. It is the biggest day of the year for gambling (about 112 million Americans bet on the 2008 Super Bowl, with most of the wagers being illegal), and it is the second biggest day in the year for food consumption (trailing only Thanksgiving). Further illustrating the magnitude of this single game: it is estimated that 350 million gallons of water were flushed in toilets during the halftime of the Super Bowl.

The Super Bowl brims with the potential for great drama, heroics, and excellence in performance, all of which are heightened by an uncertain outcome. For these and many other reasons, the game embodies all sport—and shows why the excitement of sport is so infectious to me and so many others.

But there is another side to the Super Bowl, a side that diminishes sport for me. A sports contest, a physical competition between opponents, is decided by differences in abilities, strategy, and chance. The effort to win under these conditions is the essence of sport, whether a playground basketball game, a Little League baseball game, a church league slow-pitch softball game, or a college rivalry, such as the Michigan–Ohio State annual football game, the Connecticut–Tennessee women's basketball game, or the Super Bowl. But as the level of sport becomes more sophisticated, sport shifts from play to work and from pleasurable participation to pageantry meant to please fans, owners, alumni, and other powerful people. Today, sport has become a spectacle ruled by money.

This transformation has corrupted sport. Phoenix, the host for the 2008 Super Bowl benefited from the $400 million in business generated by this mega-event. According to the American Gaming Council, Americans bet between $6 billion and $8 billion legally and illegally on this single sports event. Teams are owned either by wealthy individuals or by large corporations. Television networks pay enormous sums for the broadcasting rights to the Super Bowl and then sell advertising (at $2.7 million per thirty seconds for the 2008 Super Bowl). The NFL has a $200 million marketing contract with Nike. The sale of NFL memorabilia during Super Bowl week brings in $100 million, which is almost twenty-five times more than the athletes make cumulatively for playing this game. Some of the superstars in this game have multi-million dollar salaries. For instance, Eli Manning, the quarterback for the New York Giants, had a salary of $6.45 million in 2007, plus $5 million in endorsements. For being named the 2008 Super Bowl Most Valuable Player, Manning received a new car and an estimated $7 million in additional endorsement deals. In contrast, four of his teammates made less than $200,000 in salary and received the Super Bowl winners' share of $68,000 and a ring (of course, Manning received these also).

The expenses involved in going to the Super Bowl mean that most attendees are affluent. A ticket to the 2008 Super Bowl cost $700–$900—and around $3,000 per seat sold through brokers, plus the exorbitant costs for travel expenses, hotel accommodations, and food at rates in the host city that escalate dramatically during Super Bowl week. For example, when Boston and New York City qualified to play in the Super Bowl, airline tickets from those cities to Phoenix quadrupled. Local hotels and motels charged four to six times a typical weeknight rate, with a four-day minimum. Even if average fans could afford such a package, corporations held the bulk of the tickets, which they use to reward their top employees and key business clients and write off as business expenses for tax purposes.

Some of the players cheat by taking anabolic steroids and other banned substances that give them a chemically induced physical advantage. During the course of the game, there are cheap hits aimed at injuring an opponent. Similarly, there are numerous instances of trash talking and other intimidating behaviors. Some athletic heroes are thugs and rapists.

Racism is evident at the Super Bowl, in the race of the players at various positions, and in the dearth of African-American coaches, assistant coaches, trainers, owners, publicists, and media personnel. Likewise, the Super Bowl represents the sexist side of sport as it glorifies athletes and coaches, teams, owners, broadcasters, and newspaper writers, all but a small fraction of whom are male. Women provide supporting roles. Their bodies are used to heterosexualize the festival as cheerleaders, dancers, half-time performers, and promotional sex objects.

Winning the Super Bowl is vitally important. We Americans emphasize the outcome of games rather than the process. We glorify winners and vilify losers. Fran Tarkenton, a phenomenal quarterback whose team lost three Super Bowl attempts, carries the stigma of the Super Bowl loser. So too does Jim Kelly of the Buffalo Bills, who lost four times. As John Madden, former NFL coach and current television game analyst, has said, "The biggest gap in sports is between the winner of the Super Bowl and the loser in the Super Bowl."

Each community or region represented by a team in the Super Bowl is united in a common dream—to be victorious in this all-important event. People of various races, faiths, and classes are linked in a joint venture developing, for however brief a time, a sense of community. Evidence for this is found in the conversations at places of business, on the assembly line, in sports bars, and at family gatherings. This feeling of community is quite fragile, however. It is easily shattered by losing. One's own team, players, or coaches can become objects of contempt because of perceived bad strategy, deficient play calling, seemingly nonsensical player substitutions, or lack of effort.

Sports journalist Mark Kriegel, writing in Sports Illustrated, *described the Super Bowl as "the highest sabbath in the American religion, the annual consecration of corporate culture, an event that celebrates 30-second spots as sagas and bookmakers as theologians. The Super Bowl evokes a star-spangled yin and yang, all those equal but opposing forces that create a prime-time culture: Coke and Pepsi, Miller and Bud, McDonald's and Burger King, Disney and Fox, Bloods and Crips, AFC and NFC. Only two things you can do here at the Super Bowl: you're buying, or you're selling."*[10]

The Super Bowl symbolizes the fundamental sports paradox for me: It is both magical and materialistic, unifying and divisive, inclusive and exclusionary, expansive and exploitative. These agony and ecstasy elements of sport are the subjects of this book.

INTRODUCTION

I begin with a paradox: Sport, a seemingly trivial pursuit, is important. Sport is a fantasy—a diversion from the realities of work, relationships, and survival. Sport entertains. Why then do we take it so seriously? First and foremost, sport mirrors the human experience:

> Sport elaborates in its rituals what it means to be human: the play, the risk, the trials, the collective impulse to games, the thrill of physicality, the necessity of strategy; defeat, victory, defeat again, pain, transcendence and, most of all, the certainty that nothing is certain—that everything can change and be changed.[11]

Second, sport mirrors society in other profound ways. It shares with the larger society the basic elements and expressions of bureaucratization, commercialization, racism, sexism, homophobia, greed, exploitation of the powerless by the powerful, alienation, and ethnocentrism. American sport embodies American values—striving for excellence, winning, individual and team competition, and materialism. Parents want their children to participate in sport because participation teaches them the basic values of American society and builds character.

Third, sport is compelling because it combines spectacle (a universal human social tendency to combine sport and pageantry) with drama (an outcome that is not perfectly predictable), excellence (the most able physically), and clarity (exactly who won, by how much, and in what manner). We also know who lost and why.

Fourth, there is something transcendent about sport. Fans celebrate. Fans high-five strangers. Fans emote with cheers, jeers, screams, and tears. As Scott Simon of National Public Radio puts it: "You can tell yourself: it's just sports, nothing real; it has nothing to do with your life, no resonance in the real world of living, dying, and struggling. And you'd be right. Then, something happens. MJ leaps! Mac swings! Flutie scores! And inside, where your body cannot kid you, something takes over and it feels real."[12]

Finally, there is the human desire to identify with something greater than oneself. For athletes, this is being part of a team, working and sacrificing together to achieve a common goal. For fans, identifying with a team or a sports hero bonds them with others who share their allegiance; they belong and they have an identity. Esteemed analyst of sports Frank Deford puts it this way: "In today's world, where we are so fragmented, an arena is one place left where we come together to share. . . . That's why the creeps at games who shout loud obscenities are not merely being offensive. They're breaking a compact, which is that all us sports fans must sacrifice a little of our individuality to, for one rare modern moment, commune."[13]

Sport is a pervasive aspect of U.S. society. Participation rates are high. Most children are involved in organized sport at some time in their lives. Sport is the subject of much conversation, reading material, leisure activity, and discretionary spending. Over one-tenth of the *World Almanac* is devoted annually to sport, more than is allotted to politics, business, and science. *USA Today*, the most widely read newspaper in the United States, devotes one-fourth of its space to sport. Even the *Wall Street Journal* has a weekly sports page. A number of cable television networks provide twenty-four-hour sports coverage. Almost one-fifth of major network time is devoted to sport. Annually, the most watched television event in the United States is the Super Bowl. NBC and USA Network broadcast 1,200 hours of the 2004 Athens Olympics, but NBC devoted only six hours to the two political conventions that year. The amount of sports betting is staggering, with unknown billions wagered legally and illegally.

We sports fans read the daily sports page with a keen interest in the latest scores, win-loss records, favorite athletes, and possible new college recruits or trades that improve our beloved professional teams. We know a great deal about sport. We know point spreads, current statistics, play-off probabilities, biographical information about athletes and coaches, and more. As children, many of us learned sports information, memorizing incredible amounts of trivia. Moreover, most of us play sports, whether as individuals or on organized teams, throughout much of our lives.

But do we truly understand sport? Can we separate the hype from the reality and the myth from the facts? Do we question the way sport is organized? Unfortunately, many fans and participants alike have a superficial, uncritical attitude that takes much for granted.[14] The purpose of this book is to examine sport critically and to ask probing questions.

As a sociologist, I examine all social arrangements critically. A sociologist asks questions such as, "How does sport really work? Who has power and who does not? Who benefits under the existing social arrangements and who does not?" These questions scrutinize existing myths, stereotypes, media representations, and official dogma. The answers to these questions enable us to demystify sport and truly understand it. My inquiry is guided by critical questions. I examine sport and the beliefs surrounding it, holding them to the light of current research findings and critical thinking in order to demythologize them. I focus on showing how sport really works and, in the process, I identify a duality in it, which exists in all human institutions. In other words, sport has positive and negative outcomes for individuals and society, as we have already seen in the two preludes to this chapter. My approach will probably raise questions, doubts, resistance, and even anger among some readers, demonstrating the power of myth. In the process, though, readers will see sport from a new angle, one that brings new interpretations and insights to their experiences with sport.

PARADOXES OF SPORT

The subtitle of this book refers to the paradoxes of sport. *The Random House Dictionary of the English Language* supplies the following definition of paradox: (1) "any person, thing, or situation exhibiting an apparently contradictory nature"; and (2) "any opinion or statement contrary to commonly accepted opinion."[15]

This book is titled *Fair and Foul*[16] because sport is beset by a number of contradictions (definition 1 above), and the common understanding of sport is often guided by myth. My goal is to demythologize sport by calling into question the prevailing beliefs about this phenomenon (definition 2 above). These two dimensions of the term "paradox" constitute the organizing principle—the essence—of this book.

Sport is inherently contradictory. On the one hand, sport provides excitement, joy, and self-fulfillment for the participants. As former Olympic athlete Kenny Moore puts it: "To celebrate sport is . . . to celebrate sheer abandon, to savor moments when athletes surrender themselves to effort and are genuinely transformed. This is when sport takes loneliness, fear, hate and ego and transmutes them into achievement, records, art, and powerful example."[17]

But there is also a dark side, as Moore concedes: "[Sport also presents us with] cocaine deaths, steroid cover-ups, collegiate hypocrisies, gambling scandals, criminal agents, and Olympic boycotts. Such failings show that sport's civilizing, freeing effect on us is incomplete. Not everyone is following the rules. Not everyone is trying."[18]

Put another way, sport provides examples of courage, superhuman effort, extraordinary teamwork, selflessness, and sacrifice. Yet the images conveyed through sport—violence, greed, exploitation, selfishness, cheating, and contempt for authority—are not always uplifting.[19]

Sport is clearly appealing. We are fascinated by the competition and the striving for excellence. Sport is compelling because it transcends our everyday routine experiences with excitement, heroics, and unpredictability. But much about sport is also appalling. Paradoxically, fans often find the appalling appealing—the violence, the incredible amounts of money, and the outrageous behaviors by some athletes, coaches, and owners.

Each chapter in this book takes up a particular paradox of sport. First, sport is both unifying and divisive. Chapter 2 shows how sport can unite warring factions and bring different social classes and racial groups together. However, it can also reinforce the barricades that divide groups.

The related topics of chapter 3 are the names, mascots, logos, and rituals associated with sports teams, which evoke strong emotions of solidarity among followers. But these sports symbols have a potentially dark side as well. Many Native Americans are offended by the use of Native American names (like the Washington Redskins), war paint, tomahawks, war chants, and mascots dressed in native costume. They feel that these practices stereotype, demean, and trivialize the traditions and rituals of Native Americans. Similarly, the names given to women's teams raise parallel questions concerning stereotyping (the name Rambelles hardly refers to athletic skills) and trivialization (for example, Wildkittens as a diminutive of Wildcats). Then there is the use of the Rebel flag—the symbol of the Confederacy, racial segregation, and African American enslavement—as the rallying symbol for sports teams at some Southern schools. Proponents see the Confederate flag as an inspirational symbol of Southern heritage and Old South pride and tradition. Opponents see this symbol as sending an inflammatory message about a tradition of racial oppression and exclusion.

Sport is a rule-bound activity organized and supervised by authorities and organizations to promote fair play, as shown in chapter 4. It includes a socialization process whereby participants learn to play by the rules, commit themselves to hard work and teamwork, and practice good sportsmanship. These positive attributes of sport have given rise to the common assumption that sport builds character. Yet these attributes are counteracted by unethical coaches and players, the widespread use of performance-enhancing drugs, the pampering of athletes, hatred among opponents, and the debasement of fair play.

A fourth paradox is the subject of chapter 5: Sport is both healthy and unhealthy. Sport encourages good physical health. Obviously, the physical exercise that sports participation requires is beneficial because it promotes endurance, coordination, weight control, muscle strength, strong bones, joint flexibility, and increased aerobic (lung and heart) capacity. At the same time, however, participants get hurt during sporting activities. Sport can also damage the health of athletes through overtraining, rapid weight loss to meet weight requirements, excessive weight gain, and the use of drugs that promote muscle mass, strength, and endurance. Demanding coaches may expect too much from their athletes. Parents may drive their child athletes too hard, too fast. Elite young athletes are especially vulnerable to excessive training and even sexual abuse from adult authorities.

Chapter 6 examines two forms of children's play—peer centered and adult centered. Since the later dominates the sports experience of children today, I focus on the dark side of this phenomenon.

Chapter 7 examines the duality of sport found in its expressiveness, on the one hand, and control on the other. Social control is necessary for stability in society and all social groups. Social control, which is a central feature in sport, has two contradictory consequences. Its positive functions lead to consensus and cooperation as everyone pulls together to achieve a common goal, as well as stability on the team, in the organization, or in the society. The maintenance of the status quo, however, is not always good for everyone. Sport, for example, supports tradition, but in so doing it helps to reinforce traditional gender roles and compulsory heterosexuality. It helped to maintain racial segregation until after World War II and continues to allow considerable discrimination against racial minorities in some sports even to this day.

Chapter 8 demythologizes the prevailing notion that sport is played on a level playing field, where talent, strategy, and luck determine winners and losers. This is not the case when it comes to the participation of racial minorities in some sports (for example, automobile racing, bowling, golf, and tennis). Racial discrimination is very pronounced when considering minorities for leadership positions. Among the 119 head coaches in Division I-A football, for example, there were only five African American coaches for the 2008 season—a 4.2 percent representation in a sport in which about half of the players are African American. Another instance of an uneven playing field occurs in major league baseball. The big city/big television market teams do not share the wealth they generate with other league teams, as the National Football League does, resulting in a few teams making extraordinary money with which they buy the best talent from the poor teams. Or consider the current Bowl Championship Series (BCS), in which the top six conferences are guaranteed slots in the top four bowls (each paying about $17 million to each participating team). The two open slots are awarded to the most deserving teams. The remaining teams vie for the minor bowls that have payouts sometimes of less than $1 million per team.

Chapter 9 investigates the contradictions of big-time college athletics. Sport is an integral part of higher education in the United States. Big-time college sport supplies full-ride scholarships to athletes and generates many millions of dollars for their institutions, their communities, and corporate America. Big-time college sport unites its supporters, provides free publicity for the schools, and gives good athletes from economically disadvantaged backgrounds the chance for a college education. And it is a training ground for future professional athletes. Does it, however, fit with the educational mission of these universities?

A strong case can be made that sport is actually detrimental to academics (as chapter 9 explores). For example, most of these schools actually lose money, since scholarship money and other economic resources are channeled away from academics and toward athletics. And the athletes admitted to these schools tend to perform below the student body average on test scores and graduation rates; they are often athletes first and students second. In addition, occasional scandals hurt the image of the schools involved; the programs and resources are disproportionately geared toward the male athletes in the revenue-producing sports; gender equity is denied; and athletes are exploited under the guise of amateurism. The overarching contradiction is that big-time school sport is organized as a commercial entertainment activity within an educational environment. This arrangement may have certain positive consequences, but it compromises educational goals.

Chapter 10 asks the question: To what degree is sport a mechanism of social mobility? Athletes can parlay their skills and achievements into college scholarships, careers as professional athletes, coaching positions, and other sports-related occupations. Huge amounts of money are made by special athletes, many of whom come from lower socioeconomic backgrounds. However, the odds of any one athlete achieving these rewards are very slim.

Actually, achieving a professional sports career is extremely difficult, no matter how hard the individual works. Sport is a path out of poverty for only a very few. Racial minorities are especially vulnerable to the appeal of riches and fame through sport, but this is a false hope leading to failure for most. Women have even less chance of upward mobility through sport than men because fewer college scholarships are available to them, as well as fewer professional sport opportunities. Even those who do become professional athletes lack lifelong security.

Chapter 11 examines the link between private ownership of professional teams and public subsidies for them. Large cities either have professional sports franchises or actively seek them. In either case, the cities subsidize or offer to subsidize the teams and their wealthy owners, typically by providing arenas or stadiums, refurbishing these venues as needed, charging little or no rent, providing access roads, and giving generous percentages on concessions and parking. The rationale for such largesse is that professional teams benefit their host cities economically.

This raises some interesting questions: Who benefits financially from professional teams and who does not? Do the members of all social classes share in the benefits? Should wealthy owners and affluent athletes be subsidized by taxpayers, many of whom are not interested in sport? Do men and women in the community gain more or less equally from the arrangements? Does a city actually benefit economically from having professional teams? Is the profit margin so low for professional teams that they can only survive if subsidized by taxpayers? Is there a better alternative to professional teams being owned by affluent individuals or large corporations who threaten to move the team to a city that offers more generous subsidies?

While sport is local (that is, fans identify with their local teams and athletes), it is becoming increasing global, the subject of chapter 12. One-fifth of the players in the National Basketball Association are foreign. One-fourth of major league baseball players are not native born, instead they are mostly from Latin America. How does this new ethnic makeup of teams affect the loyalty of fans? Does it increase the hostility toward visiting teams and players? On the other hand, does the presence of foreign players on teams build bridges with other societies?

These paradoxes are considered in this book. Although each chapter focuses on a central theme, the book also explores related contradictions and myths. Issues of class, race, ethnicity, and gender are also considered in each chapter.

Do these contradictions and questions pique your interest about how sport really works? Or does their critical thrust make you defensive about sports? Both are likely reactions, indicating once again the contradictory nature of sport. My point is that anyone who truly wants to understand sport in American society must accept its inherent dualities.

Too often we focus on the bright side of the dualities present in sport, letting myths guide our perceptions and analyses. I intend to present the reality of sport, including the good and the bad. Indeed, I emphasize the negative aspects of sport in order to demythologize and demystify it. Yet I do not want to forget the magical nature of sport that is so captivating and compelling. Overcoming this basic contradiction—being critical of sport while retaining a love for it—will enable us to examine the negatives surrounding sport with the goal of seeking alternatives to improve this vital, interesting, and exciting aspect of social life.

Finally, sports organization can be changed, but this requires a plan, a strategy, and an organized effort (the topic of chapter 13). Sociologist Jay Coakley puts it this way:

The growing importance of sports in society makes it more necessary for us to take a closer and more critical look at how sports are defined, organized, and played. As we do this, some of us will call for changes in dominant forms of sports or reject those forms and call for new and alternative sports. However, we should not expect widespread, revolutionary changes to occur overnight. Social transformation is always a challenging and tedious process. It requires long-term efforts and carefully planned strategies, but it does not occur without a clear vision of possible futures and strategic efforts to turn visions into realities.[20]

Understanding sport must precede any effort to change it for the better. That is the goal of this book.

NOTES

1. Jarrett Bell, "Reaching Out, Reaching Back," *USA Today*, October 10, 2007, pp. 1C–2C; Peter King, "Making a Difference: Braylon Edwards," *Sports Illustrated*, December 31, 2007, p. 44.

2. Mark Beech, "Making a Difference: Kyle Petty," *Sports Illustrated*, December 31, 2007, p. 70.

3. Melissa Segura, "Making a Difference: Wooster Athletes," *Sports Illustrated*, December 31, 2007, p. 52.

4. Mike Sandrolini, *All the Good in Sports* (Ventura, Calif.: Regal, 2007), 126–32.

5. Richard E. Lapchick, *100 Heroes: People in Sports Who Make This a Better World* (Orlando, Fla.: NCAS Publishing, 2005), 157–59.

6. Sandrolini, *All the Good in Sports*, 11.

7. Some articles summarizing the athletic scandals of 2007 include: Richard Hoffer, "The Year Cheaters Paid the Price," *Sports Illustrated*, December 31, 2007, pp. 18–19; Jim McCauley, "No Fun in Games: Off-Field Problems Dominate Top National Stories," Associated Press, December 22, 2007; Robert Lipsyte, "Four Sports Scandals that Gave Bush Cover," *AlterNet*, October 13, 2007, online: www.alternet.org/module/printversion/64819; Jim Litke, "2007 was a Year of Breaking Rules, Not Records," Associated Press, December 26,

2007; and Dave Zirin, "Taking Back Sports in '08," *Edge of Sports*, January 1, 2008, online: www.edgeofsports.com/2008-01-01-307/index.html.

8. *USA Today*, "Home Run Hitter Gets Lift from Opponents," May 1, 2008, p. 13C.

9. A few of the sources used for his discussion of the 2008 Super Bowl are: Scott Wong, "Patriots, Giants to Draw Big Crowds," *The Arizona Republic*, January 22, 2008, online: www.azcentral.com/sports/superbowl/articles/0122superfolo0122.html; S. L. Price, "Big Game Hunter," *Sports Illustrated*, January 28, 2008, p. 76; and Dave Zirin, "The Super Bowl: Who Stole the Soul?" *Common Dreams*, February 2, 2008, online: www.commondreams.org/archive/2008/02/02/6799.

10. Mark Kriegel, "Where Have You Gone, Joe Namath?" *Sports Illustrated*, August 9, 2004, p. 44.

11. "Why Sports?" *The Nation*, August 10–17, 1998, p. 3.

12. Scott Simon, *Home and Away* (New York: Hyperion, 2000), 15.

13. Frank Deford, "Why We Love Sports," *CNN Sports Illustrated*, December 29, 1999. See also, David Shaw, "The Roots of Rooting," *Psychology Today* 11 (February 1978): 48–51; Eric Miller, "Why We Love Football," *Christianity Today* 51 (September 2007): 26–30; William S. Nack, "Behind the Thrill of Victory," *Time*, January 17, 2005, pp. A44–A45; and Michael Elliott, "Hopelessly Devoted," *Time*, June 20, 2005, p. 76.

14. David L. Andrews, "Rethinking Sports in America," *Center News* 14 (Spring 1996): 3. *Center News* is published by the Center for Research on Women at the University of Memphis.

15. Jess Stein, ed., *Random House Dictionary of the English Language*, unabridged ed. (New York: Random House, 1966), 1046.

16. For an examination of another social institution using paradoxes as an organizing theme, see Judith Lorber, *The Paradoxes of Gender* (New Haven, Conn.: Yale University Press, 1994).

17. Kenny Moore, "Uplifted, Gently, by Sport," *Sports Illustrated*, November 15, 1989, p. 234. See also George H. Sage, "Sports Participation as a Builder of Character?" *The World & I* 2 (October 1988): 641.

18. Kenny Moore, "Uplifted, Gently, by Sport," 234.

19. John Meyer, "Great Escapes . . . and Other Fantasies," *Rocky Mountain News*, January 9, 1982, p. 2B.

20. Jay J. Coakley, *Sport in Society: Issues and Controversies*, 7th ed. (New York: McGraw-Hill, 2001), 504.

AP/Wide World

2

SPORT UNITES, SPORT DIVIDES

Sports are what they are, and the best thing they are is a common memory, a shared experience that knits a community together, from the smug to the desperate, from the prosperous to the penniless, from the incoherently adolescent to the irretrievably adult.

—Bernie Lincicome, sportswriter for the *Rocky Mountain News*

To play this game you must have fire in you, and there is nothing that stokes fire like hate.

—Vince Lombardi, legendary coach of the Green Bay Packers

On the morning of September 11, 2001, four commercial planes were taken over by hijackers who piloted the planes to new destinations, and the course of history was changed. Two of the planes rammed into the World Trade Center in New York City, another plunged into the Pentagon. The fourth plane failed in its mission, presumably because of heroic passengers attacking the hijackers, crashing instead in rural Pennsylvania. About three thousand people were killed in this attack and the subsequent rescue attempts, about the same number of Americans who died at Pearl Harbor in 1941.

Following this attack by Islamic extremists, the stunned nation came together, rallying around the flag. Sports played an important role in building this patriotic unity. At first, the various sports leagues and teams postponed games out of respect for those who died. Then, as the rescheduled games began, from high school games to professional games, each was preceded by a variety of unifying symbolic acts—moments of silence to reflect on the fallen and the heroic, patriotic songs, the presentation of the flags (some as huge as a football field), military flyovers, and spontaneous chants of "U.S.A.! U.S.A.!" These patriotic displays brought the thousands of people in the stadiums and in the television audiences together in a cause larger than themselves. The first Super Bowl after the September attack, on February 3, 2002, in New Orleans, outdid itself in nationalistic fervor. For the gathering of 131 million U.S. households, the largest assemblage of Americans since 9/11, television networks and the NFL took the opportunity to celebrate all things American. Fox's three-hour pregame show had as its theme "Hope, Heroes, and Homeland," which it advertised in USA Today as a "celebration of football and the American spirit." Included in the event was a reenactment of the signing of the Declaration of Independence with famous athletes reciting words from that document, former presidents reading passages of Abraham Lincoln's speeches, Barry Manilow singing "Let Freedom Ring," and Paul McCartney singing his song "Freedom," with military personnel, firefighters, police holding flags, and young women dressed as Statues of Liberty. The pageantry before the game also included a huge flag and Mariah Carey singing the national anthem. At halftime, the NFL presented the band U2, who sang several songs on a stage in front of a huge unfurling scroll listing those whose lives were lost on September 11. "The American military-industrial-sports-entertainment complex took a bow before the world. . . . [The] message was the nexus of politics and sports, football and nationhood."[1] And to top off this orgy of football and nationalism, the winning team, in a huge upset, was the New England Patriots! And, as the team was presented the trophy, the field was inundated with red, white, and blue confetti.

THE ROLE OF SPORT IN UNITY
AND DIVISION AMONG NATIONS

Two opposing forces are at work throughout the world today: increasing intolerance, ideological purity, tribalism, exclusion, and conflict, as well as many signs of tolerance, cooperation, compromise, acceptance of differences, and inclusion. Just as the world is moving toward becoming a global community, it is torn by parochial hatreds dividing nations and regions into warring ethnic enclaves.[2] Sport, too, embodies these contradictory elements as it increasingly pulls people apart on the one hand and pulls them together on the other.

Sport Unites

International events bring together people from different countries and different racial, ethnic, and religious backgrounds, promoting understanding and friendships across these social divides. The U.S. government uses athletes to promote international goodwill. The State Department, for example, sponsors tours of athletes to foreign countries for these purposes. Sport has also been used to open diplomatic doors. In the 1970s, when Communist China and the United States did not have diplomatic relations, the leadership of the two nations agreed that their athletes could compete in each country. After this "ping-pong" diplomacy broke the ice, the two countries eventually established normal relations. In 1998, U.S. wrestlers were invited to participate in a seventeen-nation tournament in Iran, the first American athletic team to visit Iran since the 1979 Islamic revolution. Wrestling is Iran's national sport, and Iran's president at that time, Mohammed Khatami, encouraged this breakthrough to crack "the wall of distrust between the two nations." Thomas Omestad described an important symbolic act that may help to bridge the antagonism between Iran and the United States that has existed for over two decades:

> It was only a small, spontaneous gesture. But it worked emotional magic. After winning a silver medal . . . American Larry "Zeke" Jones waved a hand-sized Iranian flag, and the 2,000 fans packed into a Tehran arena went wild with delight. "America! America!" They chanted in response—a sudden, unscripted reversal of the ritual "Death to America!" chorus that Iranians usually chant at public events.[3]

Thus sport was a wedge helping to break down the hostility between these two countries. Perhaps it is a prelude to normalizing relations between the United States and a former enemy. In June 1998, Iran upset the United States in a first-round World Cup soccer match in Lyon, France.[4] The Iranians celebrated their unexpected victory wildly but not (and this is crucial) with taunts directed at the United States. President Bill Clinton congratulated the Iranians, and the Iranian president was a gracious winner. (Clinton's gesture was facilitated because soccer is not yet an important sport to Americans.)

Since India was divided into two nations—India and Pakistan—in 1948, they have gone to war three times, with millions killed. The tension between these two nuclear powers is enormous and unrelenting, unleashing religious hatred, as India is Hindu and Pakistan is Muslim. However, in 2004 the two nations came together in a series of cricket matches, as the team from India, for the first time in fourteen years, toured Pakistan for thirty-nine days.

The phrase *sporting event* can't begin to contain the religious extremism, unforgiven deeds, and rabid jingoism that swirl around each India-Pakistan cricket match; the game is haunted by battle dead, and the air is charged with the ongoing dispute between the two countries over control of Kashmir. For generations cricket has been a proxy for war between the two nations.[5]

Temporarily, at least, sport brought these two warring nations together, promising either better relations between the two countries—or an explosion of violence.

Sport can be used to unite groups within one country, as Adolf Hitler used the 1936 Olympic Games in Berlin to unite the German people through the accomplishments of Germany's athletes on the world stage. According to Richard D. Mandell in his book *The Nazi Olympics*, the Olympic festival was a shrewdly propagandistic and brilliantly conceived charade that reinforced and mobilized the patriotism of the German masses.[6] The successes of the German athletes at those Olympics (they won eighty-nine medals, twenty-three more than U.S. athletes and more than four times as many as any other country) was "proof" of German superiority.

Similarly, success in international sports competition can trigger pride across divisions within a country. For example, even in war-ravaged Iraq, with its ethnic and sectarian divides, unity was achieved briefly in 2007 when the national Iraqi soccer team, composed of Shiites, Sunnis, and Kurds, won its first ever Asian Cup, defeating Saudi Arabia. Spontaneous celebrations occurred following the victory with people dancing in the streets and waving Iraqi flags.[7]

Cuba provides another contemporary example of the great potential sport has as a mechanism for promoting domestic unity.[8] Fidel Castro, Cuba's leader, has decreed that sport is a right of the people. No admission is ever charged to a sporting event. The most promising athletes are given the best coaching and training. The Communist leadership in Cuba uses sport to unite its people through pride in its athletic achievements. Cuba devotes 3 percent of its national budget to a sports ministry that encourages and trains elite athletes. In the Pan American Games, Cuban athletes, from a country with a third the population of California, win many times more medals than US athletes on a per capita basis. In fact, *Sports Illustrated* declared that Castro "willed [Cuba] into the best pound-for-pound program on the planet."[9] The Cuban athletes are sports heroes and heroines, evoking intense nationalistic pride in the Cuban people and, indirectly, support for the ruling elite.

Racially, South Africa is a nation deeply divided. Sport has helped to break down this division, at least in part, in two ways. First, when the whites in South Africa held an election to decide whether to dismantle apartheid, 69 percent voted to give up their privilege, marking a rare peaceful transition of power. One reason for the favorable vote was South African President F. W. de Klerk's warning that failure to pass the measure would return the country to isolation in business and sport.[10] South Africa had last participated in the Olympics in 1960 and had been barred since then from international competition. Its apartheid racial policies had made it a pariah country in everything from politics to sports for three decades. With apartheid dismantled, South Africans could once again show their athletic prowess. This was a compelling argument for many whites. Subsequently, South Africa has been allowed to compete in the Olympics and in other worldwide competitions, especially in rugby, which is very important to its people.

After the formal fall of apartheid and the election of Nelson Mandela, the sports world accepted South Africa. The World Cup in rugby was held in South Africa in 1995. President Mandela used the rugby World Cup as an opportunity to bring the races somewhat closer together within his country. The national rugby team, the Springboks, and rugby itself had symbolized white South Africa, so Mandela encouraged black Africans to think of this team as their team. In speaking to a black audience, Mandela, wearing a Springbok cap, said, "This Springbok cap does honor to our boys. I ask you to stand by them tomorrow because they are our kind." Mandela inspired *Sports Illustrated* to comment:

> *Our kind.* Not [black]. Not white. South African. The rugby team became a symbol for the country as a whole. . . . Given the right time and place, sport is capable of starting such a process in a society. It is only a start, of course. The hard work lies ahead, after the crowds have dispersed and the headlines have ceased. South Africa's racial and economic woes are not behind it. Far from it. But thanks to the common ground supplied by a rugby pitch, those problems appear less imposing than they did only a month ago.[11]

The Springboks, by the way, went on to win the World Cup, defeating the world's two rugby powers—Australia and New Zealand—in the process. For the first time in South Africa's troubled history, whites and blacks found themselves unified by a sport. Of course, this kind of unity is superficial and temporary, but it is nevertheless an instrument that can promote the achievement of unity in an otherwise divided country.

After the defeat of the Taliban in Afghanistan in 2002, a soccer game was organized pitting a team from the International Security Assistance Forces (ISAF), which provided security for the interim government, and a team of Afghanistan's best players. This match served several unifying functions for Afghanistan. First, it was the first time since 1979 that an Afghan soccer team played at home against a team from another country. This contest helped bring Afghans together in a common cause, a difficult achievement given the different tribes and warring factions within that country. Second, the game symbolized the working together of the ISAF and the Afghanistan government. Third, the game gave Afghans, all Afghans, a sense of pride as their country was recognized throughout the sports world. Finally, Akmed Zia Muzaffary, secretary general of the Federation of Afghanistan football, said: "[I am hopeful] that the soccer game will bring invitations for Afghanistan to play in other countries. That would help us rebuild our relations with the world as much as any politics."[12]

Sport Divides

But sport also has the capacity to divide peoples. Phillip Goodhart and Christopher Chataway argue that there are four kinds of sport: sport as exercise, sport as gambling, sport as spectacle, and representative sport. Representative sport is

> limited conflict with clearly defined rules, in which representatives of towns, regions, or nations are pitted against each other. It is primarily an affair for the spectators: they are drawn to it not so much as the mere spectacle, by the ritual, or by an appreciation of the skills involved, but because they identify themselves with their representatives. . . .
>
> Most people will watch [the Olympic Games] for one reason only: there will be a competitor who, they feel, is representing them. That figure in the striped singlet will be their man—running, jumping, or boxing for their country. For a matter of minutes at least, their own estimation of themselves will be bound up with his performance. He will be the embodiment of their nation's strength or weakness. Victory for him will be victory for them; defeat for him, defeat for them.[13]

This keen identification with national athletes frames the contest as a symbolic battleground between "us" and "them." This attitude, of course, is exclusionary rather than inclusionary.

Sport can encourage division rather than unity. Tensions generated in sports matches, such as those that erupted between El Salvador and Honduras and between Gabon and the Congo after soccer matches, have contributed to the outbreak of war. A full-scale war between El Salvador and Honduras followed the clash between fans at the elimination round of the 1970 World Cup and concluded with bombing raids, troop movements, and, eventually, two thousand dead. Obviously, the matches themselves did not start these conflicts, since the matches occurred in an already tense context over land disputes and other contentious issues. A sports event between two quarreling countries can (and occasionally does) provide the catalyst for actual war between them.

Losing an international match can cause deep internal division, whereas unity typically accompanies victory. When Colombia lost a recent World Cup, riots occurred in the country because the people were distressed over their team's play. Incredibly, a player who had inadvertently scored a goal for the opposition was murdered, presumably for his failure in sport.

An interesting development to watch is the emergence of a European economic community with a common currency, open borders, and transgovernmental units to oversee commerce among the member nations. Will sporting events among these nations drive a wedge between them, making cooperative transnational efforts difficult or impossible? Will sport inflame nationalistic impulses, causing fragmentation rather than unity? Or can sport help these nations transcend their nationalistic tendencies by somehow enhancing the goals of transnational unity among these countries?

UNITY AND DIVISION THROUGH SPORT IN THE UNITED STATES

Does sport unify or divide Americans? Distinguished sports commentator Frank Deford makes a strong case for the negative: "It is time to recognize the truth, that sports in the United States has, in fact, never been so divisive. Uniquely today, sports has come to pit race against race, men against women, city against city, class against class and coach against player."[14]

Let's examine how sport unites and divides the United States, looking at the three major hierarchies in society: class, race, and gender. Does sport lead to greater harmony within these systems of social stratification? Or does sport increase division? As we shall see, it has the potential to work both ways. I emphasize the divisive nature of sport because that goes counter to the prevailing myth.

Class

The lines dividing the social classes in the United States are quite fuzzy, except for those that delineate the very rich and the very poor. Money separates. The affluent tend to live in enclaves that are barricaded, at least symbolically, from those with whom they do not want to associate. They tend to send their children to private schools rather than public schools, which restricts their interaction with people who possess fewer economic resources. Even in the public schools, class segregation occurs when tests privileging the mainstream culture are used to determine what courses students take. Class segregation for the affluent also occurs at play. The wealthy play golf, tennis, and swim in exclusive country clubs and ski and sail at expensive resorts. Does sport break down these economic and social barriers between social unequals, or does it reinforce them?

When in 1990 Ronald Reagan accepted the Theodore Roosevelt Award, the highest honor bestowed on an individual by the National Collegiate Athletic Association, he said:

> When men and women compete on the athletic field, socioeconomic status disappears. African American or white, Christian or Jew, rich or poor . . . all that matters is that you're out there on the field giving your all. It's the same way in the stands, where corporate presidents sit next to janitors . . . and they high-five each other when their team scores . . . which makes me wonder if it [status] should matter at all.[15]

This observation, of course, is incredibly naive. It reinforces the myth that sport is egalitarian. According to the prevailing myth, sport provides opportunity for those with ability regardless of class origins and because it promotes interaction across the social classes. Let me, as sociologists are wont to do, demythologize.

Reagan asserts that sport provides opportunity for those with athletic ability regardless of class origin. Does it? The answer is a little yes but mostly no. First, sociologists know that upward mobility is limited to a few athletes (see chapter 10). Athletes of humble social origins can become incredibly wealthy. Golfer Tiger Woods, for example, makes $120 million or so annually from his achievements plus endorsements and personal appearances. Many young males, especially African American males, believe that they will become professional athletes if they work hard enough. How reasonable is this expectation? In two words, extremely improbable, as I will demonstrate in chapters 8 and 10.[16]

Second, sociologists know that opportunity for upward mobility is limited to a few sports. Children from families with limited economic resources tend to participate in sports that require little equipment and are publicly funded, such as community youth programs and school sports. Thus they tend to excel in football, basketball, baseball, track, and boxing. Children of the affluent, on the other hand, have access to golf courses, tennis courts, and swimming pools, as well as coaching in those sports, through private country clubs, neighborhood associations, and parental subsidies. Moreover, some sports, such as gymnastics and ice skating, require considerable money for coaching, access, equipment, and travel (young elite ice skaters, for example, spend as much as $75,000 annually). Ironically, most professional opportunities for women athletes are in sports in which the affluent have a tremendous advantage from childhood.

Ronald Reagan's remarks also suggested that sport encourages interaction across class lines. Does it? Again, the answer is that sport works both ways. Yes, people of all sorts talk to each other about sports. Past or upcoming sports events are topics that transcend class lines. People in public places often shed the barriers of social class as they discuss past or future big games with strangers, acquaintances, and fellow workers.

Yes, players on teams may develop friendships with those from different social backgrounds, thus transcending social class. Yes, players from humble origins may be upwardly mobile, increasing their interaction with people across class boundaries. Certainly obtaining a college education, which athletic participation facilitates, increases interaction across classes.

But sport scholarships are for the very few. And attending college on an athletic scholarship does not necessarily lead to graduation. Athletes in the revenue-producing sports are less likely to graduate than their nonathlete peers (discussed further in chapter 9).

Historically, sport has been pursued mainly by the affluent, who alone had the time and the money for such non-income-producing activities. The notion of the sports "amateur" was a nineteenth-century invention that the affluent used as a mechanism of class separation.[17] The major competitions in Europe, including the Olympics, were limited to those who could afford the necessary travel, equipment, and coaching, and had the leisure to pursue athletic excellence. More than having the ability to participate, class origins precluded international competition for many. John Kelley, a world-class rower, was barred from the 1928 Olympics because as a bricklayer he had a physical advantage over those who either did not work at all or did not do manual labor. Ironically, the well-to-do in this case used their athletic prowess in international competitions as "proof" of their superiority over the lesser classes.

Unfortunately, the social classes are not proportionately represented at professional sports events. The cost of attending sports contests is too high for many. In 2008, a family of four attending a major league baseball game paid an average of $191.75 for tickets, parking, snacks, and a souvenir. The Boston Red Sox represented the highest average cost for this mythical family of four ($320.71; average ticket price $47.71).[18] Five NFL teams have an average cost for a ticket of over $100 (Washington was the highest in 2007 at $136.75).[19] Obviously, these amounts are prohibitive for many families. The cost for a family of four to attend an NBA, NFL, or NHL game amounts to more than 30 percent of the average household's weekly earnings. Among those who do attend, contrary to Reagan's blurred vision, CEOs and janitors do not sit side by side. Seating is segregated by cost, in a very stratified arrangement. The very rich enjoy luxury suites that cost as much as $300,000 for a season or $150,000 for a tournament (e.g., the U.S. Open tennis tournament). At basketball games, the affluent may sit in $3,000 courtside seats, while the less well-to-do are dispersed by the cost of seating, with the cheapest seats farthest from the action. The poor, of course, are not in the seats or at the golf tournament at all. If they do attend, they likely are there as vendors, janitors, or parking attendants.

John Underwood, writing in the *New York Times*, lamented the high cost of attending sports events:

> The greatest damage done by this new elitism is that even the cheapest seats in almost every big-league facility are now priced out of reach of a large segment of the population. Those who are most critically in need of affordable entertainment, the underclass (and even the lower-middle class), have been effectively shut out. And this is especially hateful because spectator sport, by its very nature, has been the great escape for the men and women who have worked all day for small pay and traditionally provided the biggest number of a sport's core support. As it now stands, they are as good as disenfranchised—a vast number of the taxpaying public who will never set foot inside these stadiums and arenas.[20]

Race

Progress in race relations has been slow and in some instances seems to be slipping. Cities are becoming more racially segregated. Schools are becoming more racially concentrated. The gap between whites and

African Americans and Latinos is widening in terms of income, wealth, education, and employment. With growing immigration and economic hard times for the working poor, racial discord increases. Racial discrimination in housing, lending policies, job opportunities, and the criminal justice system infuriates minorities. What they believe to be the pathologies of racial minorities, such as crime, welfare dependency, teenage pregnancy, and drugs, motivate fearful whites to build walls, real and symbolic, that separate them physically from racial minorities and to support harsh political policies toward these minorities. The question here is, given these racial realities in U.S. society, does sport reduce or exacerbate racial tensions? Is the playing field open or does it reinforce racial inequality?

In regard to racial harmony, sport works both ways. Clearly, white and African American teammates make friends across racial lines through sport. Research has found that attitudes toward race are enhanced (1) when players from both races contribute more or less equally to team success and (2) when the team is successful.[21] Thus, on integrated teams in which each race needs the other to succeed and the team does succeed, members of both races have positive feelings toward each other.

In many sports, minority athletes are heroes cheered by their fans of all races. That is, fans tend to appreciate the athletes on their own teams, regardless of race. The three most popular athletes in the United States (or even the world) are African American: Muhammad Ali, Michael Jordan, and Tiger Woods (who has an African American father and an Asian mother). But fans who adore their minority athletes may vent racial hatred on the minority athletes of opposing teams.

A strong case can be made that sport divides the races as well. Historically, desegregating a sport has intensified racial hostilities. Because of America's persistent racial divide, sport sometimes provides the context for episodes of racial hostility (in schools, parks, playgrounds, prisons). Similarly, games that involve teams representing white schools and teams representing African American or predominantly Latino schools often provide a setting for racial taunts and violence by players and fans. This occurs with some regularity in metropolitan areas when mostly white suburban high schools play against high schools from the inner city that have a mostly African American or Latino student body. It also occurs in small-town America.

Race tends to be a factor in the choices that athletes make. That is, on integrated teams, players often segregate themselves voluntarily for meals, travel arrangements, and leisure activities, and they tend to select roommates of the same race. As whites and racial minorities compete for positions on a team, each group may feel that the other race is getting special treatment, leading to various manifestations of "racial paranoia."

Integrated teams may be segregated by position, which is called "stacking." In football, whites are more likely to play on offense and at thinking and leadership positions that more often determine the game's outcome. African Americans overwhelmingly play on defense and at positions that require physical characteristics such as size, strength, speed, and quickness. This means that the members of one race spend most of their practice time with players of the same race (see chapter 8 for a more elaborate account of stacking).

Most African American college athletes play for schools that are predominantly white (with African Americans constituting only 5 percent or so of the student body). They differ from the rest of the student body in color and size. They may also differ in academic preparation. They often differ in economic resources. Consider, for instance, a six-foot, ten-inch poor African American basketball player from the inner city of Detroit. Although he took high school courses that did not prepare him for college, he is recruited to play at Tulane University, where the student body is mainly from a southern, rural background, 98 percent white, affluent, and with average SAT scores of 1100. He is marginal in a number of dimensions in this setting. This marginality from the rest of the student body is likely to drive him further into not just the athletic ghetto but, most particularly, the African American athletic ghetto (see chapter 9).[22] Moreover, African American athletes are often segregated in athletic ghettos on campus (dorms, meals, courses, majors) and interact with other athletes but rarely with other students.

In November 2004, a National Basketball Association game between the Indiana Pacers and the Detroit Pistons ended in a brawl between players and fans. Preceding the violence were profane taunts by the Detroit fans aimed at the visiting Pacer players. The verbal aggression progressed in intensity with objects thrown and players going into the stands to fight the alleged perpetrators. There are many reasons for this extreme case of violence (e.g., an increasingly uncivil society, alcohol, media attention to violence), but let's limit the discussion here to the racial implications. About 75 percent of the NBA players are African American, and the fans are mostly white. In this riot, "it was not just a case of players going into the stands. It was black players going after white fans."[23] NBA players are extremely wealthy with an average salary in 2007–2008 of $5.36 million. The ten highest-paid players in the NBA, all African Americans, range in salary from $23.75 million to $16.4 million plus endorsements. There is fan resentment toward these rich young men for their outlandish wealth and their behavior, which many consider boorish, selfish, inappropriate, and disrespectful. Their tattoos, cornrows, hip hop, and "look at me" strutting are seen through the eyes of whites as reinforcing old racial stereotypes. As black sociologist Harry Edwards puts it: "Race is always an issue in America. When the national TV screens continuously play out a scene of black players and mostly white fans coming to blows, the racial context is clear. Race played an aggravating role in this, whether consciously or not on the part of both sides."[24]

Gender

Ours is a patriarchal society. Women are second to men in power, earnings, and job opportunities. With few exceptions, women occupy secondary roles at home, in corporations, in colleges and universities, and in voluntary associations. Women experience discrimination by lenders, by employers, and by the Social Security system, to name a few.[25]

Does sport reinforce this imbalance, or does it work to break down gender inequities? As with class and race, a case can be made for both sides on this question. On the integrating side, there is the passage of Title IX in 1972, which states that no person in the United States can be excluded, on the basis of sex, from participation in, can be denied the benefits of, or can be subjected to discrimination in any educational program or activity receiving federal financial assistance. As a result of this landmark legislation, there has been a boom in women's participation in school athletics. High school programs for girls went from about 300,000 participants in 1971 to 2.95 million in 2006 (there were over 4 million boys). During those years the number of women in college sports more than quintupled. The money for women's sports programs in college went from virtually nothing before Title IX to about 38 percent of the athletic budgets. Before Title IX, women received no athletic scholarships, compared to 45 percent of all athletic scholarships in 2006.[26]

But the implementation of Title IX on many campuses has pitted men against women. To meet the regulations, the various athletic departments have typically added women's teams but to offset the new expenses have dropped non-revenue-producing men's sports such as wrestling, gymnastics, and swimming. In response, for example, college wrestling advocates have sued the Department of Education arguing that Title IX promotes sexual bias by eliminating men's teams and scholarships (reverse discrimination). That argument fails to acknowledge that men's football and basketball are excluded from the equation. Football especially is very expensive, but its expenses are not trimmed to move money to women's programs, making it impossible to bring equality to men's and women's sports.

Although progress has been slow, a few women's teams have been successful in winning support from their schools and the fans. In some programs, women's teams actually have better support than men's teams (e.g., in women's basketball, Louisiana Tech). The 2004 NCAA women's national championship was watched by more people than any single basketball game—college or pro, men or women—in the twenty-five-year history of ESPN.

Women's professional tennis has at least as much fan support as men's tennis, as measured by attendance and television viewing. Women's professional golf is gaining popularity, although it does not generate the interest that men's golf does. Women's gymnastics and ice skating are more popular than men's gymnastics and skating. When the women's Olympic ice skating champion turns professional, she receives much more money than her male counterpart.

Sport, however, continues to perpetuate male dominance in society. What could be more striking than the shift in leadership that has occurred in women's athletics in only a few years? Ironically, after Title IX brought greater public attention and wider participation in women's sports, control over the teams shifted dramatically to men. Before Title IX, 90 percent of collegiate women's teams were coached by women; in

2006 only 42.4 percent were. Male coaches of female teams also receive higher salaries than female coaches of female teams. Finally, in 1972 more than 90 percent of women's intercollegiate programs were administered by a woman, but now less than 19 percent are.[27]

Major inequities remain, despite the progress since Title IX. For example, whereas women in 2007 comprised 57 percent of college student populations, they received only 43 percent of participation opportunities, which is 56,110 fewer participation opportunities than their male counterparts.[28] Despite this obvious disparity, the male-dominated athletic establishment defines the situation as gender equity, since they do not include football (see chapter 9).

Sport also perpetuates male dominance through the media. The media guides compiled by athletic departments of various universities provide some useful hints. These guides (for example, basketball guides) give more attention to the men's team than to the women's team (in terms of number of pages and length of descriptions for coaches and players), use better-quality paper, and include more photographs and different types of photographs (action pictures for men and stills for women). The descriptions of the players differ, with men much more likely than women to be characterized as aggressive. Women's sports activities are viewed as secondary and relatively unimportant. *Sports Illustrated* and *USA Today* have the best record of the major journalistic outlets in providing coverage for women's sports, although they devote much less than half of their coverage to it. But even *Sports Illustrated* errs by giving too much emphasis to the nonathletic side of women. For example, in 1993 the fifty-two magazine covers included only six featuring women. Who these women were and what they represent is quite instructive. The annual swimsuit cover objectifies feminine beauty of a nonathletic kind. The cover featuring tennis player Monica Seles showed a knife in her back. The third and fourth women were the nonathlete widows of Cleveland Indians pitchers Steve Olin and Tim Crews. The fifth was tennis player Mary Pierce, whose father beat her. The sixth was skater Nancy Kerrigan, who was clubbed on the knee by an assailant. Thus, in one year, *Sports Illustrated* displayed on its cover one beautiful model in a swimsuit and five women who were victims.[29] The media also treat men and women differently in their broadcasts. The play-by-play announcers and those providing the analysis are almost exclusively men.

A few women roam the stadium looking for human interest stories or interviewing coaches, athletes, wives of the participants, and the like.

The announcers also refer to women differently than men. A study of play-by-play television commentary of women's and men's basketball and tennis by Michael A. Messner, Margaret Carlisle Duncan, and Kerry Jensen found some interesting and important differences.[30] In basketball, men's games were referred to as universal (the NCAA championship game, the Final Four) whereas women's games were always referred to as the NCAA women's national championship game or the women's Final Four: "The men's games and tournament were presented as the norm, the universal, while the women's were continually marked as the other, derivative (and, by implication, inferior) to the men's."[31]

Messner and colleagues also found a gendered hierarchy of naming. Both in basketball and tennis (and I would add figure skating), the commentators commonly referred to women as girls, as young ladies, and as women. Men, on the other hand, were never referred to as boys but rather as men or young men. This difference tends to infantilize women linguistically while granting adult status to men. Similarly, when athletes were named, the commentators used women's first names far more often than men's. Both of these practices—referring to women as girls and by their first names—in effect make men the dominants and women the subordinates. In doing so, they both reflect and reconstruct gender inequality.

Male dominance is also perpetuated through the names given to women's teams. Some of these names make women athletes either invisible (i.e., are subsumed under a male name given the men's teams, such as Tomcats), or they are trivialized (e.g., the Pink Panthers rather than the Panthers).[32] This form of sexism is discussed in detail in the next chapter.

Sport also perpetuates male dominance by celebrating beautiful and sexy women. Women are used as entertainers at sports events. It is a rare sports event that does not feature majorettes, cheerleaders, and dancers dressed in sexy outfits who prance, shake, and titillate. The press coverage of sports disproportionately emphasizes the beauty of female athletes rather than their athletic attributes and accomplishments. When Anna Kournikova was playing tennis, she had the highest income of any woman athlete ($11 million annually from endorsements and public appearances). Ms. Kournikova does not command high fees because of her tennis prowess (she never won a tournament on the professional circuit) but because of her physical attractiveness.[33]

For the most part, men in sport are viewed as the achievers, the doers; women support them as cheerleaders, girlfriends, or spouses, achieving status from the men's exploits rather than their own. Women are passive, men are aggressive; women are dependent, men are independent.

Male dominance is maintained when communities build very expensive stadiums and arenas to keep their professional teams or to entice other teams to move there (see chapter 11). These stadiums, costing a quarter to half a billion dollars in tax revenue, are for men. They are for male owners, male athletes, male coaches, male trainers, male media, male-controlled corporations, and mostly male fans. The symbolic message is clear: Men count for much more than women.

IS THE UNITY ACHIEVED THROUGH SPORT ALWAYS GOOD?

Most discussions of sport implicitly assume that unity is good and division is bad. This is not always the case.[34] The Nazi Olympics of 1936, for example, unified the Germans in their contempt for Jews, Gypsies, people of color, homosexuals, and non-Germans. This unity was achieved by separating the German people into superior/inferior categories. Soccer wars divide nations precisely because of soccer's ability to unite the people within national boundaries. The infamous black power fist statement by Tommy Smith and John Carlos on the victory stand during the playing of the national anthem in the 1968 Olympics was viewed by most Americans as a divisive gesture pulling white and black athletes apart. Many blacks and antiracists, however, interpreted this symbolic act as a powerful, unifying political statement. Depending on the audience, this act was divisive or unifying, unpatriotic or progressive. Thus it is not simply a matter of sport either uniting or dividing but how and under what circumstances sport unites and/or divides and with what consequences.

Sport does have a unifying function. This can be accomplished with progressive consequences if it is organized to make full participants of the members of all social classes, races, and genders. Sport does this to some degree, but for the most part sport reinforces the inequalities in society. Consider, for example, the statement by Mariah Burton Nelson from her book, *The Stronger Women Get, the More Men Love Football*: "We need to take sports seriously—not the scores or the statistics, but the process. Not to focus on who wins, but on who's losing."[35] By my count, the losers in sport have been and continue to be the poor, racial minorities, and women. And, as long as these folks lose, sport will more likely divide than unify.

NOTES

1. Joanne Ostrow, "Patriotism Takes Over Airwaves on Super Sunday," *Denver Post*, February 4, 2002, p. 11D.

2. Benjamin R. Barber, "Jihad vs. McWorld," *Atlantic Monthly* 269 (March 1992): 53–63; and Benjamin R. Barber, "Beyond Jihad vs. McWorld," *The Nation*, January 21, 2002, pp. 11–18.

3. Thomas Omestad, "Wrestling with Tehran: U.S., Iran Go to the Mat in a Replay of Ping-Pong Diplomacy," *U.S. News & World Report*, March 2, 1998, p. 44.

4. For the political background of this event, see Ian Thomsen, "Political Football," *Sports Illustrated*, June 1, 1998, pp. 66–69.

5. S. L. Price, "Diplomacy by Other Means," *Sports Illustrated*, May 10, 2004, p. 56.

6. Richard D. Mandell, *The Nazi Olympics* (New York: Macmillan, 1971).

7. Grant Wahl, "What a Ball Can Do," *Sports Illustrated*, August 6, 2007, p. 23; Stephen Farrell and Peter Gelling, "With Eyes Fixed on a Distant Soccer Field, Iraqis Leap at a Reason to Celebrate," *New York Times*, July 30, 2007, online: www.nytimes.com/2007/07/30/world/middleeast/30iraq.html?_r=1&oref=slogin&ref.

8. Steve Wulf, "Running on Empty: Cuba Maintains a Rich Sports Tradition Despite Shortages of Everything but Pride," *Sports Illustrated*, July 29, 1991, pp. 60–70.

9. S. L. Price, "The Big Red Machine," *Sports Illustrated*, March 3, 2008, p. 14.

10. "Rugby over Race," *Sports Illustrated*, March 30, 1992, p. 10.

11. E. M. Swift, "Bok to the Future," *Sports Illustrated*, July 3, 1995, p. 33.

12. Quoted in Tim Friend, "Afghans Welcome Fun and Game," *USA Today*, February 15, 2002, p. 9C.

13. Phillip Goodhart and Christopher Chataway, *War without Weapons* (London: Allen, 1968), 3.

14. Frank Deford, "Seasons of Discontent," *Newsweek*, December 29, 1997–January 5, 1998, p. 74.

15. Ronald Reagan, quoted in "Athletics a Great Equalizer, Reagan Tells NCAA," *NCAA News* 10 (January 1990): 1.

16. Wilbert M. Leonard II, "The Odds of Transiting from One Level of Sports Participation to Another," *Sociology of Sport Journal* 13.3 (1996): 288–99.

17. D. Stanley Eitzen, "The Sociology of Amateur Sport: An Overview," *International Review for the Sociology of Sport* 24.2 (1989): 95–105.

18. *Boston Globe*, "Major League Baseball Average Ticket Prices," Boston.com, March 28, 2008, online: www.boston.com/sports/baseball/articles/2008/03/28/average_teams.

19. *Dallas Morning News*, "Hot NFL Tickets," *Dallasnews*.com, October 27, 2007, online: http://www.dallasnews.com/sharedcontent/dws/spt/columnists/rgosselini.

20. John Underwood, "From Baseball and Apple Pie, to Greed and Sky Boxes," *New York Times*, October 31, 1993, p. 22.

21. McKee J. McClendon and D. Stanley Eitzen, "Interracial Contact on Collegiate Basketball Teams: A Test of Sherif's Theory of Super-Ordinate Goals," *Social Science Quarterly* 55 (March 1975): 926–38.

22. Patricia A. Adler and Peter Adler, *Backboards and Blackboards: College Athletes and Role Engulfment* (New York: Columbia University Press, 1991).

23. Frank Deford, "Quo Vadis, NBA?" Commentary on National Public Radio, December 2, 2004, online: www.sportsillustrated.cnn.com/2004/writers/frank—deford/12/02/race.

24. Harry Edwards, quoted in Erik Brady, "The Great Fan Divide," *USA Today*, November 23, 2004, p. 2C. See also, Todd Boyd, "Did Race Play a Role in Basketbrawl?" *Los Angeles Times*, November 26, 2004, online: www.latimes.com/news/opinion/commentary/la-oe-boyd26nov26.

25. See D. Stanley Eitzen, Maxine Baca Zinn, and Kelly Eitzen Smith, *Social Problems*, 11th ed. (Boston: Allyn and Bacon, 2009), especially chapter 9.

26. Donna Lopiano, "Pay Inequity in Athletics," Women's Sports Foundation, 2007.

27. R. Vivian Acosta and Linda J. Carpenter, *Women in Intercollegiate Sport: A Longitudinal Study—Twenty-Nine Year Update: 1977–2006* (West Brookfield, Mass.: Carpenter/Acosta, 2006).

28. Lopiano, "Pay Inequity."

29. Lynda Truman Ryan, "Swimsuit Models or Victim Stories, Who Will Cover for Me?" *New York Times*, February 2, 1994, p. 20.

30. Michael A. Messner, Margaret Carlisle Duncan, and Kerry Jensen, "Separating the Men from the Girls: The Gendered Language of Televised Sports," *Gender and Society* 7 (1992): 121–37.

31. Messner, Duncan, and Jensen, "Separating the Men from the Girls," 125.

32. D. Stanley Eitzen and Maxine Baca Zinn, "The De-athleticization of Women: The Naming and Gender Marking of Collegiate Sport Teams," *Sociology of Sport Journal* 6 (December 1989): 362–70.

33. Michael A. Messner, *Taking the Field: Women, Men, and Sports* (Minneapolis: University of Minnesota Press, 2002), chapter 4.

34. My thanks to Mike Messner, who made these points in his review of the initial draft of this project.

35. Mariah Burton Nelson, *The Stronger Women Get, the More Men Love Football: Sexism and the American Culture of Sports* (New York: Harcourt Brace, 1994), 8.

3

NAMES, LOGOS, MASCOTS, AND FLAGS: THE CONTRADICTORY USES OF SPORTS SYMBOLS

What's in a name?

—William Shakespeare

Words are tools of thought. We can use words to maintain the status quo or to think in new ways—which in turn creates the possibility of a new reality.

—Sherryl Kleinman, sociologist

The two teams that played in the 1995 World Series were the Atlanta Braves and the Cleveland Indians. Inside the stadium, the fans of the Braves did the "tomahawk chop" and enthusiastically shouted "Indian" chants. Similarly, the fans of the Indians united behind their symbol, Chief Wahoo, waved foam tomahawks, and wore war paint and other pseudo-Native American symbols. Outside the stadium, Native American activists carried signs in protest of the inappropriate use of their symbols by Anglos. Symbols have the power to both unite followers and divide groups into "us" and "them." They also can be interpreted as symbolic of past and continued oppression.

SYMBOLS AND SPORTS

A symbol is anything (word, gesture, or object) that carries a particular meaning for the members of a group. A raised finger (which one is important!), a green light, a whistle, a handshake, and a raised fist are all symbols with meaning. Some symbols, such as a wink, are trivial; others, such as the American flag, are vitally important.

A group's symbols serve two fundamental purposes—they bind together the individual members of a group, and they separate one group from another. Each of the thousands of street gangs in the United States, for example, has a group identity that is displayed in its name, code words, gestures, distinctive clothing, and colors. The symbols of these gangs promote solidarity and set them apart from rivals. These symbols are so important that the members may risk their lives in their defense.[1]

Using symbols to achieve solidarity and community is a common group practice, as the French sociologist Émile Durkheim showed in his classic analysis of primitive religions.[2] Durkheim noted that preliterate people in a locality believed that they were related to some totem, which was usually an animal but could be some other natural object as well. All members of a common group were identified by their shared symbol, which they displayed as the emblem of their totem. This identification with an animal, a bird, or another object is common in U.S. schools. Students, former students, faculty members, and others who identify with the school adopt nicknames for the school's teams, display the school colors, wave the school banner, wear special clothing and jewelry, and engage in ritual chants and songs. These behaviors usually center around athletic contests. Sociologist Janet Lever connects these activities with Durkheim's notion of totemism: "Team worship, like animal worship, makes all participants intensely aware of their own group membership. By accepting that a particular team represents them symbolically, people enjoy ritual kinship based on a common bond. Their emblem, be it an insignia or a lapel pin or a scarf with team colors, distinguishes fellow fans from both strangers and enemies."[3]

A school's nickname is much more than a tag or a label. It conveys symbolically, as Durkheim suggests, the characteristics and attributes that define the institution. In an important way, the school's symbols represent the institution's self-concept. Schools may have names that signify the school's ethnic heritage (e.g., the Bethany College Swedes), state history (University of Oklahoma Sooners), religion (Oklahoma Baptist College Prophets), or founder (Whittier College Poets). Most schools, however, use symbols of aggression and ferocity for their athletic teams (birds, such as hawks; animals, such as bulldogs; human categories, such as pirates; and even the otherworldly, such as devils).[4] Although school names and other symbols evoke strong emotions of solidarity among followers, there is also a potential dark side to their use. The names, mascots, logos, and flags chosen by some schools may be derogatory to some groups. The symbols may dismiss, differentiate, demean, and trivialize marginalized groups, such as African Americans, Native Americans, and women. Thus they serve to maintain the dominant status of powerful groups and subordinate those groups categorized as "others." That may not have been the intent of those who decided on the particular names and mascots for a particular school, but their use diminishes these "others," thus retaining the racial and gender inequities found in the larger society.[5] School symbols in sports, then, have power not only to maintain in-group solidarity but also to separate the in-group from the out-group and perpetuate the hierarchy between them. Three conspicuous examples of this phenomenon are the use of the Confederate flag at the University of Mississippi, the use of Native American names (Redskins, Scalpers) and other racial symbols (war paint, tomahawks, Native American dances), and the sexist names given to women's athletic teams.

Symbols of the Confederacy

At Nathan Bedford Forrest High School in Jacksonville, Florida, young African American athletes wear the Confederate army's colors on their uniforms. They call themselves the Rebels. And the school they play for is named after the slave-trading Confederate general who became the original grand wizard of the Ku Klux Klan.[6]

There is a neo-Confederate culture in much of the South.[7] There are organizations dedicated to promoting the heritage of the Confederate States of America. They fight to retain Confederate symbols, such as the Rebel battle flag, that have had a prominent place in many Southern states, most notably Alabama, Georgia, South Carolina, and Mississippi. The neo-Confederate culture and its symbols have two distinct meanings. One promotes the South's heritage. In this regard, Bob Chance of Selma, Alabama, says:

> I strongly oppose efforts to ban or to at least discourage the use of the Confederate battle flag. We southerners have as much right to our heritage as anyone else has to theirs. The flag in question was a battle flag which led Confederate soldiers into battle. Now it leads the Ole Miss Rebels into battle. That should be all there is to it. The so-called Rebel flag is the flag of the South—the symbol of many good things about our culture and history that are dear to the hearts of Southerners. It becomes racist only in the hands of a racist.[8]

The opposing view is that the Confederate flag symbolizes "antebellum slavery, Old South patriarch, Jim Crow segregation, Civil Rights lynching, and numerous other forms of oppression."[9]

The Rebel battle flag, which some individuals and groups feel should still fly over state buildings, is an object of controversy. Several states have abandoned it after considerable struggle, but South Carolina continues to use the Rebel flag as its official flag.

The University of Mississippi displays the Rebel battle flag and sings "Dixie" at football games.[10] This practice began in 1948 after the Dixiecrats, rebelling against a strong civil rights plank in the Democratic platform, walked out of the Democratic convention. In that year the University of Mississippi adopted the Rebel flag, designated "Dixie" the school's fight song, and introduced a mascot named "Uncle Reb," a caricature of an Old South plantation owner. These symbols proclaimed its support for racial segregation (its sports teams were officially designated the Rebels in 1936). In 1962 James Meredith, despite the strong opposition of Governor Ross Barnett and other white leaders in the state, became the first black student at the school. There were demonstrations at that time that supported the governor and demonstrations that opposed the racial integration of the school. Through it all, the Rebel flag and the singing of "Dixie" were symbols of defiance used by the supporters of segregation.

Over the ensuing years, the use of these symbols at the University of Mississippi caused considerable debate. On the one hand, they represented the state's heritage and as such were a source of pride, inspiration, and unity among citizens of the South. The opposing position was that these symbols represented a history of oppression against African Americans, noting that the Rebel flag was also a prominent symbol of the Ku Klux Klan. Since almost one-third of Mississippians are African Americans (among the states, Mississippi has the nation's largest African American population), the flagship university of that state should not use symbols that recall the degradation and demeaning of their ancestors. Is it proper, they ask, to use the key symbol of the Confederacy and African American enslavement as a rallying symbol for the University of Mississippi's sports teams—teams composed of whites and African Americans?

As a compromise, in 1983, twenty-one years after the University of Mississippi integrated, its chancellor ruled that the Rebel flag was no longer the official banner for the school. Chancellor Porter L. Fortune Jr. made it clear, however, that students would have the right to wave the flag at football games. And that they have done. Sports team names such as "Rebels," as well as songs such as "Dixie," have continued as official school symbols. The Uncle Reb mascot has been retired, however.

The debate continues, as summarized by Charles W. Eagles, a University of Mississippi history professor: "For some of us—those who believe in the University of Mississippi—the symbols prevent the university from being everything it can be. Others—those that are faithful to Ole Miss [the traditionalists]—think that if you took the symbols away, there wouldn't be anything there. The symbols are seen as a real burden for the University. But they're the backbone of Ole Miss."[11]

This debate demonstrates vividly the power of symbols, not only the power to unite or divide but also the hold these symbols have on people, as seen in their resistance to change and in the organized efforts to change those symbols interpreted as negative.

The Use of Native American Names and Ceremonial Acts

Ray Franks conducted an exhaustive study of the names of athletic teams at all U.S. community colleges, colleges, and universities. He found that names associated with Native Americans predominated in popular use.[12] It is estimated that about three thousand of the nation's high schools have Native American names. Major professional teams have also adopted Native American names—in baseball, the Atlanta Braves and the Cleveland Indians; in football, the Washington Redskins and the Kansas City Chiefs; in basketball, the Golden State Warriors; and in hockey, the Chicago Blackhawks.

Native American names used for sports teams can be generic (Bryant College Indians, Rio Grande College Redmen), tribal (Florida State Seminoles, University of Alaska at Fairbanks Nanooks, Central Michigan Chippewas, Eastern Michigan Hurons, Mississippi College Choctaws, Utah Utes), or they can focus on some attribute (Bradley Braves, Marquette Warriors, Lamar High School [Colorado] Savages) or some combination of names (University of Illinois Fighting Illini, North Dakota Fighting Sioux).[13]

Defenders of Native American names, logos, and mascots argue that their use is a tribute to the indigenous peoples. Native Americans, the argument goes, are portrayed as brave, resourceful, and strong. Native American names were chosen for sports teams precisely because they represent these positive traits.

Other defenders claim that the use of Native American names and mascots is no different from the use of names and mascots that represent other ethnic groups, such as the Irish or the Vikings or the Norse. Because members of these ethnic groups accept the use of their names, Native Americans should also be proud of this recognition of their heritage.

But Native American leaders object to their symbols being used by athletic teams. Since the early 1970s individuals and organizations, such as the American Indian Movement and the National Coalition on Racism in Sports and the Media, have sought to eliminate the use of Native American names, mascots, and logos by sports teams.[14] They use several key arguments, foremost, racist stereotyping. Names such as Indians, Braves, and Chiefs are not inherently offensive, but some names, logos, and mascots project a violent caricature of Native Americans (such as scalpers and savages). The official booster club of Florida State University, for example, is called "The Scalphunters." Teams that use Native American names commonly employ the tomahawk chop, war paint, and mascots dressed as Native Americans. This depiction of Native Americans as bloodthirsty warriors distorts history, since whites invaded Native American lands, oppressed native peoples, and even employed and justified a policy of genocide toward them.

Some mascots are especially demeaning to Native Americans. Consider Chief Wahoo, "the red-faced, big-nosed, grinning, drywall-toothed moron who graces the peak of every Cleveland Indians cap."[15] Is such a caricature appropriate? Clyde Bellecourt, national director of the American Indian Movement (AIM), summarizes the complaints:

> If you look up the word "redskin" in both the Webster's and Random House dictionaries, you'll find the word is defined as being offensive. Can you imagine if they called them the Washington Jews and the team mascot was a rabbi leading them in (the song) Hava Nagila, fans in the stands wearing yarmulkes and waving little sponge torahs? The word Indian isn't offensive. Brave isn't offensive, but it's the behavior that accompanies all of this that's offensive. The rubber tomahawks. The chicken-feather headdresses. People wearing war paint and making these ridiculous war whoops with a tomahawk in one hand and a beer in the other. All of these things have significant meaning for us. And the psychological impact it has, especially on our youth, is devastating.[16]

Another problem is the imitation or misuse of symbols that have religious significance to some Native American peoples. Using dances, chants, drumming, and other rituals at sporting events clearly trivializes their meaning.

Also problematic is the homogenization of Native American cultures. Native Americans are portrayed uniformly, without regard for the sometimes enormous differences among tribes. Thus, through the use of Native American names of mascots, society defines who Native Americans are instead of allowing Native Americans to determine how society thinks of them.

There is a dispute concerning the degree to which Native Americans object to the use of Indian symbols for sports teams. On the one hand, a survey by *Indian Country Today* found that 81 percent of respondents "indicated use of American Indian names, symbols, and mascots are predominantly offensive and deeply disparaging to Native Americans."[17] This finding is contradicted by the survey reported in *Sports Illustrated*, which found that, while Native American activists are virtually united in their opposition to the use of Indian nicknames and mascots, some

83 percent of Native Americans said that professional teams should not stop using Indian nicknames, mascots, or symbols.[18]

Native American activists dismiss such opinion as misguided ("There are happy campers on every plantation," says Suzan Harjo, president of Morning Star Institute, an Indian-rights organization in Washington, D.C.) or as evidence that Native Americans' self-esteem has fallen so low that they don't even know when they're being insulted.[19] Similarly, Native Americans have been immersed in a society that demeans them and socializes them to accept their secondary status in society.

After more than forty years of protest, about seven hundred high schools and colleges throughout the nation have changed their former Native American names and mascots. Most notably, colleges and universities such as Dartmouth, Marquette, Stanford, Eastern Michigan, Eastern Washington, University of Massachusetts, Oklahoma City, St. Bonaventure, Siena, Miami of Ohio, and St. John's have taken these objections seriously and done so.

Similarly, a number of "Native American" mascots have been retired. For example, the Kansas City Chiefs retired their horse mascot "Warpaint"; the Atlanta Braves got rid of "Chief Noc-A-Homa," who used to come out of a teepee after an Atlanta home run and do a ceremonial dance; and after a long and very contentious debate the University of Illinois retired Chief Illiniwek, a mascot who pretended to be an Indian by dressing in a war bonnet and war paint.[20]

Yet many high schools and colleges resist changing their Native American nicknames and mascots to ones that do not demean a minority group. Ironically, they insist on retaining the Native American symbols even though their schools do not have a Native American heritage or significant Native American student representation. The members of these schools and their constituencies insist on retaining their Native American names because they are part of their collective identities. This allegiance to their school symbols seems to have higher priority than sensitivity to the negative consequences produced by inappropriate depictions of Native Americans.

Sexist Names for Women's Teams[21]

Many studies have shown the varied ways in which language acts in the defining, deprecation, and exclusion of women.[22] Names do this, too. Naming women's and men's athletic teams is not a neutral process. The names chosen are often badges of femininity and masculinity, inferiority and superiority. To the degree that this occurs, the names of women's and men's athletic teams reinforce a basic element of social structure: gender division and hierarchy. Team names reflect this division as well as the asymmetry that is associated with it. Despite advances made by women in sport since the implementation of Title IX, widespread naming practices continue to mark female athletes as unusual, aberrant, or invisible.

My colleague Maxine Baca Zinn and I examined the names and accompanying logos and mascots of sports teams for women and men at 1,185 coeducational four-year colleges and universities.[23] We identified eight gender-linked practices associated with names/logos that diminish and trivialize women.

First, physical markers. One common naming practice emphasizes the physical appearance of women, such as the Angelo State Rambelles or the Bellarmine College Belles (the men are the Knights). As Casey Miller and Kate Swift argue, this practice is sexist because the "emphasis on the physical characteristics of women is offensive in contexts where men are described in terms of achievement."[24]

Second, the terms "girl" or "gal." The use of "girl" or "gal" stresses the presumed immaturity and irresponsibility of women, such as the Elon College Golden Girls. "Just as boy can be blatantly offensive to minority men, so girl can have comparable patronizing and demeaning implications for women."[25]

Third, feminine suffixes. This is a popular form of gender differentiation found in the names of athletic, social, and women's groups. The practice not only marks women but also denotes a feminine derivative by establishing a "female negative trivial category."[26] The devaluation is accomplished by tagging words with feminine suffixes such as "ette" and "esse." At Dillard University, the men's team is the Blue Devils, and the women's team is the Devilettes; at Albany State, the men are the Golden Rams and the women are the Rammettes; at Duquesne University and James Madison University, the men are the Dukes and the women the Duchesses.

Fourth, the term "lady." This label has several meanings that demean women as athletes. "Lady" is used to "evoke a standard of propriety, correct behavior, and elegance,"[27] characteristics that are decidedly unathletic. Similarly, "lady" carries overtones recalling the age of chivalry. "This makes the term seem polite at first, but we must also remember that these implications are perilous: they suggest that a 'lady' is helpless, and cannot do things for herself."[28] The use of "lady" for women's teams is common, for example, the University of Florida Lady Gators or the University of Arkansas Lady Razorbacks. At Kenyon College the men are the Lords and the women are the Ladies, and at Washington and Jefferson College the men are Presidents and the women are First Ladies. In both of these instances, the names for the women's teams clearly mark their status as inferior to that of the men.

Fifth, male as a false generic. This practice assumes that the masculine in the language, word, or name choice is the norm while ignoring the feminine altogether. Miller and Swift define this procedure as "terms used of a class or group that are not applicable to all members."[29] The use of "mankind" to encompass both sexes has its parallel among men's and women's athletic teams that have the same name, for example, the Rams (Colorado State University), Stags (Concordia College), Norsemen (Luther College), the Tomcats (Thiel College), and the Hokies (a hokie is a castrated turkey) (Virginia Tech). Dale Spender has called the practice of treating the masculine as the norm "one of the most pervasive and pernicious rules that has been encoded."[30] Its consequence is to make women invisible as well as secondary to men, since they are robbed of a separate identity.

Sixth, male name with a female modifier. This practice applies the feminine to a name that usually denotes a male, giving females lower status.[31] Examples among sports teams are the Lady Friars of Providence College, the Lady Statesmen of William Penn College, the Lady Penmen of New Hampshire College, the Lady Centaurs of Columbia College, the Lady Gamecocks of the University of South Carolina (a gamecock is a fighting rooster), and the Lady Horsemen of St. Michaels's High School in Santa Fe. Using such oxymorons "reflects role conflict and contributes to the lack of acceptance of women's sport."[32]

Seventh, double gender marking. This occurs when the name of the women's team is a diminutive of the men's team name combined with "belle" or "lady" or other feminine modifier. For example, the men's teams at Mississippi College are the Choctaws, and the women's teams are designated as the Lady Chocs. At the University of Kentucky the men's teams are the Wildcats, and the women's teams are the Lady Kats. The men's teams at the University of Colorado are the Buffalos, and the women's teams are the Lady Buffs. At Augusta College the women are the Lady Jags, whereas the men are the Jaguars. Similarly, at both the University of Nebraska–Omaha and the University of Texas–Arlington, the men are the Mavericks and the women the Lady Mavs. Compounding the feminine intensifies women's secondary status. Double gender marking occurs "perhaps to underline the inappropriateness or rarity of the feminine noun or to emphasize its negativity."[33]

Eighth, male/female paired polarity. Women's and men's teams can be assigned names that represent a female/male opposition. When this occurs, the names of the men's teams embody competitiveness and other positive traits associated with sport, whereas the names for women's teams are lighthearted or cute. The essence of sport is competition, and physical skills largely determine outcomes. Successful athletes are believed to embody such traits as courage, bravura, boldness, self-confidence, and aggression. When the names that are given to men's teams imply these traits but the names for women's teams suggest that women are playful and cuddly, then women are trivialized and de-athleticized. For example, the men at the College of Wooster are called the Fighting Scots, and the women are the Scotties; Mercer University men's teams are the Bears, and the women the Teddy Bears; at the Albany College of Pharmacy the men are the Panthers, and the women the Pink Panthers; and at Fort Valley State College the men's teams are named the Wildcats, and the women's teams are the Wildkittens.

Another grouping occurs when names that could be included in one of the above categories also incorporate race. This occurs especially with teams using Native American symbols. The men's teams at Southeastern Oklahoma State University are the Savages and the women's teams are the Savagettes, using the diminutive feminine suffix combined with a negative stereotype for the racial category. Similarly, at Montclair State College the men are the Indians and the women are the Squaws. The word "squaw" also refers to a woman's pelvic area and means prostitute in some native languages. Vernon Bellecourt of the American Indian Movement says, "The issue itself is clear. . . . The word 'squaw' has got to go in all its forms. It's demeaning and degrading to Indian women and all women."[34]

Our survey found that approximately three-eighths of U.S. colleges and universities employ sexist names, and slightly over half have sexist names and/or logos for their athletic teams. Thus the identity symbols for athletic teams at those schools contribute to the maintenance of male dominance within college sports. Since the traditional masculine gender role matches most athletic qualities better than the traditional feminine gender role, the images and symbols are male. Women do not fit into this scheme. They are "other" even when they do participate. Their team names and logos tend to perpetuate and strengthen the image of female inferiority by making them secondary, invisible, trivial, or unathletic.

RESISTANCE TO CHANGE

It is important to note that many schools do not have team names, mascots, and logos that are racist or sexist. They use race-neutral and gender-neutral names, such as Bears, Eagles, Seagulls, Cougars, Wasps, Mustangs, Royals, Saints, Big Green, or Blue Streaks. Schools that currently employ racist or sexist names could change to neutral ones that embody the traits desired in athletic teams such as courage, strength, and aggressiveness.[35] For some, such a change would be relatively easy—dropping the use of "lady" or "ette" as modifiers, for example. Teams with Native American names or male names (stags, rams, hokies, centaurs) must adopt new names to eliminate the racism or sexism inherent in their present names. A few schools have made these changes. Most schools, however, resist changing names with passion because a name change negates the school's traditions.

The athletic teams at my school, Colorado State University, are called the Rams. Is it appropriate for the women's teams to be called Rams (rams are male sheep)? This question has been raised from time to time by the Faculty Women's Caucus and a few male professors, but strong resistance from journalists, student government leaders, and the Committee on Intercollegiate Athletics, as well as silence by the women athletes and the coaches of women's teams, have worked to maintain the status quo.

The naming issue at Colorado State University reveals a contradiction. Many students, including women student-athletes, express a lack of interest in the issue, yet it evokes strong emotions among others. These responses seem to originate in several sources at Colorado State and, by implication, elsewhere. These arguments parallel resistance to changing sexist language in general.[36]

Tradition, above all, is always a barrier to change. Students, alumni, faculty, and athletes become accustomed to a particular name for their university and its athletic teams, and it seems "natural." This is the argument made on behalf of the many teams that continue to use Native American names and symbols for their teams despite the objections of Native Americans. So too with names that are sexist. But even if a school name has the force of tradition, is it justified to continue using it if it is racist or sexist? If a sexist team name reinforces and socializes sexist thinking, however subtly, then it must be changed. If not, then the institution is publicly sexist.

Many see the naming issue as trivial. In 2005, after the California state legislature passed a bill banning the use of "Redskins" as a public school nickname, Governor Schwarzenegger vetoed it, saying it was a trivial issue. However, it is not trivial to the group being demeaned, degraded, and trivialized. Some progressives argue that there are more important issues to address than changing racist or sexist names of athletic teams. This illustrates the contradiction that the naming of teams is at once trivial and important. For African Americans, whether the University of Mississippi fans sing "Dixie" and wave Confederate flags is not as important as ending discrimination and getting good jobs. Similarly, for Native Americans, the derogatory use of their heritage surrounding athletic contests is relatively unimportant compared to raising their standard of living. For women, the sexist naming of athletic teams is not as significant as pay equity or breaking the "glass ceiling" or achieving equity with men in athletic departments in resources, scholarships, and media attention. Faced with a choice among these options, the naming issue would be secondary. But this sets up a false choice. We can work to remove all manifestations of racism and sexism on college campuses. Referring to language and relevant to the team names issue as well, the Association for Women in Psychology Ad Hoc Committee on Sexist Language has addressed and refuted the "trivial concern" argument: "The major objection, often even to discussing changing sexist language, is that it is a superficial matter compared with the real physical and economic oppression of women. And indeed, women's total oppression must end; we are not suggesting any diversion of energies from that struggle. We are, however, suggesting that this is an important part of it."[37]

The opposite point—that the naming issue is crucially important—is the third argument. Symbols are extremely compelling in the messages they convey.[38] Their importance is understood when rebellious groups demean or defame symbols of the powerful, such as the flag. Names and other symbols have the power to elevate or "put down" a group. If racist or sexist, they reinforce and therefore maintain the secondary status of African Americans, Native Americans, or women through stereotyping, caricature, derogation, trivialization, diminution, or making them invisible. Most of us, however, fail to see the problem with symbols that demean or defame the powerless because these symbols support the existing power arrangements in society. Despite their apparent triviality, the symbols surrounding sports teams are important because they can (and often do) contribute to patterns of social dominance.

Colleges and universities, for the most part, are making major efforts to diversify their student bodies, faculties, and administrations by race, ethnicity, and gender. This laudable goal is clearly at odds with the existence of racist and sexist names and practices for their athletic teams. The leadership in these schools (boards of regents, chancellors, presidents, and faculty senates) must take a stand against racism and sexism in all its forms and take appropriate action. Removing all racist and sexist symbols such as names, mascots, flags, logos, and songs is an important beginning to this crucial project.

NOTES

1. See, for example, Martin Sanchez Jankowski, *Islands in the Street: Gangs and American Urban Society* (Berkeley: University of California Press, 1991).

2. Émile Durkheim, *The Elementary Forms of Religious Life*, trans. Joseph Ward Sivain (New York: Free Press, 1947). This classic was first published in 1915.

3. Janet Lever, *Soccer Madness* (Chicago: University of Chicago Press, 1983), 12.

4. See John R. Fuller and Elisabeth Anne Manning, "Violence and Sexism in College Mascots and Symbols: A Typology," *Free Inquiry in Creative Sociology* 15 (1987): 61–64.

5. Margaret Carlisle Duncan, "Representation and the Gun That Points Backwards," *Journal of Sport and Social Issues* 17 (April 1993): 42–46.

6. Dennis Cauchon, "A Slave-Holding Past: Search for Perspective," *USA Today*, March 9, 1998, p. 8A.

7. Brian Britt, "Neo-Confederate Culture," *Z Magazine* 9 (December 1996): 26–30.

8. Bob Chance, "Ole Miss" (October 26, 1997), online: www.zebra.net/~bchance/rebel.html.

9. Joshua I. Newman, "Old Times There Are Not Forgotten: Sport, Identity, and the Confederate Flag in the Dixie South," *Sociology of Sport Journal* 24 (September 2007): 262.

10. The following is taken from several sources: Newman, "Old Times There Are Not Forgotten, 261–82; William Nack, "Look Away, Dixie Land," *Sports Illustrated*, November 3, 1997, p. 114; Douglas S. Lederman, "Old Times Not Forgotten: A Battle over Symbols," in *Sport in Contemporary Society*, ed. D. Stanley Eitzen, 6th ed. (New York: Worth, 2001), 109–14; and Paula Edelson, "Just Whistlin' Dixie," *Z Magazine* 4 (November 1991): 72–74.

11. Lederman, "Old Times Not Forgotten," 132.

12. Ray Franks, *What's in a Nickname? Exploring the Jungle of College Athletic Mascots* (Amarillo, Tex.: Ray Franks, 1982).

13. The names and mascots for schools used in this essay are taken from Ray Franks, *What's in a Nickname?* This comprehensive compilation of information, although dated, is the most current listing. Therefore, some of the schools named in the chapter may have subsequently changed the names of their athletic teams.

14. This section is taken primarily from: Laurel Davis, "Protest against the Use of Native American Mascots: A Challenge to Traditional American Identity," *Journal of Sport and Social Issues* 17 (April 1993): 9–22; Ward Churchill, "Crimes against Humanity," *Sport in Contemporary Society*, ed. D. Stanley Eitzen, 6th ed. (New York: Worth, 2001), 115–22; C. Richard King and Charles Fruehling Springwood, "Fighting Spirits: The Racial Politics of Sports Mascots," *Journal of Sport and Social Issues* 24 (August 2000): 282–304; Carol Spindel, *Dancing at Halftime: Sports and the Controversy over American Indian Mascots* (New York: New York University Press, 2000);

and a four-part series on Indian Mascots in the *Greeley Tribune* (Colorado), January 20–23, 2002.

15. Rick Telander, "These Nicknames, Symbols Should Offend All Americans," *Chicago Sun-Times*, October 20, 1995, p. 143.

16. Quoted in Bob Kravitz, "Aim of Native Americans' Protest Is True," *Rocky Mountain News*, January 21, 1992, p. 39.

17. *Indian Country Today*, August 8, 2001.

18. S. L. Price, "The Indian Wars," *Sports Illustrated*, March 4, 2002, pp. 64–72. For a critique of this *Sports Illustrated* article, see C. Richard King, Ellen J. Staurowsky, Lawrence Baca, Laurel R. Davis, and Cornel Pewewerdy, "Of Polls and Prejudice," *Journal of Sport and Social Issues* 26 (November 2002): 381–402.

19. Price, "Indian Wars," 69.

20. J. Wolburg, "The Demise of Native American Mascots: It's Time to Do the Right Thing," *The Journal of Consumer Marketing* 23.1 (2006): 4.

21. This section is based in part on D. Stanley Eitzen and Maxine Baca Zinn, "The De-athleticization of Women: The Naming and Gender Marking of Collegiate Sport Teams," *Sociology of Sport Journal* 6 (December 1989): 362–70; D. Stanley Eitzen and Maxine Baca Zinn, "The Sexist Naming of Athletic Teams and Resistance to Change," *Journal of Sport and Social Issues* 17 (April 1993): 34–41; D. Stanley Eitzen and Maxine Baca Zinn, "Never Mind the Braves; What about the Lady Rams?" *Baltimore Sun*, November 3, 1991, p. 3D; and D. Stanley Eitzen and Maxine Baca Zinn, "The Dark Side of Sports Symbols," *USA Today: The Magazine of the American Scene* 129 (January 2001), 48–51.

22. Barrie Thorne, Cheris Kramarae, and Nancy M. Henley, "Language, Gender, and Society: Opening a Second Decade of Research," in *Language, Gender, and Society*, ed. Barrie Thorne and Nancy M. Henley (Rowley, Mass.: Newbury House, 1985), 7–24; Nancy M. Henley, "This New Species That Seeks a New Language: On Sexism in Language and Language Change," in *Women and Men in Transition*, ed. Joyce Penfield (Albany: State University of New York Press, 1987), 3–27.

23. Eitzen and Baca Zinn, "Sexist Naming of Athletic Teams."

24. Casey Miller and Kate Swift, *The Handbook of Nonsexist Writing* (New York: Lippincott and Crowell, 1980), 87.

25. Miller and Swift, *Handbook of Nonsexist Writing*, 71.

26. Casey Miller and Kate Swift, *Words and Women: New Language in New Times* (Garden City, N.Y.: Doubleday-Anchor, 1977), 58.

27. Miller and Swift, *Words and Women*, 72.

28. Robin Lakoff, *Language and Woman's Place* (New York: Harper & Row, 1975), 25.

29. Miller and Swift, *Handbook of Nonsexist Writing*, 9.

30. Dale Spender, *Man Made Language* (London: Routledge and Kegan Paul, 1980), 3.

31. Dennis Baron, *Grammar and Gender* (New Haven, Conn.: Yale University Press, 1986), 112.

32. Fuller and Manning, "Violence and Sexism," 64.

33. Baron, *Grammar and Gender*, 115.

34. Quoted in Lois Tomas, "What's in a Name?" *In These Times*, October 19, 1997, p. 11.

35. Daniel P. Starr, "Unisex Nicknames One Way of Skirting Gender Problem," *NCAA News*, March 20, 1991, p. 4.

36. Maija S. Blaubergs, "An Analysis of Classic Arguments against Changing Sexist Language," *Women's Studies International Quarterly* 3 (1980): 135–47.

37. Association for Women in Psychology Ad Hoc Committee on Sexist Language, "Help Stamp Out Sexism: Change the Language!" *APA Monitor* 6.11 (1975): 16.

38. Sherryl Kleinman, "Why Sexist Language Matters," *Qualitative Sociology* 25.2 (2002): 299–304.

AP/Wide World

SPORT IS FAIR, SPORT IS FOUL

When the One Great Scorer comes
to write against your name—
He marks—not that you won or lost
—but how you played the game.

—Grantland Rice, sportswriter

Cheating is not merely countenanced in baseball, it is loved.

—John Thorn, baseball historian

Serious sport has nothing to do with fair play. It is bound up with
hatred, jealously, boastfulness, disregard of all the rules and sadistic
pleasure in witnessing violence; in other words it is war minus the
shooting.

—George Orwell, author

Winning isn't everything, it is the only thing.

—Vince Lombardi, coach

In 1940 Cornell won a football game with Dartmouth 7–3. A review of the films established that Cornell had received a fifth down on its winning drive. The Cornell coach and the university president left it up to the players to decide what to do. The Cornell players, faced with the ethical dilemma, awarded Dartmouth a 3–0 victory.

Fifty years later, the University of Colorado scored its winning touchdown against Missouri on a drive that included a fifth down that officials did not notice until after the game. Colorado refused to forfeit and at the conclusion of the season was declared national cochampion.

We celebrate sport for many good reasons. It excites and inspires us. We identify with athletic teams and our sports heroes. We savor the great moments of sport, when an athlete does the seemingly impossible or when the truly gifted athlete makes the impossible routine. We exult when a team or an athlete overcomes great odds to succeed. We are touched by genuine camaraderie among teammates. We are uplifted by the biographies of athletes who have used sport to get an education that otherwise would have been denied to them because of economic circumstances. Others have used sport to overcome delinquency and drug addiction.

Sport promotes fair play, and an ethical high road is sometimes taken. A month or so after Rockdale County (Georgia) won the state basketball championship in 1987, the coach, Cleveland Stroud, found that he had unknowingly used an ineligible player. Although the player in question was in the game for only a minute or two and had not scored, Stroud notified the authorities of the infraction. As a result, the school forfeited the only state championship it had ever won. Coach Stroud said, "You've got to do what's honest and right. People forget the scores of basketball games; they don't ever forget what you're made of."[1]

Fair play was also exhibited in a Colorado state high school Class A championship basketball game when Agate played Stratton. Because of a mix-up over keys, Agate was not able to dress in time for the game. The referees called a technical foul, allowing Stratton to begin the game with two free throws. The Stratton coach, feeling that this was unfair to his opponent, instructed his player to miss the shots. In a similar vein, Andy Herr of Bloomington, Indiana, chose to hold up and finish second in a 10K race in Toledo because the leader had accidentally taken a wrong turn.[2] This unwillingness to accept a tainted victory is found often in professional golf, when players call penalties on themselves, as Greg Norman did when he disqualified himself for a minor rule violation when leading a 1990 tournament. Tom Kite, playing in the 1993 Kemper Open, told his playing partner Grant Waite that Waite was about to commit a rules infraction that would result in a one-stroke penalty. Waite corrected his mistake and went on to beat Kite by one stroke. Kite's sportsmanship cost him about $100,000.[3] In the 2008 Master's Tournament two players called one-stroke penalties on themselves.

There are countless examples in sport of competitors showing respect for one another. In the 1995 Prefontaine Classic, the two-mile competition featured two premier runners, Bob Kennedy and Todd Williams. After a fierce battle (won by Kennedy), the two competitors embraced and then jogged a lap together. Winner Kennedy said, "We're friends but we were both racing to win, and we wound up taking each other to a higher level."[4] Or, consider the ethics of cyclists in the Tour de France. In 2003 Lance Armstrong, after overtaking the leaders, fell. The leaders, including Armstrong's main rival, Jan Ullrich, slowed to wait for Armstrong. Two years earlier Armstrong had done the same for Ullrich when he crashed. "It was proper for me to do what I did and proper for Jan to do what he did," Armstrong said. "I appreciate it"[5]

When Jake Porter was a player on the Northwest high school football team in McDermott, Ohio, because he was mentally challenged he had never run the ball in three years. His coach arranged with the visiting coach to let Jake play one play at the end of the game, just taking a knee. But the visiting coach told his players to let Jake run the ball and score a touchdown. Jake went in the game and scored with a forty-nine-yard run. "Imagine having 21 teammates on the field. In the stands mothers cried and fathers roared. Players on both sidelines held their helmets to the sky and whooped."[6]

But for all of the honor and integrity found in sport, there is also much about sport that disregards the ideals of fair play. The Colorado State University football team upset Louisiana State University in 1992. On CSU's winning drive there was a fumble. An LSU player fell on the ball, but in the ensuing pileup, a CSU player ended up with the ball illegally. The player, Geoff Grenier, was quoted in the newspaper as saying that he elbowed and kicked a player to get the ball. The referees did not see this action and awarded the ball to CSU. CSU coach Earle Bruce said, "One player who should get credit for the victory is Geoff Grenier. If we had lost the ball, the game was over. Geoff found a way to get the ball."[7]

THE DUALITY OF SPORT

A widely held assumption of parents, educators, banquet speakers, and editorial writers is that participating in sport prepares children and youth for success in a competitive society. According to folk wisdom, these young people will take on a number of desirable character traits from sport. They will learn to strive for excellence, to persevere, to sacrifice, to work hard, to follow orders, to work with others, and to be self-disciplined. But are these the lessons that young people actually learn from sport? The answer is complex and paradoxical. Philosopher Charles Banham has observed that many do benefit from the sports experience, but for many others, sport "encourages selfishness, envy, conceit, hostility, and bad temper. Far from ventilating the mind, it stifles it. Good sportsmanship may be a product of sport, but so is bad sportsmanship."[8]

Sport psychologist Terry D. Orlick also points to the contradictory nature of sport:

> For every positive psychological or social outcome in sports, there are possible negative outcomes. For example, sports can offer a child group membership or group exclusion, acceptance or rejection, positive feedback or negative feedback, a sense of accomplishment or a sense of failure, evidence of self-worth or a lack of evidence of self-worth. Likewise, sports can develop cooperation and a concern for others, but they can also develop an intense rivalry and a complete lack of concern for others.[9]

Thus there is a fundamental paradox in sport. On the one hand, sport inspires as it fosters the admirable traits of courage, determination, hard work, fairness, respect, sacrifice, selflessness, and loyalty. But sport also promotes rule breaking, selfishness, greed, contempt for opponents, and violence on the field as well as deviant behaviors off the field.

The Dark Side of Sport

Sport has a dark side. Big-time sport has corrupted academe by su-perseding academics, engaging in recruiting violations, and exploiting athletes (as elaborated in chapter 9). Coaches sometimes engage in outrageous behaviors such as brutalizing and publicly belittling their players. But if they win, they are rewarded handsomely (discussed in chapter 8). The media glorify gratuitous violence. Some athletes take drugs. Some athletes have been convicted of gang rape and spouse abuse. Many athletes cheat to achieve a competitive edge. Sports or-ganizations exploit athletes. Many believe that the problems in sport result from bad people. Others believe that the problems stem from a morally distorted sports world in which winning supersedes all other considerations and moral values have become confused with the bottom line. In this in-your-face, whip-your-butt climate, winning at any price has become the prevailing code of conduct.

Americans demand winners in school, business, politics, and sport.[10] Coaches are fired if they are not successful; teams are booed if they play for ties. Super Bowl losers are defined as losers, not as the second best team in professional football. A grotesque example of exalting first place and debasing second place is demonstrated by a football team composed of fifth-graders that was undefeated going into the Florida state cham-pionship game several years ago. They lost that game in a close contest. At a banquet for these boys following that season, each player was given a plaque on which was inscribed a quote from Vince Lombardi: "There is no room for second place. I have finished second twice at Green Bay and I never want to finish second again. . . . It is and always has been an American zeal to be first in anything we do and to win and to win and to win." The quote from Lombardi told the boys not to accept second place. Second is losing. The only permissible placement is first.

If second is unacceptable and all the rewards go to the winners, then some will do whatever it takes to be first. It may require using steroids or human growth hormone, trying to injure a competitor, altering a re-cruit's transcript so that he or she can play (illegally), or falsifying a birth certificate so that one might "qualify" to play at a younger age (such as in the case of Danny Almonte, who in 2001 played against twelve-year-olds in the Little League World Series, pitching a no-hitter, although later he was found to actually be fourteen years old). These unethical practices are an integral part of sport. This being the case, what lessons are being taught in the sports world? How is the character of athletes being shaped in the process?

The Debasement of Fair Play

The essence of sport is competition. The goal is to win. But to win ethically requires a spirit of fair play. Fairness tends to prevail in certain sports, such as golf; in other sports, the prevalent mood is to achieve an unfair advantage over an opponent. Unfairly gaining such a competitive edge is viewed by many in these sports as "strategy" rather than cheating. Thus some illegal acts are accepted as part of the game. In basketball, for example, it is common for a player to pretend to be fouled in order to receive an unmerited free throw and penalize the opponent with an undeserved foul. Commonly, rebounders nudge or shove their opponents out of position. About Dennis Rodman, the best rebounder in professional basketball at the time, *Sports Illustrated* said, "Like every successful rebounder, Rodman has certain tricks he uses to help him gain advantage. . . . He particularly likes to pin his opponent's arm between his own arm and his body, making it impossible for the opponent to jump. He gets called for this fairly often but not nearly as often as he gets away with it."[11]

In soccer it is common for a player to feign an injury "caused" by an opponent, hoping that an out-of-position official will award his team an undeserved penalty kick with a relatively high certainty of scoring.

Football players are often coached to use illegal techniques to hold or trip opponents without detection. Some offensive linemen grease their jerseys (an illegal act) so that blockers will have more difficulty holding them (another illegal act). To show how accepted these forms of cheating are, consider the commentary during an NFL game between the Denver Broncos and the Los Angeles Raiders. A replay showed that a Denver offensive lineman grabbed and held a defensive lineman. Upon seeing this blatant infraction of the rules, the sportscaster said, "It's only illegal if he gets caught."[12] Former professional football player Tim Green echoes this sentiment:

I don't know an NFL cornerback that doesn't consider bumping a receiver beyond the 5-yard chuck rule a matter of survival. And I'll confess that as a player I thought nothing of grabbing an opponent's jersey to complete a pass rush stunt but wasn't called for it once. You cheat to win, and because you can. Most illegal blocks, pass interference, holding and hands-to-the-face penalties go uncalled. In football, you're not wrong unless you're caught.[13]

According to Green, his former coach Jerry Glanville told his team each week, "If you ain't cheatin', you ain't trying."[14]

Pitchers in baseball sometimes achieve an illegal advantage by scuffing the ball or by putting a foreign substance (spit or Vaseline) on it so that it drops suddenly when pitched. Catchers sometimes help in this nefarious activity by doctoring the ball for their pitchers, using thumbtacks in their shin guards to rough up a ball or using Vaseline that was applied to their forearm. Batters counter by illegally corking their bats as Sammy Sosa did in 2004. Gaylord Perry, a Hall of Fame pitcher who won 314 games, said, "I became an outlaw in the strictest sense of the word—a man who lives outside the law, in this case the law of baseball. . . . A pitcher who can slick one up effectively has twice the advantage."[15] These vignettes reveal that the culture of some sports is to get a competitive advantage over the opponent even if it means taking an unfair advantage. When this occurs, sport is sending a message that winning is more important than playing fair.

Violence

Another area of concern has to do with normative violence. Many popular sports demand aggressive moves, such as body checking, blocking, and tackling, but the culture of these sports sometimes goes beyond what is needed to move or take down an opponent. Players are taught to deliver a blow to the opponent, not just to block or tackle him. They are taught to gang tackle, to make the ball carrier "pay the price." The assumption is that physically punishing the other player increases the probability of the opponent fumbling, losing his concentration, and executing poorly the next time, or being replaced by a less talented substitute.

Coaches sometimes reward athletes for extra hard hits. *Sports Illustrated* noted three types of helmet decals that were awarded at that time (1985). At Florida, a lineman receives a "dead roach" if he knocks his opponent so hard that he lies prone with his legs and arms in the air; at Wisconsin, the athlete receives a "decleater" when he stands up to "dee opponent and knocks him off dee cleats"; and at Miami, a player is awarded a "slobber knocker" if he hits an opposing player so hard that saliva is expelled from his mouth.[16] In the past, the Denver Broncos coaching staff (like other NFL teams yet contrary to league rules) gave monetary awards each week to the players who hit their opponents the hardest. In 1997 a Kansas City Chiefs player said on a radio show that coach Marty Schottenheimer offered to pay off any fines his team incurred for breaking the jaws of or knocking down any Denver player.[17] Unethical violence is such a part of the game that a Buffalo Bills player in a 1993 playoff game put a splint on the outside of his good leg so that opponents would concentrate on that leg rather than on his bad leg.

This emphasis on intimidating violence is almost universal among football and hockey coaches, players, and fans. The object is not just to hit but to punish and even to injure. The late sociologist Michael Smith argued that violence in hockey, as in war, is a socially rewarded behavior. The players are convinced that aggression (body checking, intimidation, and the like) is vital to winning.[18] Sportswriter John Underwood concludes that: "Brutality is its own fertilizer. From 'get by with what you can' it is a short hop to the deviations that poison sport. . . . But it is not just the acts that border on criminal that are intolerable, it is the permissive atmosphere they spring from. The 'lesser' evils that are given tacit approval as 'techniques' of the game, even within the rules."[19]

Drugs to Enhance Performance

Some athletes use drugs to increase their intensity, endurance, or strength despite the fact that they are illegal and entail harmful side effects (see chapter 5). The most commonly used drugs are anabolic steroids and human growth hormone, which make athletes bigger, stronger, and faster. Various studies have found that 7 percent of high school male athletes and 2.4 percent of high school female athletes use anabolic steroids, as do 15 percent of male college athletes and

6 percent of female college athletes. Former NFL players claim that up to 75 percent of the players in that league use or have used steroids (offensive and defensive lines and linebackers, who play the power positions in professional football, are the most likely to have used them). Elite athletes in weight lifting, body building, and weight throwing (shot put, discus, hammer, javelin) are almost required to take steroids if they want to be successful. Canadian weightlifter Jacques Demers explained why he felt it necessary to use steroids: "To go to international competitions, you have to meet international standards and those are based on what the Russians and Bulgarians do. They are the best weightlifters in the world . . . and they take steroids. So if I go to the Olympics, I must take steroids."[20]

The use of performance-enhancing drugs corrupts the essence of fair sporting competition—it is cheating. What lessons are being taught when some athletes (e.g., Barry Bonds, Marion Jones) take drugs, find ways to conceal their actions, and then are honored and rewarded handsomely for setting records and winning?

Disrespecting Opponents

Disrespect for opponents takes several forms. One is to humiliate a team by running up the score. Crushing an opponent is clearly evident in big-time college football, since scores affect team rankings, which, in turn, determine participation in bowl games (depending on the prestige of the bowl, teams receive anywhere from $150,000 to $17 million for playing). But humiliation of an opponent occurs at other levels as well. For example, a Laramie, Wyoming, girls' junior high school basketball team won a game by a score of 81–1, using a full-court press throughout the game. In 1997 Long Island University, a Division I school, played Medgar Evers College, a Division III school, and won by 117 points (179–62), the largest victory margin in NCAA history. Long Island pressed its hapless opponents for the entire game.[21] Similarly, in 2001 Camden (New Jersey) High School crushed Gloucester Township Technical 157–67, using full-court pressure and keeping their leading scorers in the game, with one scoring 100 points. On that same night in Texas, Heritage Christian Academy of Texas City defeated Banff Christian School by a score of 178–28, with one player scoring 101 points.

Another part of sport these days, not in golf but clearly in basketball at all levels, is trash talking, wherein one player talks to another player in an excessively boastful or scornful manner. This intimidating form of gamesmanship is tolerated by many coaches and is commonly practiced by players.[22] By definition, this practice does not promote mutual respect among competitors.

Spectators also show disrespect for opponents, even to the point of encouraging violence. They cheer an opponent's injury or engage in blood-lust cheers such as, "Kill! Kill! Hate! Hate! Murder! Murder! Mutilate!"

Sometimes fans try to distract opponents by yelling racial and other slurs. When Patrick Ewing played at Georgetown, he was confronted by T-shirts that said "Ewing Kant Read Dis," a banner at Providence College that read "Ewing Can't Read," and Villanova fans holding up a bedsheet with the words "Ewing Is an Ape."[23] Several years ago, Arizona State fans chanted "P-L-O" at Arizona's Steve Kerr, whose father had been assassinated by terrorists in Beirut.[24]

The Behavior of Coaches

Coaches are important role models for their athletes. Many coaches take this responsibility seriously, insisting on fair play, respect for opponents, and humane treatment of their athletes. Others cheat. Some have lied on their resumes, as did former Georgia Tech football coach and coach at Notre Dame (for five days), and current coach at Central Florida, George O'Leary, who in applying at Notre Dame claimed to have lettered at a college where he never played and to have a master's degree, which he never earned. Some deceive their players, fans, and employers by promising to remain as coach, yet all the while looking and often taking other opportunities. Some throw tantrums. Others discourage sportsmanship. Pat Riley, when coach of the Miami Heat professional basketball team, fined his players $1,500 if they helped an opposing player get off the floor. Some male coaches are sexist and homophobic, calling their male players "pussies" or "fags" if they are not aggressive enough. Bob Knight, while the coach at Indiana, for example, once put a tampon in the locker of a player as a means of letting him know that Knight thought he was a wimp.[25]

Because winning is so important, some coaches drive their athletes too hard, take them out of the classroom too often, and encourage them to use performance-enhancing drugs. They may also abuse their athletes physically and mentally. Verbal assaults by coaches are routine at all levels of sport (see chapter 7). *Newsweek* carried a mother's description of how one girl was treated by her Little League coach: "His narrowed eyes burn like hot little coals, and he screams through clenched teeth, his face thrust into hers. . . . She leans back a bit from time to time to avoid the spray of spit he spews as he spells it out for her: she's stupid, lazy and worthless, and if she doesn't shape up someone else will soon be doing her job."[26]

Coaches may encourage violence in their players. Green Bay Packers coach Vince Lombardi once said, "To play this game, you have to have that fire within you, and nothing stokes that fire like hate."[27] Some coaches whip their players into a frenzy that can lead to excessive violence. A North Carolina football coach tried to fire up his squad for their 1939 game with rival Wake Forest by mailing each of his players anonymous threatening letters. Mississippi State football coach Jackie Sherrill had a bull castrated in front of his players at the end of the last practice before they were to play the Texas Longhorns. A high school coach in Iowa, playing a team called the Golden Eagles, spray-painted a chicken gold and had his players stomp it to death in the locker room before the contest. Libertyville, Illinois, football coach Dale Christensen, during a pep talk prior to a state playoff game, tried to break up a fake fight he had arranged between two youths. Shots rang out from a starter pistol that fired blanks, and Christensen fell, with fake blood spreading across his shirt. Another coach bit off a toad's head in front of his players in an effort to motivate them to be more aggressive.

What lesson is a coach teaching when he openly asks a player to cheat? A few years ago, the Pretty Prairie (Kansas) High School basketball coach had twin boys on his team. One of the twins was injured but suited up for a game in which his brother was in foul trouble at halftime. The coach had the twins change jerseys so that the foul-plagued twin would begin the second half with no fouls charged to the player's number he was now wearing. A high school football coach in Portland sent a player into the game on a very foggy night. The player asked, "Who am

I going in for?" "No one," the coach replied, "the fog is so thick the ref will never notice you."[28]

Big-time college coaches are rewarded handsomely when they win. In addition to generous salary raises, successful college coaches receive lucrative contracts from shoe companies, endorsements, media deals, summer camps, speaking engagements, country club memberships, insurance annuities, and the like. With the potential income of college coaches sometimes exceeding $4 million at the highest levels, the temptations are great to offer illegal inducements to prospective athletes or to find illicit ways to keep them eligible (phantom courses, surrogate test-takers, altered transcripts). These scandals make a mockery of higher education and also make cynics of the so-called student-athletes (see chapter 9). These athletes know that they are athletes first and students second. They soon realize that winning is the important thing, not how they play the game.

Ethics and Administrative Decisions

College administrators are not always ethical when they hire and fire coaches strictly on their won-lost record. For the most part, school administrators do not fire coaches guilty of shady transgressions if they win.

Immorality is not just a matter of breaking or bending the rules—the rules themselves may be unfair or even immoral. Powerful organizations, such as universities, leagues, Little League baseball, and the International Olympic Committee, have denied equality to women and have exploited athletes. Until the mid-1970s, Little League, a baseball organization that operated twenty thousand leagues for children from eight to twelve years of age, had a males-only policy as part of its federal charter. Similarly, the International Olympic Committee banned women participants early in the twentieth century and then relented, allowing them to participate in nonendurance events. Many professional leagues, historically, had whites-only clauses (e.g., major league baseball, NFL, Professional Golf Association, American Bowling Congress). Informally, there remain racial barriers in automobile racing and leadership (coaching and administrative roles) throughout sports.

The exploitation of athletes is exemplified by the rules of the NCAA, which are consistently unfair to college athletes. NCAA rules require that athletes commit to a four-year agreement with a school, yet schools make only a year-by-year commitment to athletes. This means that players can lose their scholarships at the whim of their coaches, yet they cannot move to another school without waiting a year before they are eligible to play (two years if the coach does not formally approve of the player's transfer). This rule ties the athlete to the school even if the new recruit has not started school and the coach who signed him has left the school. Full-ride scholarship athletes in the revenue-producing sports of men's basketball and football receive room, board, tuition, and books while generating millions of dollars; their coaches make many hundreds of thousands, sometimes millions. The players in big-time programs must wonder about the fairness of such a system.

Disloyalty

One of the traits that sport hopes to transmit to its participants is loyalty—allegiance to teammates, coaches, school, fans, and locality. But loyalty is becoming passé in sport. College coaches often exhibit an absence of loyalty by breaking one contract to coach elsewhere; unlike players who move, they are eligible to coach immediately. A few athletes repeal their commitment to their school by leaving to play at the professional level before their eligibility expires.

Problems with loyalty are even greater at the professional level. With free agency, professional athletes usually follow the money, leaving behind their teammates and fans. As a result, the average major league baseball player changes teams every 3.3 years; only 13 percent of the players play for the same teams they did four years ago.[29] Greed in sport is more obvious when owners of profitable professional teams move their franchises to other cities for lucrative financial packages (see chapter 11). The Cleveland Browns' move to Baltimore is an especially egregious example of callous disregard for the longtime bond between a team and its fans. This and other franchise moves, real or threatened, show the bottom-line mentality in sport that makes loyalty an outmoded concept.

CONSEQUENCES FROM THE LESSONS LEARNED

Given the contradictions found in sport, the consequences are not uniform for all participants. Sociologist Jay Coakley argues that (1) sports can be constructed in different ways in different situations; (2) people who participate in sports can have a variety of different experiences; and (3) sport experiences take on different meanings, depending on the circumstances and relationships associated with participation. Coakley concludes that "Neither good nor bad socialization outcomes occur automatically in connection with sport participation. In fact, the impact of all our experiences in sports is mediated by the social and cultural context in which we live."[30] With this important caveat in mind, let's examine three areas of concern regarding the effects of sports participation: (1) the behavior of athletes off the field, (2) the moral development of athletes, and (3) the possibility of character building through sport.

Athletes and Off-the-Field Deviance

Research comparing high school athletes with their nonathletic peers shows consistently that athletes are less likely to be adjudicated for delinquency.[31] This finding, however, does not prove that sports participation reduces the likelihood of delinquency. There are two major reasons for this. First, delinquency-prone individuals very likely do not try out for athletic teams, or if they do, they are likely to be cut from teams because they do not conform to the coach's orders or team norms. Second, athletes may receive preferential treatment, which keeps them out of the courts when they get in trouble. Thus it is difficult to say whether high school athletes are any more or less deviant than their peers of comparable backgrounds.

Media accounts seem to indicate that college and professional athletes are more prone than nonathletes of the same age and social class to engage in assault, domestic violence, rape, recreational drugs, stealing, and other forms of deviance. There is an obvious problem with interpreting these incidents because the deviant behaviors of high-profile athletes are much more likely to be publicized than similar acts by noncelebrities. Nevertheless, a strong case can be made that male athletes in football and basketball are overrepresented in crimes, especially sexual assaults (see chapter 9).[32]

What might account for male athletes being more likely than nonathletes to engage in criminal behaviors? There are several possible explanations. First, male athletes at the highest levels are different from their nonathletic male peers. They are bigger, stronger, and more aggressive because sport, at least the aggressive kind, is the result of a selection process that selects for aggressive, risk-taking, dominant personalities. They are expected to act aggressively on the field. Can this macho persona be turned off for other social settings? This is especially difficult for athletes when they are verbally abused in bars and other settings (for example, African American athletes are commonly subjected to racial slurs). Second, like military units, youth gangs, and college fraternities, athletic teams foster a spirit of exclusivity, camaraderie, and solidarity. The result is a prolonged adolescence and an exaggerated male bonding that celebrates male dominance, physical and verbal aggression, and daring behaviors and accords them status.[33]

This male world, epitomized by the locker room, has been studied by sociologist Timothy Jon Curry. He found that the talk among athletes focused on aggression and on women as objects, taking the form of loud, profane performances for other men.[34] As Mariah Burton Nelson says, "The locker room is a place where men discuss women's bodies in graphic sexual terms, where they boast about 'scoring' and joke about beating women."[35] Thus the athletic subculture that emerges actually legitimizes rape and aggression in general.

Third, the celebrity status of athletes results in preferential and deferential treatment. They receive special treatment that exempts them from the rules that others must follow. This results in a sense of entitlement—a sense that they can take anything they want without asking, including sex. Ken Dryden, Hall of Fame goalie who is now a lawyer, says, "It's really a sense of power that comes from specialness, reputation, money, whether it's an athlete, businessman, or entertainer—anyone who finds himself at the center of the world they're in has a sense of impunity."[36]

According to Jeff Benedict, no fewer than 112 college athletes were charged with sexual assault or incidents of domestic violence during

1995 and 1996. Yet few have been successfully prosecuted, much less jailed for these crimes. According to Benedict, this is how it works: "Often in packs, like wolves on a deer, college and pro athletes bring down a woman as they would sack a quarterback, play with her, physically hurt her and then toss her away. Should she complain, the college or pro team pays for a lawyer whose standard ploy is to contrast the popularity and value of the defendant with the contemptible star-chasing sexuality of the victim."[37]

Benedict's research led him to conclude that professional athletes have, as a result of their profession, undergone a socialization process which, in addition to stripping away virtually all off-the-field accountability, churns out an image of women as sexually compliant. Because of the availability of sex partners and the casualness of their encounters, athletes ultimately have problems distinguishing between force and consent.[38]

Steroid use is a fourth reason for the disproportionate number of athletes involved in cases of sexual aggression. Research shows that aggressiveness and a heightened sexual drive are among the side effects of anabolic steroid use.[39] These characteristics are chemically induced, but they also result from the "steroid culture" that values physicality.

Although athletes are disproportionately guilty of crimes and sexual aggression, only a relatively small number of athletes are involved. Thus sports participation does not cause sexual aggression in the vast majority of athletes. Yet it seems reasonable that sport does contribute to the aberrant behavior of a few.

Moral Development

The "winning-at-all-costs" philosophy pervades sport at every level and leads to cheating by coaches and athletes, the dehumanization of athletes, and their alienation from themselves and their competitors. Under these conditions, it is not surprising that research consistently reveals that sport stifles moral reasoning and moral development.

From 1987 to the present, physical educators Sharon Stoll and Jennifer Beller have studied over ten thousand athletes from the ninth grade through college. Their findings include the following:[40]

1. Athletes score lower than their nonathlete peers on moral development.
2. Male athletes score lower than female athletes in moral development. However, the average score for female athletes has been declining over the past few years.
3. Moral reasoning scores for athletic populations steadily decline from the ninth grade through university age, whereas scores for nonathletes tend to increase.

This last point is significant: The longer individuals participate in sport, the less able they are to reason morally. According to Stoll and Beller, "While sport does build character if defined as loyalty, dedication, sacrifice, and teamwork, it does not build moral character in the sense of honesty, responsibility, and justice."[41]

Not only is the length of time in sport relevant but so, too, is the level. That is, athletes at the Division I level in college are less ethical than those at Division III. In this regard, a recent survey by the Men's and Women's College Basketball Coaches Association produced the following results:[42]

1. In response to the statement "My teammates would expect me to cheat if it meant the difference in winning a game," 46.7 percent of Division I men agreed, compared to 26.6 percent of Division III men.
2. In response to the statement "Trash talking is an acceptable part of being competitive," 45.9 percent of Division I men agreed, compared to 31.4 percent of Division III men.

The unethical practices so common in sport have negative consequences for the participants. Gresham's law would seem to apply to sport—bad morality tends to defeat good morality; unfairness tends to encourage unfairness. Sociologist Melvin Tumin's principle of "least significant morality" also makes this point:

In any social group, the moral behavior of the group as an average will tend to sink to that of the least moral participant, and the least moral participant will, in that sense, control the group unless he is otherwise restrained and/or expelled. . . . Bad money may not always drive out good money, though it almost always does. But 'bad' conduct surely drives out 'good' conduct with predictable vigor and speed.[43]

The irony, as sport psychologists Brenda Jo Bredemeier and David Shields have pointed out, is that many athletes, coaches, and fans believe that "to be good in sports, you have to be bad."[44] You must take unfair advantage and be overly aggressive if you want to win. The implications of this are significant. Moral development theorists agree that the fundamental structure of moral reasoning remains relatively stable from situation to situation. When coaches and athletes corrupt the ideals of fair play in their zeal to succeed, they are likely to employ or condone similar tactics outside sport. They might accept the necessity of dirty tricks in politics, the manipulation of foreign governments for our benefit, and business practices that include using misleading advertising and selling shoddy and/or harmful products. The ultimate goal in politics, business, and sport, after all, is to win. And winning may require moving outside the established rules. Unfortunately, this lesson is learned all too often in sport.

Does Sport Build Character?

Is there proof for the assertion that sports participation builds character? Studies comparing male athletes and male nonathletes (few studies compare women) yield little evidence to support the idea that sport is necessary for complete and adequate socialization or that involvement in sport results in character-building moral development, good citizenship, or valued personality traits. Athletes and nonathletes are comparable on various personality traits and value orientations. Sports participation has no general effect on self-image—it does not reduce prejudice; it is not necessary for leadership development; and it does not enhance social adjustment.[45]

The widespread conclusion by sport sociologists is that when an apparent socialization effect is found, it is actually the result of a selection process that attracts and retains children and youth in sport who already have or are comfortable with the values and behavioral traits that coaches demand and that lead to success in sport.[46] Those without these desired values and traits either show no interest in sport or leave sport voluntarily (i.e., they drop out) or involuntarily (i.e., they are removed by coaches). In other words, young people who have such traits as perseverance, achievement orientation, a hard work ethic, and obedience to authority do well in sport when compared to those who are not as strong on these attitudinal and behavioral traits. After studying more than sixty thousand athletes at all levels, sports psychologists Thomas Tutko and Bruce Ogilvie concluded:

> We found no empirical support for the tradition that sport builds character. Indeed, there is evidence that athletic competition limits growth in some areas. It seems that the personality of the ideal athlete is not the result of any molding process, but comes out of the ruthless selection process that occurs at all levels of sport. Athletic competition has no more beneficial effects than intense endeavor in any other field. Horatio Alger success—in sport or elsewhere—comes only to those who already are mentally fit, resilient and strong.[47]

In effect, then, sports participation does not build character, discipline, self-esteem, and other achievement-related qualities in young men and women. Rather, it provides an outlet for those already imbued with these positive traits. As this chapter points out, the opposite occurs. That is, athletes (not all, but many) learn bad sportsmanship and engage in various forms of cheating to gain an edge over opponents.

Matthew Goodman notes a fundamental contradiction of sport that negatively affects character development:

> The very qualities a society tends to seek in its heroes—selflessness, social consciousness, and the like—are precisely the opposite of those needed to transform a talented but otherwise unremarkable neighborhood kid into a Michael Jordan or a Joe Montana. Becoming a star athlete requires a profound and long-term self-absorption, a single-minded attention to the development of a few rather odd physical skills, and an overarching competitive outlook. These qualities may well make a great athlete, but they don't necessarily make a great person.[48]

ENNOBLING SPORT

Sport has the potential to ennoble its participants. Athletes strain, strive, and sacrifice to excel. But if sport is to exalt the human spirit, it must

be practiced within a context guided by fairness and humane considerations. Sports competition is great, but it can go too far. It has gone too
far when a coach fines his players for helping a competitor off the floor.
Competition has gone too far when a high school league in Southern
California eliminates the mandatory postgame handshake because trash
talking in the handshake line leads to shoving and fistfights.[49] Competition has gone too far when the quest to win corrupts organizations,
coaches, and players.

Sport teaches and participants learn. But the current sports climate is
teaching disrespect for opponents and the use of unfair means to trump
those who play by the rules. When moral boundaries are trampled,
then sport, instead of achieving its ennobling potential, has the contrary
effect. If sport is to achieve its promise, then those involved must be
guided by the fundamental premise that to win by breaking the rules
and the spirit of fair play is not really winning at all.

NOTES

1. Quoted in Rick Reilly, "Too Many Spoilsports: The World Seems Over-
run by Athletes, Coaches and Fans Eager to Take the Best Out of Our Games,"
Sports Illustrated, January 1, 1993, p. 68.

2. Reilly, "Too Many Spoilsports," 68.

3. Jeff Thoreson, "The Integrity of Golf," *The World & I* 11 (July 1996):
311.

4. Quoted in *Sports Illustrated*, June 8, 1995, p. 43.

5. Quoted in Sal Ruibal, "Armstrong Stumbles, Pulls Away," *USA Today*,
July 22, 2003, p. 9C.

6. Rick Reilly, "The Play of the Year," *Sports Illustrated*, November 18,
2002, p. 108.

7. Quoted in Jim Benton, "Bruce Says Upset Saved by Grenier," *Rocky
Mountain News*, October 2, 1992, p. 3C. For a number of examples of good and
bad sportsmanship, see the three-part series "The Changing Face of Sportsmanship," *The Boston Globe*, December 28–30, 2001.

8. Charles Banham, "Man at Play," *Contemporary Review* 207 (August
1965): 62.

9. Terry D. Orlick, "The Sports Environment: A Capacity to Enhance—A
Capacity to Destroy" (paper presented at the Canadian Symposium of Psycho-
Motor Learning and Sports Psychology, 1974), p. 2.

10. Robert H. Franks and Philip J. Cook, *The Winner-Take-All Society* (New York: Free Press, 1995); William McGowan, "The Hustle-Butt Society," *Business and Society Review* 61 (Spring 1987): 52–54.

11. Phil Taylor, "Tricks of the Trade," *Sports Illustrated*, March 4, 1996, p. 36.

12. NBC Sports broadcast, December 11, 1994.

13. Tim Green, "Cheating to Win Is Rule of Thumb for Teams' Survival," *USA Today*, November 6, 1997, p. 4C, emphasis added.

14. Green, "Cheating to Win," 4C.

15. Quoted in Ira Berkow, "A Spitter, a Hustler and the Hall of Fame," *New York Times*, July 28, 1991, p. 26.

16. *Sports Illustrated*, September 4, 1985, p. 29.

17. Adam Schefter, "Chiefs Players Confirm What the Coach Won't," *Denver Post*, November 22, 1997, p. 7C.

18. Michael D. Smith, *Violence in Sport* (Toronto: Butterworths, 1983).

19. John Underwood, *Spoiled Sport* (Boston: Little, Brown, 1984), 85.

20. Quoted in Skip Rozin, "Steroids: A Spreading Peril," *Business Week*, June 19, 1995, p. 177.

21. "179–62 Score Raises Eyebrows," *Denver Post*, November 28, 1997, p. 14C.

22. Phil Taylor, "'Crackin', Jackin', Woofin' and Smackin'," *Sports Illustrated*, November 23, 1992, pp. 83–85; Mark Starr, "Yakety-Yak: Do Talk Back," *Newsweek*, December 21, 1992; Phil Taylor, "Flash and Trash," *Sports Illustrated*, May 30, 1994, pp. 20–22; and Peter Brewington, "Sportsmanship: Rulemakers Blow Whistle on Taunting," *USA Today*, March 7, 1995, pp. 1C–2C.

23. Leslie Visser, "Indecencies Ewing Faces Shouldn't Be Tolerated," *Denver Post*, February 14, 1983, p. 5F.

24. Reilly, "Too Many Spoilsports."

25. Rick Telander, "Not a Shining Knight," *Sports Illustrated*, May 9, 1988, p. 122.

26. Rosemary Parker, "Learning by Intimidation?" *Newsweek*, November 8, 1993, p. 14.

27. Quoted in Jerry Kramer, ed., *Lombardi: Winning Is the Only Thing* (New York: Pocket Books, 1970), x.

28. John E. Vawter, letter to the editor, *Sports Illustrated*, February 6, 1989, p. 4.

29. Erik Brady, "Big Money, Big Trades Changing Face of the Game," *USA Today*, July 2, 1998, p. 1A.

30. Jay J. Coakley, *Sport in Society: Issues and Controversies*, 8th ed. (New York: McGraw-Hill, 2004), 109.

31. See, for example, Jeffrey O. Segrave, "Do Organized Sports Programs Deter Delinquency?" *Journal of Physical Education, Recreation and Dance* 57.1 (1986): 16–17.

32. See, for example, Todd W. Crosset, James Ptacek, Mark A. McDonald, and Jeffrey R. Benedict, "Male Student-Athletes and Violence against Women," *Violence against Women* 2 (June 1996): 163–79.

33. John W. Loy, "The Dark Side of Agon: Fratriarchies, Performative Masculinities, Sport Involvement, and the Phenomenon of Gang Rape," *International Sociology of Sport: Contemporary Issues*, ed. Karl-Heinrich Bette and Alfred Rutten (Stuttgart: Verlag Stephanie Naglschmid, 1995), 263–81; Jill Neimark, "Out of Bounds: The Truth about Athletes and Rape," *Mademoiselle*, May 1991, pp. 196–99, 244–46; David Leon Moore, "Athletes and Rape: Alarming Link," *USA Today*, August 27, 1991, pp. 1C–2C; Jeff Benedict, *Public Heroes, Private Felons* (Boston: Northeastern University Press, 1997); and Jeff Benedict and Don Yaeger, *Pros and Cons: The Criminals Who Play in the NFL* (New York: Warner Books, 1998).

34. Timothy Jon Curry, "Fraternal Bonding in the Locker Room: A Profeminist Analysis of Talk about Competition and Women," *Sociology of Sport Journal* 8 (June 1991): 119–35. See also Timothy Jon Curry, "Beyond the Locker Room: Campus Bars and College Athletes," *Sociology of Sport Journal* 15.3 (1998): 205–15.

35. Mariah Burton Nelson, "Bad Sports," *New York Times*, June 22, 1994, p. 11A. See also Janet Singleton, "Athletes and Abuse: Is Spirit Grown in Locker Room?" *Denver Post*, March 9, 1995, pp. 1E–2E; and Ian O'Conner, "Male Locker Room Has Long Way to Go," *USA Today*, July 25, 2001, p. 3C.

36. Quoted in Gerald Eskenazi, "When Athletic Aggression Turns into Sexual Assault," *New York Times*, June 3, 1990, pp. 27, 30.

37. Quoted in Robert Lipsyte, "Violence, Redemption and the Cost of Sports," *New York Times*, October 19, 1997, p. 30Y. See Jeffrey R. Benedict, "Colleges Must Act Decisively When Scholarship Athletes Run Afoul of the Law," *The Chronicle of Higher Education*, May 9, 1997, pp. 6B–7B; and Jeffrey R. Benedict and Alan Klein, "Arrest and Conviction Rates for Athletes Accused of Sexual Assault," *Sociology of Sport Journal* 14.1 (1997): 86–94.

38. Quoted in Robert Lipsyte, "Many Create the Climate for Violence," *New York Times*, June 18, 1995, p. 21.

39. See the National Institute of Mental Health study reported in Doug Levy, "Steroid Mood Effect 'Dramatic,'" *USA Today*, June 2, 1993, p. 1A; study found in the *Journal of the American Medical Association*, reported in "Teen-Age Steroid Users Likely to Be Aggressive"; Steve Woodward, "Steroids: A Dose of Danger," *USA Today*, April 6, 1989, p. 10C; and John R. Fuller and

Marc J. LaFountain, "Performance-Enhancing Drugs in Sport: A Different Form of Drug Abuse," *Adolescence* 22 (1987): 969–76.

40. Jennifer M. Beller, personal communication with author, April 9, 1993. See Jennifer M. Beller and Sharon Kay Stoll, "Sportsmanship: An Antiquated Concept?" *Journal of Physical Education, Recreation and Dance* 64 (August 1993): 74–79.

41. Beller, personal communication.

42. Reported in "Attitude," *Sports Illustrated*, May 12, 1997, p. 23.

43. Melvin Tumin, "Business as a Social System," *Behavioral Science* 9.2 (1964): 127.

44. Brenda Jo Bredemeier and David L. Shields, "Values and Violence in Sports Today," *Psychology Today* 19.10 (1985): 22.

45. For a summary, see James H. Frey and D. Stanley Eitzen, "Sport and Society," *Annual Review of Sociology* 17 (1991): 503–22.

46. For summaries by sociologists of the arguments in the character-building debate, see especially George H. Sage, *Power and Ideology in American Sport*, 2nd ed. (Champaign, Ill.: Human Kinetics, 1998), chap. 9; and Coakley, *Sport in Society*, chap. 4.

47. Bruce C. Ogilvie and Thomas A. Tutko, "Sport: If You Want to Build Character, Try Something Else," *Psychology Today* 5 (October 1971): 61.

48. Matthew Goodman, "Where Have You Gone, Joe DiMaggio," *Utne Reader* 57 (May–June 1993): 103.

49. E. M. Swift, "Give Young Athletes a Fair Shake: When We Eliminate Postgame Handshakes, We Fail to Teach the Main Lesson of Sports," *Sports Illustrated*, May 2, 1994, p. 76.

5

SPORT IS HEALTHY, SPORT IS DESTRUCTIVE

What I miss most [about playing football] is the violence.

—Dick Butkis, Hall of Fame linebacker

Pitcher Curt Shilling thinks twice before giving a teammate the traditional slap on the butt for a job well done. "I'll pat guys on the ass, and they'll look at me and go, 'Don't hit me there man. It hurts.' That's because that's where they shoot the steroid needles."

—Quoted in *Sports Illustrated*, June 3, 2002

BENEFITS OF SPORTS

The exercise required of sports participants is good for them. It promotes coordination, stamina, strength, strong bones, joint flexibility, and heart and lung capacity. Exercise diminishes the ill effects of diseases such as diabetes. It reduces hypertension (high blood pressure), lowers bad cholesterol, and raises good cholesterol. Physical activity is an important part of controlling weight. Without exercise, bones become brittle, muscles atrophy (including the heart muscle), the efficiency of blood circulation diminishes, plaque in the arteries builds up rapidly, and the aging process accelerates. The positive effects of physical exercise cannot be denied. The health benefits of exercise are the motive for requiring physical education and sports programs in schools, youth sports, community adult recreation, and corporation-sponsored sports teams.

Sports and Women's Health

As an example of the health benefits of sport, let's examine the consequences of participation for girls and women. Until recently, the commonly held assumption was that certain types of sports participation were harmful to the health of females. Physical exertion and the encouragement of aggressive behavior were seen as the main culprits. As a result, historically women were not permitted to run, swim, or cycle long distances. Girls' basketball teams were divided into offensive and defensive players, who played one end of the court only and were limited to no more than two dribbles at a time to minimize physical effort. The title of an article chronicling the history of women's sport captures the reason for not permitting girls and women to engage in strenuous activities: "Nice Girls Don't Sweat."[1]

Young girls were channeled into sports that emphasized graceful movement (diving, gymnastics, and ice skating) and limited physical contact with opponents. The most popular women's sports often separated the athletes by a net (tennis, badminton, volleyball). According to sociologist Nancy Theberge, "Women have been discouraged or prevented from participating in sport by a complementary set of exclusionary practices and cultural ideals that viewed them as fragile and unsuited to strenuous physical activity."[2]

Since the 1970s, these barriers to participation in all types of sports have weakened. The numbers of women participants in high school sports, college sports, and adult running and fitness activities have risen dramatically. From 1970, the participation of girls in high school sports has increased from one in twenty-seven to less than one in three. Along with this dramatic increase in sports participation have come important health benefits for girls and women.

Traditionally, it was widely assumed that women do not have the mental toughness for athletic competition and that such activities damage them psychologically. Research shows this belief to be a myth. Theberge has summarized the demythologizing findings.[3] Compared to nonathletes, female athletes are more achievement-motivated, independent, poised, and inner-controlled. They have higher self-confidence, higher energy levels, better health, and a general well-being. They have more positive attitudes toward life, more positive psychological well-being (in good spirits, satisfied with life, happy), and a more positive body image. In addition, current research shows that regular and strenuous exercise results in a lower lifelong risk of breast cancer.

Research also shows that when teenage girls involved in sport are compared with teenage nonathletes, the athletes are less likely to drop out of school, smoke cigarettes, and use illicit drugs, and are more likely to be virgins. If sexually active, they are more likely to have begun intercourse at a later age, to engage in sex less often, and to have fewer sex partners, as well as being less likely to become pregnant.[4] A likely explanation for these differences is that sport may provide girls with the self-esteem necessary to ward off peer pressure to have sex and to use illicit drugs.[5]

THE DESTRUCTIVE ASPECTS OF SPORT

Running, jumping, lifting, throwing, swimming, skiing, skating, cycling, rowing, and calisthenics enhance the physical and emotional health of female and male participants. But athletes can also be injured during these sporting activities. Behind the popular myth that sport is a healthy activity is the reality that many aspects of sport are unhealthy—physical injuries, mental abuse from coaches or parents, drugs, eating disorders, overtraining, and even the sexual abuse of athletes by authorities. These latent tragedies of sport are its dark side, often hidden from view. Because they usually do not make the headlines of the sports section, they are emphasized here. Let's begin with injuries that occur in the normal course of engaging in a sport, followed by drug use and dietary dangers. The next chapter will explore emotional damage to child athletes and the sexual abuse of girls and women.

Sports Injuries

Football is a collision sport. The average National Football League player will take 130,000 full-speed hits over a seven-year period.[6] In a typical season, about one-fifth of NFL players will be hurt seriously enough to miss at least one game. "I hate to say it," says Barry Sanders, the former Detroit Lions' superb—and relatively durable—running back, "but one of the first things you notice in this league is how steadily people step in and out of the lineup because of injuries. After a while you hardly notice it anymore. You just go on."[7] Injuries are part of that sport, and the sprains, muscle tears, broken bones, and concussions that the players endure may have lasting physical consequences. Surely that will be the case of former Denver Bronco guard Mark Schlereth, who has had twenty-nine surgeries, including a combined twenty on his knees. "Routine actions become mission impossible. Schlereth cannot bend down to line up a putt. He cannot bend down to catch when his son, Daniel, tries to pitch to him. He cannot sleep through a night without waking up as many as a dozen times because his knee hurts, his back aches, or his body throbs."[8] A 1990 study commissioned by the NFL Players Association surveyed 870 ex-players and found that nearly two-thirds had a permanent disability from football.[9] The problem, of course, is also found at the high school and collegiate levels. In 2004, for example, the Colorado State University football team had seventeen players that required surgery.

Team doctors and trainers may compound the injury problem. Prescribing painkillers that allow players to participate before they are physically ready can lead to a greater likelihood of permanent damage. Yet athletes may insist on this because they (1) are socialized to accept pain and injury as part of the game and to "play hurt"; (2) fear losing a starting position or even a place on the team; (3) want to keep their careers going as long as possible; (4) feel the pressure of teammates or coaches to play; or (5) want to sacrifice themselves for the good of the team. Team doctors may also inject painkillers such as Novocaine, cortisone, or anti-inflammatories because their primary task is to keep players on the field, not in the training room. These doctors and trainers are in a bind between doing what is medically appropriate for a player and doing what benefits their employer.[10] Hall of Fame linebacker Dick Butkis was given cortisone and other drugs by the Chicago Bears' team doctor during the last two years of his career to deaden the pain in his knees. Butkis argued that the doctor had put the short-term needs of the team over his long-term health. He sued for $1.6 million and received $600,000 in an out-of-court settlement.

Serious injuries in football are increasing. This is because the players are getting bigger without sacrificing speed. Using the Pittsburgh Steelers as the example, in 1964 the offensive line averaged 241 pounds. This increased to 260 pounds in 1980 and 309 pounds in 2004. Similarly, the defensive line increased from 255 in 1964 to 305 pounds in 2004.[11] This increase in mass results in not only greater collisions but also in too much weight on the joints, especially the ankle and knee. Moreover, according to a *New England Journal of Medicine* report, primarily because of their large size, NFL football players are five times more likely than other men their age to suffer from sleep apnea, which can lead to heart disease and stroke.[12]

Sports injuries are not limited to contact sports (football, rugby, hockey, wrestling, and boxing). Sociologist Howard Nixon surveyed nearly two hundred male and female athletes in eighteen varsity sports at an NCAA Division I school. Nixon found that over 75 percent reported sustaining significant injuries, and nearly all of those had played while hurt. Also, over 45 percent experienced long-term effects from these injuries.[13]

Sport poses special dangers to young bodies, including Little League elbow, tennis elbow, gymnast's back, swimmer's shoulder, ligament tears, shin splints, and stress fractures (see the next chapter).[14]

Athletes of any age who train seriously every day year-round engage in what sport sociologists call "positive deviance." This concept refers to "cases of conformity that are so intense, extensive, or extreme that they go beyond the conventional boundaries of behavior. They are cases of overconformity rather than counterconformity, but they are deviant because of their extreme nature." Positive deviants in sport take the sport ethic to the extreme—subordinating other interests for the sake of sport, being dedicated to becoming number one, accepting risk and playing through pain, and believing that there are no limits for someone who is dedicated enough.[15] Athletes who aspire to stardom as swimmers, distance runners, bodybuilders, cyclists, and triathletes often are positive deviants. They follow this ethic without question to the point of risking their own safety and well-being. This may lead to self-injurious overtraining, eating disorders, rigid training schedules, uncritical commitment to playing through pain and injury, and problems with family relationships and school and work responsibilities.

Intensive sports training has detrimental effects for both males and females, but it creates some special health dangers for women. The most prominent is amenorrhea (cessation of menstrual function without menopause). This condition occurs when rigorous training causes the body to stop producing the hormones that make estrogen. Without the normal amount of estrogen, irregularities in the menstrual cycle occur, which results in a lack of bone density and, if left untreated, osteoporosis and a relatively high susceptibility to fractures.[16]

Drug Use

Athletes use restorative drugs, such as painkillers, anti-inflamma-tories, and muscle relaxants, to help them overcome injuries. Used properly, with adequate time to restore health before vigorous exercise, these drugs are helpful. They may, however, as noted before, be used to return athletes to play before their bodies are healthy, leading to long-term health problems. Athletes may use other drugs, such as alcohol, marijuana, and cocaine, to mask pain or to help them deal with anxiety and stress. There are dangers in using these drugs, among them drug dependency. Also, these drugs can lead to problems with the criminal justice system (underage drinking, possession, and, perhaps, the mar-keting of a banned substance), jail time, and a criminal record.

A more important drug issue is athletes' use of additive drugs, espe-cially drugs that improve performance. Some examples are beta blockers (used by golfers, archers, and those in the shooting sports), which slow down the heart, steady the nerves, and calm performance anxiety, and so-called brake drugs, such as cyproterone acetate, that delay puberty (used by female gymnasts and ice skaters). Human growth hormones increase strength and size (weight lifters, football linemen); amphet-amines get players fired up and keep them stimulated and aggressive (football and rugby players). Prescription drugs are also misused. Ap-proximately 10 percent of the population has some degree of asthma, but 60 percent of Olympic athletes use a prescription drug for asthma, presumably not because they have asthma but because it increases the lung capacity for endurance athletes.[17] Similarly, in 2007 some 103 major league baseball players, four times as many as in 2006, sought "therapeutic exemptions" that would allow them to take controlled substances such as Ritalin and Adderall. These are drugs used for ADD (attention deficit disorder). *USA Today* editorialized that since ADD is not contagious, the players may be faking a medical condition to get around the ban on amphetamines that went into effect in 2006.[18] The hormone erythropoietin (EPO) is chosen by endurance athletes, such as distance runners and cyclists, because it stimulates the production of red blood cells, thereby increasing the oxygen-carrying capacity of the blood. Anabolic steroids, along with human growth hormone, constitute the most commonly abused performance-enhancing drugs used by athletes. Most recently, clandestine laboratories have created a steroid, called "Clear," that cannot be detected by current methods.

There are also dangerous practices that increase athletic performance. Female endurance athletes, for example, can get pregnant in order to have an abortion to benefit from the natural increase in certain hormones. Wrestlers and boxers use diuretics for weight loss to compete at lower weight classes, and drug-using athletes often use diuretics to minimize detection of other drugs by diluting the urine. Blood doping (removing a pint of blood, allowing the blood volume to return to normal, and then transfusing the blood back into the blood supply in order to enhance the body's oxygen-carrying capacity) is thought to increase fitness by as much as 20 percent. In a fit, elite athlete, blood doping appears to add 1 to 3 percent, which translates into running a 1,500-meter race three seconds faster than would be possible without the extra oxygen-carrying blood.

There are legal nutritional supplements that increase performance. The current supplements of choice for athletes are ephedrine and creatine. Ephedrine opens bronchial tubes, stimulates the central nervous system, and increases heart rate and blood pressure. Creatine is a muscle-building compound. An NCAA survey of 21,000 female and male college athletes in 2001 found that nearly 58 percent were using ephedrine and that most had started in high school or even junior high school.[19] A 2001 survey commissioned by Blue Cross and Blue Shield found that about one million children between the ages of twelve and seventeen were taking dietary supplements and/or performance-enhancing drugs to make them better athletes.[20]

When it comes to teenagers, many doctors, nutritionists, coaches, and some players themselves wonder whether taking sports supplements now will haunt them later, perhaps in the form of damaged kidneys or malfunctioning livers. They worry that the products could mess up an adolescent's churning hormones. They fear that gung-ho young body-builders will assume that if one daily dose is good, five is even better. And with creatine, there's no research to see how the supplement affects the turbulent teenage body now or in the future.[21]

The most common illegal drugs used to enhance sports performance are anabolic steroids, a group of compounds that are related to the male hormone testosterone. The adjective "anabolic" refers to protein building, since the steroids promote dramatic increases in muscle bulk, strength, and power. Synthetic steroids were first developed in 1935, and weight lifters began using them in the early 1950s. The practice spread rapidly among athletes whose performance was improved by increased size and strength. An unofficial poll taken by a U.S. athlete at the 1972 Munich Olympics revealed that over two-thirds of the track and field athletes used some form of steroids in preparing for the games.[22] Some governments, as a matter of public policy, used performance-enhancing drugs as building blocks to international sports success (indirectly demonstrating the superiority of their culture). After the breakup of the Soviet empire and the fall of East Germany, documents were found showing that 1,000 to 1,500 scientists, physicians, and trainers ran controlled experiments on East German athletes in an effort to boost athletic performance while avoiding detection. This was confirmed by twenty former East German coaches who admitted that anabolic steroids had been used for over two decades as East German women dominated international swimming.[23] Apparently, China and Bulgaria have had similar state-sponsored programs. But drug violations are not limited to Communist countries. Many individuals from the West have been disqualified for drug violations in international competitions in various sports, e.g., skiing, speedskating, hockey, snowboarding, swimming, canoeing, cycling, track (mostly sprinters), and field (throwing weights—shot, discus, hammer).

U.S. athletes take these drugs by choice, not as a matter of state policy. They want to be bigger, stronger, and faster, which may lead to a college scholarship, all-star status, a professional career, or success in international sports. Boys and girls as young as ten take illegal steroids to perform better in sports. Various studies have found that 7 percent of high school male athletes and 2.4 percent of high school female athletes use anabolic steroids, as have 15 percent of male college athletes and 6 percent of female college athletes. As many as 75 percent of NFL players and as many as 50 percent of major league baseball players use or have used steroids.[24] Elite athletes in weight lifting, bodybuilding, and weight throwing are almost required to take steroids if they are to compete successfully internationally.

Drug scandals once again took prominence in late 2004 when an investigation of BALCO, a California nutritional company and its founder Victor Conte, and a subsequent grand jury investigation revealed that a number of prominent athletes (in baseball and track) had received anabolic steroids, human growth hormone, EPO, and ways to mask their detection by authorities.

The use of anabolic steroids has serious health consequences.[25] Prolonged use can damage the liver. It increases total cholesterol and decreases good forms of cholesterol, thus increasing the risk of coronary heart disease. It causes the body to retain sodium, potassium, and water, which increases the chances of congestive heart failure. Like other muscles, the heart often becomes enlarged, raising the risk of sudden heart attacks and blood clots. The tendons, which connect muscle to bone, become less resilient as bigger muscles put more pressure on them. Anabolic steroids cause testicular atrophy and breast enlargement in males, and menstrual cycle difficulties, deepening of the voice, and increased body hair growth in women. Acne is common in both sexes. Mood swings and an increase in aggressive behavior are also by-products of steroid use.[26] A study of fifty steroid-using weight lifters revealed that one common side effect was sexual aggression.[27]

Consider what happened to University of South Carolina lineman Tommy Chaiken when he first took anabolic steroids:

I went from about 210 pounds to a lean 235 in eight weeks. My bench press went from the upper 300s to 420 and my squat from 400 to 520. I watched my diet and I was really cut—big arms, chest and legs, great definition. . . . Besides the muscle growth, there were other things happening to me. I got real bad acne on my back, my hair started to come out. I was having trouble sleeping, and my testicles began to shrink—all the side effects you hear about. But my mind was set. I didn't care about the other stuff. . . . In fact, my sex drive during the cycle was phenomenal, especially when I was charged up from all the testosterone I was taking. I also had this strange, edgy feeling—I could drink all night, sleep two hours and then go work out. In certain ways I was becoming an animal. And I was developing an aggressiveness that was scary.[28]

Chaiken ended up with tumors and clinical depression that nearly drove him to suicide. There are other extreme examples of the apparent consequences of prolonged steroid use. Steve Courson, an NFL player who used steroids for eleven years, needed a heart transplant.[29] Aside from the side effects from steroids, their use increases the chances for injury. The increased aggression ("roid rage") contributes to excessive violence on and off the field, including sexual assault.[30]

As noted earlier, football players are, on average, heavier each year. For example, in 1991 there were eighty-three National Football League players weighing at least 300 pounds. In 2001, the number was 290.[31] This trend is found in colleges as well. At the University of Colorado, for example, the average weight of offensive linemen (tackle to tackle) was 189 pounds in 1950, 246 in 1980, and 307 in 2000.[32] The extra weight of contemporary football players is probably not only the consequence of better diet and weight training but of steroid or other drug use. When players put on more weight than their frames were meant to hold, this puts extra stress on ligaments and joints, leading to more sprains, strains, and ligament tears. The additional bulk without loss of speed makes collisions all the more violent, leading to an increase in the number and severity of injuries. The added weight also places additional strain on the heart during exertion, especially when the weather is hot. This is a possible cause of the death of lineman Korey Stringer, weight 338 pounds, who died of heatstroke during preseason conditioning drills with the Minnesota Vikings in 2001.

Despite the many dangers associated with performance-enhancing chemicals, their use continues and even increases. The motive is obvious—an extreme desire to excel. A 1995 poll of sprinters, swimmers, power lifters, and other U.S. Olympians or aspiring Olympians asked the following questions.

Scenario I: You are offered a banned performance-enhancing substance, with two guarantees:

(1) You will not be caught. (2) You will win. Would you take the substance?

One hundred and ninety-five athletes said yes; three said no.

Scenario II: You are offered a banned performance-enhancing substance that comes with two guarantees: (1) You will not be caught. (2) You will win every competition you enter for the next five years, and then you will die from the side effects of the substance. Would you take it?

More than half the athletes said yes.[33]

The use of artificial means to improve performance presents a paradox—while improving performance, it diminishes that performance. That is, if a world record is accomplished by an athlete known to use illicit drugs, is that a world record? Ken Caminiti admitted that he used steroids in 1996, the year he was selected as the National League most valuable player. Similarly, if Barry Bonds, one of those accused of steroid use, is found guilty, will his home run records be recognized or tainted? Should he be kept out of baseball's Hall of Fame? In response, an editorial in *USA Today* stated:

Steroids are banned in sports. Using them is cheating. . . . Clean players are put at an unfair disadvantage, tempting them to cheat to keep up. . . . Fans, young and old, are cheated out of seeing a game honestly played. . . . Records become lies. Take Bonds' record-shattering performances in recent years. Since turning 35, he's doubled the rate at which he hits home runs. That's a time when nearly all athletes' performances turn down, but for Bonds, it was the time that his physique visibly bulked up. Should he hold a place in the record books above Babe Ruth and Roger Maris [and Hank Aaron]?[34]

And what about horses that are injected with anabolic steroids? In 2008 the winner of the Triple Crown was a horse named "Big Brown." It is legal in Kentucky to give horses steroids, so no law was violated, and racing horses are commonly given these drugs. But Big Brown was given the same anabolic steroid that Canadian sprinter Ben Johnson took before the Seoul Olympics (he was later stripped of his gold medal). It's also the steroid that baseball player Rafael Palmeiro took. Anabolic steroids enhance athletic performance. Should not Big Brown's achievements be nullified or at least receive an asterisk?[35]

Dietary Dangers

Women and girls in certain sports (figure skating, gymnastics, tennis, swimming, diving, and distance running) are advantaged if they are slim. Thus, by choice or by coercion from parents or coaches, many severely limit their diets. The extreme forms of this are anorexia nervosa (self-imposed starvation) and bulimia nervosa (cyclical binging and purging).[36] The prevalence of anorexia nervosa among athletes appears to be about the same range as that reported for nonathletes, while bulimia nervosa is found more often among athletes than nonathletes.[37] According to studies of collegiate women athletes, between 20 and 33 percent of female athletes reported disordered eating. In one study, 43 percent said that they were terrified of being or becoming too heavy, and 55 percent reported experiencing pressure to achieve or maintain a certain weight.[38] A 1992 University of Washington study of 182 female college athletes found that 32 percent practiced some radical form of weight control (vomiting and using laxatives, diuretics, or diet pills). Among college gymnasts, the rate was 62 percent.[39]

For males, eating disorders are most prevalent among wrestlers and boxers, athletes who need to make a weight category to compete. Dangerous weight loss has long been the norm in wrestling. To meet lower weight requirements, wrestlers limit calories and engage in a number of questionable activities such as minimizing liquid intake and using diuretics, laxatives, saunas, and exercising in rubber suits in overheated rooms to promote rapid weight loss. Wrestler Jeff Reese died after shedding seventeen pounds in two days. He spent his last two hours of life wearing a plastic suit and riding a stationary bike in a room that had been heated to ninety-two degrees.[40]

Serious problems occur with excessive dehydration, especially when it is combined with substances such as creatine. During a thirty-three-day span in late 1997, three college wrestlers died while trying to sweat off pounds. Since no college wrestler had died in the previous fifteen years, some experts wonder if the addition of this new supplement was responsible, since it can contribute to dehydration.[41]

The drastic methods used to lose weight in wrestling have been widely accepted by athletes, coaches, and sports organizations.[42] Worse yet, these practices have gone unregulated. However, the deaths of the three college wrestlers stunned NCAA officials, who quickly announced rule changes. First, rubber suits, saunas, and diuretics were banned from competition preparation. Second, official weigh-in times were moved from twenty-four hours before matches to no more than two hours before (thus making it much more difficult to recover from rapid weight loss).

Although the NCAA's quick action was commendable, it is akin to locking the barn door after the horse is gone, since the NCAA was negligent in allowing unhealthy practices to flourish unhindered until three athletes died of them.

At the other end of the weight continuum, some sports require heaviness. Sumo wrestlers in Japan eat enormous amounts of foods and supplements to achieve a weight of 400 pounds or more. The prevailing view is that football linemen are more effective if heavy. It is not uncommon for high school football players to weigh in excess of 250 pounds. But what is the impact of such corpulence on the heart, blood pressure, circulation, and weight-bearing joints?

CONCLUSION

Sport encapsulates a fundamental duality—it is healthy yet unhealthy. Some sports are inherently dangerous. In others, overtraining may lead to injury. The nature of sport is such that to be good requires commitment and dedication. Sometimes this dedication to achieving a goal leads to ethical distortions such as taking dangerous drugs, engaging in unsafe practices such as taking diuretics, perhaps even trying to hurt an opponent. To achieve success by unethical means is shallow, cheap, and undeserved. Should not sports organizations and schools be guided by the principle that the ends do not justify the means? Putting this principle into practice requires sponsoring organizations to monitor coaches for abusive behaviors or other demands with unhealthy consequences for their athletes. Athletes, coaches, and parents must be educated about the unhealthy consequences of performance-enhancing drugs. There must be random drug testing and zero tolerance for violators if sport is to be a healthy activity.

Although sport can never be entirely free of injury, it needs to be structured to enhance the safety of the participants. Schools, communities, and organizations need to put sport programs in perspective. To maximize the health of the athletes, one operating principle should prevail—the outcome of the athlete (physically and emotionally) is infinitely more important than the outcome of the game.

NOTES

1. William H. Beezley and Joseph P. Hobbs, "Nice Girls Don't Sweat: Women in American Sport," *Journal of Popular Culture* 16 (Spring 1983): 42–53.

2. Nancy Theberge, "Women's Athletics and the Myth of Female Frailty," in *Women: A Feminist Perspective*, ed. Jo Freeman, 4th ed. (Mountain View, Calif.: Mayfield, 1989), 507.

3. Theberge, "Women's Athletics," 334–35. See also Tucker Center for Research on Girls & Women in Sport, *Developing Physically Active Girls: An Evidence-Based Multidisciplinary Approach* (Minneapolis: College of Education and Human Development, University of Minnesota, 2007).

4. Reported in Steven S. Woo, "Teen Girl Athletes Less Sexually Active," *Rocky Mountain News*, May 14, 1998, p. 36A; *USA Today*, "Sports Lower Teen Pregnancy," July 13, 1998, p. 1C; Women's Sports Foundation, "Sport and Teen Pregnancy: Executive Summary," July 9, 1998; and Kathleen E. Miller, Donald F. Sabo, Michael P. Farrell, Grace M. Barnes, and Merrill J. Melnick, "Sports, Sexual Behavior, Contraceptive Use, and Pregnancy among Female and Male High School Students: Testing Cultural Resource Theory," *Sociology of Sport Journal* 16.4 (1999): 366–87.

5. Although these findings show consistently positive effects in athletic participation for women, there is a methodological problem in studies that compare athletes with nonathletes (female and male). We do not know whether (1) participation in sport causes the differences, or (2) there is a selectivity bias. In short, people who are physically and psychologically healthier are more likely than the less favored to participate in sports or to stay in sports longer than those who do not participate, drop out, or are pushed out at an early age.

6. Mark Kram, "If You Think Pro Football Is All Broken Noses and Shattered Knees, You're Wrong. It's Worse. No Pain, No Game," *Esquire*, January 1992, p. 75. See also two articles, one by Pat Toomay and the other by Tim

Green under the overarching title, "Football Pain: Dancing with the Devil," *Chicago Tribune*, September 9, 2001, Section 2, p. 6.

7. Cited in Peter King, "The Unfortunate 500," *Sports Illustrated*, December 7, 1992, p. 23.

8. Adam Schefter, "World of Hurt," *Denver Post*, November 12, 2000, p. 1K. See also Adam Schefter, "Working Through Pain," *Denver Post*, December 7, 2003, pp. 1J, 6J.

9. Cited in a four-part series on injuries by Brian Hewitt, *Chicago Sun-Times*, September 19–22, 1993. See also William Nack, "The Wrecking Yard," *Sports Illustrated*, May 7, 2001, online: www.sportsillustrated.cnn.com/si—online/news/2002/0k9/11/wrecking—yard/.

10. Joseph Nocera, "Bitter Medicine," *Sports Illustrated*, November 6, 1995, pp. 74–88. See also Gerald Eskenazi, "Team Doctors: Operating in a Quandary," *New York Times*, April 15, 1987, p. 44. This observation that team doctors are part of the problem was made to me in a personal conversation with a former member of the Jacksonville Jaguars (February 21, 2002).

11. Peter King, "Painful Reality," *Sports Illustrated*, October 11, 2004, p. 61.

12. Cited in Jack McCallum, "The Incredible Bulk," *Sports Illustrated*, February 3, 2003, p. 21.

13. Howard L. Nixon II, "Accepting the Risks of Pain and Injury in Sport: Mediated Cultural Influences on Playing Hurt," *Sociology of Sport Journal* 10 (1993): 183–96.

14. Howard L. Nixon II and James H. Frey, *A Sociology of Sport* (Belmont, Calif.: Wadsworth, 1996), 103.

15. Robert Hughes and Jay J. Coakley, "Positive Deviance among Athletes: The Implications of Overconformity to the Sport Ethic," *Sociology of Sport Journal* 8.4 (1991): 307–25. See also Jay J. Coakley, *Sport in Society: Issues and Controversies*, 9th ed. (New York: McGraw-Hill, 2007), 157–69.

16. L. A. Marshall, "Amenorrhea," in *Women in Sport*, Volume VIII of the *Encyclopaedia of Sports Medicine*, ed. Barbara L. Drinkwater (Oxford, UK: Blackwell Science, 2000), 377–90; and Dylan B. Tomlinson, "Too Much of a Good Thing," *Denver Post*, February 24, 1998, p. 10D.

17. CBS Evening News, February 22, 1994.

18. "Baseball's ADD Epidemic," *USA Today*, January 17, 2008, 16A.

19. Reported in *USA Today*, "Coaches, Congress Put Young Athletes at Risk," August 16, 2001, p. 14A.

20. Reported in Jenny Deam, "Sports Craze," *Denver Post*, September 9, 2001, p. 4K. See also Jerry Adler, "Toxic Strength," *Newsweek*, December 26, 2004, pp. 45–52.

21. Bill Briggs, "Sports Supplements Pervasive in Schools," *Denver Post*, May 17, 1998, pp. 1A, 14A.

22. Terry Todd, "Anabolic Steroids: The Gremlins of Sport," in *Sport in America: From Wicked Amusement to National Obsession*, ed. David K. Wiggins (Champaign, Ill.: Human Kinetics, 1994), 285–300.

23. Michael Janofsky, "Women Swimmers Used Steroids, 20 German Coaches Acknowledge," *New York Times*, December 3, 1991, p. 1B; John Meyer, "Profile in Courage: Harvey Took on East German Sports Machine," *Denver Post*, October 21, 2001, pp. 1C, 11C; and Steven Ungerleider, *Faust's Gold: Inside the German Doping Machine* (New York: St. Martin's, 2002).

24. See Charles B. Cordin et al., "Anabolic Steroids: A Study of High School Athletes," *Pediatric Exercise Sciences* 6 (1994): 149–58; Jeffrey A. Pottieger and Vincent G. Stilger, "Anabolic Steroid Use in the Adolescent Athlete," *Journal of Athletic Training* 29 (1994): 60–64; Skip Rozin, "Steroids: A Spreading Peril: Thousands of Young U.S. Athletes Are Risking Their Health," *Business Week*, June 19, 1995, pp. 138–41; Associated Press, "Steroid Use on Rise with Teenage Girls," *Denver Post*, December 15, 1997, p. 5C; Rick Telander, "In the Aftermath of Steroids," *Sports Illustrated*, January 27, 1992, p. 103; Scott E. Lucas, *Steroids* (Hillside, N.J.: Enslow, 1994); and Tom Verducci, "Totally Juiced," *Sports Illustrated*, June 3, 2002, pp. 34–48.

25. The following information on steroids and their consequences is from R. H. Barry Sample, "An Overview of Anabolic/Androgenic Steroids," *NCAA Sport Sciences* (Spring 1992): 3–4. See also *USA Today*, December 6, 2004, p. 11C.

26. William Nack, "Muscle Murders," *Sports Illustrated*, May 18, 1998, pp. 96–106.

27. John R. Fuller and Marc J. LaFountain, "Illegal Steroid Use among Fifty Weightlifters," *Sociology and Social Research* 73 (October 1988): 19–21; and John R. Fuller and Marc J. LaFountain, "Performance-Enhancing Drugs in Sport: A Different Form of Drug Abuse," *Adolescence* 22 (Winter 1987): 969–76.

28. Tommy Chaikin with Rick Telander, "The Nightmare of Steroids," *Sports Illustrated*, October 24, 1988, p. 90.

29. Steve Courson and Lee R. Schreiber, *False Glory* (New York: Longmeadow, 1992).

30. Skip Rozin, "Steroids: A Spreading Peril," *Business Week*, June 19, 1995, pp. 138–41.

31. *USA Today*, "300-Pounders," January 18, 2002, p. 1A.

32. Mike Burrows, "Agile 300-Pounders Wanted to Play Up Front," *Denver Post*, February 6, 2002, pp. 1D, 8D.

33. Reported in Michael Bamberger and Don Yaeger, "Over the Edge: Aware That Drug Testing Is a Sham, Athletes Seem to Rely More Than Ever on Banned Performance Enhancers," *Sports Illustrated*, April 14, 1997, p. 62.

34. "When Sports Fail to Confront Steroids, Cheaters Prosper," *USA Today*, December 6, 2004, p. 14A.

35. Christine Brennan, "So, Will Annals One Day Show 'Big Brown'?" *USA Today*, May 22, 2008, p. 3C.

36. For two sociological analyses of this phenomenon, see Diane E. Taub and Rose Ann Benson, "Weight Concerns, Weight Control Techniques, and Eating Disorders among Adolescent Competitive Swimmers: The Effect of Gender," *Sociology of Sport Journal* 9 (March 1992): 76–86; and David Johns, "Fasting and Feasting: Paradoxes of the Sport Ethic," *Sociology of Sport Journal* 15.1 (1998): 41–63.

37. Jorunn Sungot-Borgen, "Eating Disorders," in *Women in Sport*, Volume VIII of the *Encyclopaedia of Sports Medicine*, ed. Barbara L. Drinkwater (Oxford, UK: Blackwell Science, 2000), 364–76.

38. Katherine A. Beals, *Disordered Eating among Athletes: A Comprehensive Guide for Health Professionals* (Champaign, Ill.: Human Kinetics, 2004). See also Katherine A. Beals and Melinda M. Manore, "Disorders of the Female Athlete Triad among Collegiate Athletes," *International Journal of Sport Nutrition and Exercise Metabolism* 12.3 (2002): 281–93; and Tiffany C. Sanford-Martins et al., "Clinical and Subclinical Eating Disorders: An Examination of Collegiate Athletes," *Journal of Applied Psychology* 17.1 (2005): 79–86.

39. The studies are noted in Joan Ryan, *Little Girls in Pretty Boxes: The Making and Breaking of Elite Gymnasts and Figure Skaters* (New York: Warner Books, 1995), 63–64.

40. David Fleming, "Wrestling's Dirty Secret," *Sports Illustrated*, January 5, 1998, p. 134.

41. Karen Springer and Marc Peyser, "The New Muscle Candy," *Newsweek*, January 12, 1998, p. 68.

42. Brandon L. Alderman, Daniel Landers, John Carlson, and James Scott, "Factors Related to Rapid Weight Loss Practices among International-Style Wrestlers," *Medicine & Science in Sports & Exercise* 36 (February 2004): 249–52.

THE ORGANIZATION OF CHILDREN'S PLAY: PEER CENTERED OR ADULT CENTERED?

In the years after World War II, when the ideal of a sheltered child-hood was finally achieved by the American middle class, kids spent many weekend days playing in the sandlot with other neighborhood kids. They picked teams, made up rules, and quit at the first sight of an ice-cream truck.

—Tom Farrey, investigative journalist

It's pressure through fear. If you don't get them played, and if they're not getting any better, they're behind. Nobody wants to wait, so people go with it early, at 4 and 5 years old."

—Mother of a nine-year-old girl

A "winning is everything" notion starts in the littlest of leagues. Lessons of hard work and fair play give way to "gain an edge at any cost."

—Robert Lipsyte, sports journalist

Sometimes the preparation is so hard, so intense. . . [t]he crying, the screaming. . . . We are not in the gym to be having fun. The fun comes at the end, with the winning and the medals.

—Bela Karolyi, famed women's gymnastics coach

TWO FORMS OF PLAY

When I was growing up in Southern California in the 1940s, I did not play in an adult-organized game until I was a freshman in high school. My sports activities were limited to playground games in grade school and middle school, and most frequently to games after school with friends in vacant lots, backyards, driveways, streets, and parks. What was the norm then has been superseded by adult-organized sport for youth in recent decades. Now there are more than 52 million girls and boys (40 percent are girls) participating in organized youth sports in the United States.[1] Little League baseball involves 2.5 million participants. Pop Warner football has 400,000 children in its program. Soccer is the largest youth team sport with some 4.8 million boys and girls involved. Children still engage in unorganized peer group sports activities, but adult-organized sports are now the dominant sports form for them. The differences between these two forms of children's sports are profound. Let's examine each type, recognizing that these are generalizations and may not always apply to all situations.

Organization

In adult-organized sports for children, the games are modeled after professional sports (teams typically have names and logos of professional teams), with uniforms, standard practice and game facilities, practice and game schedules, tournaments, referees, rules, and coaches who teach strategy and skills to players who listen passively. Players are assigned to teams either by neighborhood or by tryouts followed by a draft in which coaches select players. Decisions are made by ruling bodies, referees, and coaches rather than the participants. The emphasis in this organized setting is on the development of sport skills and winning. Games are played with spectators (most commonly, parents) present.

Peer play is player controlled. The players gather and teams are selected, rules are decided, and the playing field demarcated by consensus. The children vary the rules during play to suit the situation. Adults are missing in these settings. They neither make the rules nor watch these games.

Daniel Sanger describes the differences between these two types of play, using hockey in Canada as the sport. He begins with a description of a minor hockey league for teenagers:

> Inside an arena, inside cumbersome equipment, most of the players sit on the bench most of the time, behind which a pacing, anxious coach barks out orders, behind whom one or more idiot fans or parents take it way, way too seriously. The players are said to be *playing* hockey, but judging by the limited laughter and smiling, there is little play involved. Rather, organized hockey is about following instructions, executing set plays, confronting opponents, scoring, and winning. Open-air pickup hockey on the other hand, is a game of endless variety, spontaneity, adaptation, and unspoken rituals. With no coaches telling players what to do and no prescribed way to play, it lends itself to an often beautiful creativity. With no referees and few hard-and-fast rules, it insists on self-regulation and, in so doing, encourages accommodation and tolerance. Pickup hockey is always unpredictable and almost always instructive, even edifying, in a life-lessons kind of way. . . . [These players are] engaged in a pleasurable pursuit together. [They are] playing.[2]

Process

In peer group sport the games begin quickly without warm-ups. Players have to negotiate rule interpretations or when a player is "safe" or "out." A consensus often occurs but when it doesn't the decision may be to play it over. Kids want action. Instead of a situation common in adult-centered baseball for example, where the action is mainly with a pitcher either striking out or walking batter after batter, in peer group sports, a dominant player may not be allowed to pitch, or they may shout "let him hit it." The emphasis is on action, not winning.

Kids prefer close scores, not blowouts. So they divvy up the talent more or less equally, and sometimes place handicaps on the better players. Less skilled players are granted "do-overs" and "interference" calls to compensate for deficiencies or mistakes, minimizing the embarrassment that could cause them to walk off—and leave the game short on players. Abuse of such special exemptions is regulated by teasing. Rules go ignored provided that it doesn't interrupt the flow of the action. In baseball, called strikes are verboten so that everyone gets a chance to hit (and there are more balls to field). In football, every kid is eligible to receive a pass on any play.[3]

In contrast, the process in adult-organized youth sports emphasizes order, punctuality, respect for authority, obedience to adult directions, and a strict division of labor. Practices start and end by a coach's decision. Coaches may interrupt practice to discuss mistakes, demonstrate the proper skill, or punish misbehavior. The players become so accustomed to following orders in an organized sport setting that they frequently cease play altogether if the coach is absent or not directly supervising.[4]

Typically, winning is the overriding goal of organized youth sports programs. Games can be very lopsided. A team in a league may be dominant, but the adults make no effort to equalize the teams. Moreover, "By striving for league standings, by awarding championships, by choosing all-star teams, such programs send the not-so-subtle message to youngsters that the most important goal of sports is winning."[5]

Impetus

The impetus for peer play comes entirely from the players. They begin and terminate a game based on player interest. They participate to have fun. Conversely, the impetus for play in organized sports programs comes from the coaches. Practices are scheduled by coaches. Games are scheduled by a league authority and played in a very rigid time frame. Instead of fun, players do repetitive drills. They are expected to work hard. Indeed, practice is work.

Although everyone wants to win, victory seems to be most important for coaches and parents. While winning is preferable to losing—and many children will try hard to win, even crying when they come up short—they don't linger on the result. Ten minutes after the final whistle, they've moved on. It's coaches and parents who keep talking about the game at dinner. Adults exist in an adult world that dispenses rewards based on the bottom line, where the destination matters more than the journey.[6]

Analysis of Differences

Informal sports are action centered, while organized sports are rule centered. In the former, youngsters are involved, developing decision-making skills. Sociologist Jay Coakley says:

> Children must be creative to organize games and keep them going. They encounter dozens of unanticipated challenges, requiring on-the-spot decisions and interpersonal abilities. They learn to organize games, form teams, cooperate with peers, develop rules, and take responsibility for following and enforcing rules. These are important lessons, many of which are not learned in adult-controlled organized sports.[7]

Unfortunately, the number of participants in peer-organized play is declining. On the one hand, more children devote more and more of their leisure time to computer games. If interested in sport, they are lured into organized sports by the uniforms, playing in real stadiums (sometimes even "under the lights"), and the dream of becoming a star.[8]

While adult-organized sports encourage passivity by the participants and overemphasize winning, there are some benefits. Again, turning to Coakley:

> Organized sports help children learn to manage relationships with adult authority figures. Children also learn the rules and strategies used in activities that are defined as important in the culture, and through their participation, they often gain status that carries over to other parts of their lives. When they play organized sports, they learn about formal structures, rule-governed teamwork, and adult models of work and achievement.[9]

An interesting difference involves sportsmanship. In peer-centered games, unsportsmanlike behavior is not tolerated. Peer pressure demands good behavior, but if unsportsmanlike acts occur, the offender is banished from the game by his/her peers. In adult-organized sports, while dominated by fair play and playing within the rules, the pressure to win sometimes encourages unsportsmanlike behavior by coaches, players, and parents. This may involve trash talking, intimidating opponents, taunting and ridiculing opponents, and deliberately violating the rules of sport to gain an advantage and win the sporting event. Writing about adult-organized children's sports, Robert Lipsyte says:

> Lessons about the rewards of discipline, playing fair and working hard compete against lessons about the punishment-free payoffs of cheating. Dads pour illegal additives into the quarter-midget race cars of their 7-year-olds. A Little League pitcher lies about his age. A coach winks when a teenage basketball star fabricates an address to join an out-of-town team. Kids who grow up seeing grown-ups shrug, if not actually pulling the strings behind the scenes, come to think it's the way of the world.[10]

For example, a study of youth sports conducted by researchers at the University of Missouri–St. Louis, the University of Minnesota, and Notre Dame involving 803 young athletes ages 9 to 15, along with 189 parents, and 61 coaches found:[11]

- 2 in 10 athletes admitted cheating often.
- 19 percent of athletes had tried to hurt an opponent often.
- 27 percent of athletes had acted like "bad sports" after a loss.
- According to the athletes, 7 percent of their coaches had encouraged them to cheat.
- According to the athletes, 8 percent of their coaches had encouraged them to hurt an opponent.

DANGERS OF ADULT-CENTERED PLAY

The remainder of this chapter examines the intrusion of adults into children's play in more depth, focusing on the dark side. The widespread participation by children in organized, adult-sponsored sports has many beneficial consequences. The exercise is healthy. Team sports emphasize cooperation and teamwork. The children learn sports skills. They have proper equipment for safety. Individual sports foster self-reliance. Playing under adult supervision helps children stay out of trouble. And children gain acceptance from their peers for their accomplishments and contributions to the team. But accompanying these benefits are problems, sometimes serious problems.

Beginning too Early

When is it too early for a child to be in adult-organized sports? There is no definitive answer, but surely there is an age when it is inappropriate for the physical and psychosocial development of the child. Consider:

> There are 12-year-olds driving racecars. Eleven-year-olds are turning pro in skateboarding. Nine-year-olds hire professional coaches. Eight-year-olds play 75 baseball games a year. Seven-year-olds vie for power-lifting medals. Six-year-olds have personal trainers. Five-year-olds play soccer year-around. Four-year-old tumblers compete at the AAU Junior Olympics. Three-year-olds enter their third year of swim lessons. Two-year-olds have custom golf clubs.[12]

Or how about children as young as six, with the blessing of their parents, participating in "ultimate fighting," the sport sometimes characterized as "human cockfighting"? One father defended this sport for his sons: "As a parent, I'd much rather have my kids here learning how to defend themselves and getting positive reinforcement than out on the streets."[13]

What about Jani Silva, who enrolled in a prestigious tennis academy near Paris *before* he was in the first grade? Jani's parents sold their house, furniture, and cars in California and moved to France with Jani and their two other children (an older brother is also enrolled in the academy). Jani is five years old, 4 feet tall, and weighs 60 pounds. His favorite cartoon is *SpongeBob SquarePants*. Jani's parents believe that he, and perhaps his older brother, will be champions. The father says, "Best-case scenario is they both win Grand Slam titles. [Worst case] Jani wins a bunch of Grand Slam titles and Kadyn plays professional tennis but isn't as successful as he'd like to be, and then does whatever he wants." The mother says, "Everyone thinks we're crazy, but when they come and actually meet us, they are like, 'The kid loves it.' We don't have to push him."[14]

Specialization

"Kids used to play year-round alternating the sport with the season. That's not the case anymore as parents let unrealistic dreams shoehorn their children into one-sport misery. The day of the three-sport high school athlete is rapidly disappearing as coaches tell even 10-year olds who show some promise in a particular sport to stick to that sport year-round."[15]

Youth with special talent now play on "traveling teams" or "club teams." They have two- or three-hour practices three or four times a week and play single-day or in weekend tournaments with similarly skilled teams, sometimes at great distances. George Sage characterizes this phenomenon:

> For both the young athletes and their families the commitment to traveling teams is almost total. The young athletes must abandon other organized sports to concentrate on the travel team. They must commit to specializing in one sport, and often must compete with their team year-round. Family lives must be re-centered around the sports world of the traveling teams. The new breed of sports parents are road warriors who drive thousands of miles every season and spend weekends and evenings watching their kid's practice and play. And they write lots of checks because it is very expensive to support a traveling or club team athlete.[16]

The Intrusion of Organizations on Children's Sport

The actions by various organizations have enticed many parents to push their children toward athletic greatness. Some examples:

- Children's sports and the feats of elite child athletes have been glamorized in the media. *Sports Illustrated* and *USA Today* have featured youth sports, including the national ranking of high school teams and high school players. ESPN and ABC-TV (not so incidentally, both are owned by the Walt Disney Company) televises the Little League World Series.
- Corporations such as Nike and McDonald's sponsor basketball tournaments for teenagers, which are frequented by college coaches who are scouting for talent. The McDonald's all-star game is nationally televised.
- Talent evaluators such as The HoopScoop Online rank basketball prospects as young as the fourth grade. It charges $499 for a one-year subscription for its services.

- Big-time university athletic programs are now offering athletic scholarships to eighth and ninth graders. In 2008 such scholarships were offered by basketball coaches at Kentucky and the University of Southern California.[17]

Out-of-Control Parental Behavior

There are many instances of abusive behavior by parents at their child's games. This includes berating officials; mocking opponents; and using abusive language toward their own child, his/her teammates and coaches, and/or the opponents. Sometimes this verbal abuse spills over into physical assaults. Reports from over 2,000 chapters of the National Alliance for Youth Sports reveal that about 15 percent of youth games involve some sort of verbal or physical abuse from parents or coaches.[18] A survey by *Sports Illustrated for Kids* found that 74 percent of more than 3,000 respondents reported that they had witnessed out-of-control adults at their games.[19]

Excessive Parental Demands

Some parents and coaches are too demanding, making sport work instead of fun—something to be dreaded rather than enjoyed. Kids are pressured by parents who live vicariously through their children's accomplishments (the "achievement-by-proxy" syndrome). This may manifest itself in starting the children in sport too soon, narrowing the choice of sports by specialization, forcing them to train or play when injured, and being too critical of their performances. At the extreme, it can result in programming a child to become a star athlete.

Consider the case of Todd Marinovich and his father, Marv.[20] Todd's training began before he was born: His mother ate nothing but natural foods during her pregnancy. When Todd was two weeks old, Marv, a former pro football player, forced daily stretching and flexibility exercises on him. As an infant, Todd was given only natural foods. He was encouraged to crawl as long as possible because crawling improves hand-eye coordination. Throughout his youth Todd was never allowed to eat white sugar, white flour, or processed foods. He drank only fruit juices, bottled water, and raw skim milk. During Todd's formative years, Marv hired experts to work on every phase of Todd's physical condition—speed, agility, endurance, strength, and peripheral vision. For most of his young life, Todd worked out seven days a week. On his fourth birthday, he ran four miles at an eight-minute pace. He was never punished for failure, only for not trying. Once, when Todd was in the sixth grade, Marv felt that he had slacked off in basketball practice and had him run home—a distance of five miles. In high school, Todd switched schools three times because of what Marv viewed as inept coaching.

Was Marv Marinovich's experiment a success? Todd became a star high school quarterback and later a starting quarterback for the University of Southern California. He was drafted by the Oakland Raiders but lasted only two years. Since then, Todd has tried his hand at art and music. He has been busted several times for possession of illegal drugs and at age 35 was sentenced to 12 months of treatment. At age 38 he was arrested again, this time for felony possession of methamphetamines and resisting arrest. Todd's younger half-brother, Mikhail, was subjected to the same serious physical regime to become a star athlete. Mikhail, who grew to 6'6" and 210 pounds, transferred schools several times because his father was dissatisfied with the coaching. He signed to play football at Syracuse in 2006 and was arrested the next year for breaking into a sports equipment room. Bruce Ogilvie, a noted sports psychologist, has responded to Marv Marinovich's parenting:

> My goodness, what a distortion of love. When you love someone, you extend them total freedom in what they want to be. You must remain a guest in your child's life. Emotional distance is essential. When parents begin vicariously to live through their children, there is the inherent danger of stunting their children's growth. The parent starts failing to discriminate as to when the child's life begins and ends.[21]

In another celebrated instance, Marc O'Hair devoted his life to molding his son Sean into a champion golfer.[22] He enrolled Sean in the David Leadbetter Golf Academy. He pushed Sean, awakening him at 5 a.m. to run and lift weights. Once, Sean was forced to run eight miles in 93-degree heat after shooting an 80 (a mile for each shot over par). Marc berated his son in public. He admits to slapping his son. Sean's social life was curtailed by many hours of practice and watching tapes of his swing. In return for his investment in Sean, Marc made Sean sign management contracts, which specified that Sean would pay his father 10 percent of his professional earnings. Sean broke free of his father in 2002. He had limited success on the Nationwide Tour (the level below the PGA Tour) but eventually qualified for the PGA Tour. In 2005 his season earnings amounted to $2,461,482, and he won PGA Rookie of the Year honors. By 2008 he had won two PGA tour events and was a success. Sean has not paid his father any of the money that the father says he is owed.

A final example of a father pushing his son too far involves Corey Gahan, who at age 13 was a world age-group champion of in-line skating.[23] When Corey was 12, Corey's father, Jim, and his trainer started giving him shots. First the shots contained B-12 vitamins. Then human growth hormone, and later a steady dose of steroids in the form of synthetic testosterone. When Corey won, he was rewarded. When he did not, his dad would not speak to him. He did win often. At fifteen he was a national champion at 500, 1,000 and 1,500 meters. In 2006, after failing drug tests, he was suspended for two years and had to forfeit his previous wins. Corey cooperated with the authorities, resulting in his trainer and father being sentenced to prison. As of 2008, he lives with his mother and has not spoken to his father in over a year.

What consequences ensue for a child who is robbed of his/her childhood by an overzealous parent? Todd Marinovich was an athletic success but failed to meet the goals his father set for him. What emotional scars does that failure leave? What does it do to the parent-child relationship? In each of these examples, the young athletes are estranged from their fathers.

Most parents, of course, do not go the extremes of a Marv Marinovich, Marc O'Hair, or Jim Gahan to make sports stars of their children. But they may do other things that put excessive pressure on their children to succeed. They may send their child to a tennis academy for year-round training. Nick Bollettieri's camp costs around $50,000 for hands-on coaching by Bollettieri. The two hundred or so children who aspire to professional tennis careers put in daily workouts of four to five hours. Most, however, fail to achieve professional status. And, lest we forget,

Bollettieri's Tennis Academy is only one of more than three hundred such camps in the United States. The chances of success are extremely thin even for talented players with well-heeled parents.

The situation is the same for aspiring young gymnasts. About 2,500 U.S. female gymnasts train seriously, with about two hundred competing on the elite level and only twenty making the national team. Bela Karolyi has coached the most Olympic gymnastics champions in history, including Nadia Comaneci and Mary Lou Retton. He selects fifty of the most promising for his camp. The financial cost to their parents is high. The workouts are grueling. The competition at the camp is intense. The coaches are incredibly demanding. The athletes in such a setting work extremely hard, even when in pain, for fear of losing. But most of them do lose, that is, they do not become champions. At least forty-four of those excellent gymnasts at Karolyi's camp, and all the others at other camps, do not make the Olympic team, since there is only room for six on that elite squad. The successful are ecstatic, but what of the "losers"? They have sacrificed their childhoods, their home lives, their parents' financial resources, and their bodies without meeting expectations. Some, of course, handle failure with little trauma. Others experience depression and low self-esteem. Still others become antisocial and rebellious. Even the successful may experience a downside. Tennis stars Tracy Austin and Jennifer Capriati, for example, turned professional and made the cover of *Sports Illustrated* at thirteen. By age seventeen, however, both were out of the sport, experiencing severe burnout. Austin suffered physical injuries, and Capriati assumed an alternative lifestyle that included the use of illicit drugs. Capriati, however, did eventually make a successful comeback.

At a less intense but nonetheless serious level, many parents push their children to win college scholarships and become champions. They start their children at an early age, have them specialize in one sport, hire trainers and coaches, and send their children to summer camps for skills improvement. As a result, some children start as young as three in competitive swimming. Boxing can start as young as five. There are football, soccer, and other sports leagues for five-year-olds. Some children at that age compete in marathons and triathlons. Many specialize, with a passion:

Joseph [Lorenzetti] recently turned 12. With his slender limbs and un-blemished skin, he looks like a boy. But he is really a hockey machine, one as dedicated to the sport as any man-sized player. When he started playing at 3½, he was so small he couldn't hold a stick. He now trains 300 days a year, attends seven summer hockey camps, and travels 4,500 miles a year to compete, while his parents spend $6,000 a year on equipment, ice time, and hotels.[24]

Or consider the dedication of fourteen-year-old James Johnson, an aspiring basketball player:

At 6 a.m. he is at Pro Club in Bellevue, Washington, shooting for an hour and a half. After school, he goes back to Pro Club, gets instruc-tion, works on ball-handling, scrimmages and lifts weights until 6 p.m. Then he has eighth grade AAU practice until 8:30 p.m. At home, he does homework, shoots on the immaculate backyard court (which cost $38,000 to build) and goes to bed early. Every weekend, he travels to tournaments, playing at least three games. [His father says] "In today's world, if you want to be a college basketball player, you have to make a commitment at his age."[25]

These two young men (and their parents, through their children) are pursuing the American Dream. Their efforts can be characterized posi-tively as dedicated and achievement oriented, or negatively as fanatical and one-dimensional. In either case, the children are giving up the chance to develop a wide range of skills from a variety of sports, aca-demics, music, and other activities. They are also missing out on a nor-mal childhood, a time that includes periods of unstructured freedom, free from the demands of parents and other adults. Their monomania-cal devotion to achieving success may lead them to use performance-enhancing drugs or otherwise cheat. Moreover, most of these children are also being set up to fail. Even when they achieve success, will it be good enough for them (or their parents)? And what if they do not get a college scholarship, let alone become a professional athlete?

Consider the case of Kristie Phillips. Her mother entered her in a beauty pageant when she was a year old, enrolled her in modeling

classes at eighteen months, and dance school at two.[26] By the time she
was five, Kristie was training at gymnastics four hours a day. At fourteen
she was training with Bela Karolyi and was featured on the cover of
Sports Illustrated with the headline "The Next Mary Lou." Her parents
spent $180,000 over six years for Kristie to train under Karolyi. She
competed while hurt and used laxatives to control her weight. In the
1988 Olympic trials she finished in eighth place, one spot short of being
named an alternate.

> The road she had followed since she was four years old did not lead to
> the Olympics after all, but back home to Baton Rouge, where she had not
> lived since she was eight. Now she was sixteen and saw herself as a com-
> plete failure. A zero. Without gymnastics she felt she was nothing—less
> than nothing because she had disappointed everyone who had believed in
> her. Her parents were never going to see a payoff for all the money they
> had invested in her. She hated gymnastics, she hated herself, she hated
> Karolyi. She refused to watch the Olympics on television.[27]

Physical Injuries from Sports Specialization and Overuse

Sport poses special dangers to young bodies, including Little League
elbow, tennis elbow, gymnast's back, swimmer's shoulder, ligament
tears, shin splints, and stress fractures. The collisions in tackle football
and ice hockey are especially dangerous to preadolescents. According
to a study reported in the *Journal of the American Academy of Ortho-
paedic Surgeons*, in the year 2000, U.S. hospitals and doctors' offices
treated 2.2 million recreation-linked bone fractures, dislocations, and
muscle injuries to children five to fourteen years old.[28] At greatest risk
are young people striving for elite sport status. Their ambition leads to
accelerated training regimens that can include more than one workout
a day, cumulative daily workouts of six hours a day, six days a week,
year-round.

Of concern to all athletes, especially young athletes, are the so-called
overuse injuries (stress fractures, tendinitis, and bursitis) that result
from overdoing a certain action without giving the body sufficient time
to recover. Swimmer's shoulder, for example, is caused by a repetition

of shoulder strokes that can reach 400,000 for a typical male over a ten-month training season, and 660,000 for females.[29] Lyle Michel, director of sports medicine at Boston Children's Hospital, argues that sports injuries are especially serious for children:

> Sports injuries in children are serious. Growing children are predisposed to overuse injuries because of the softness of their growing bones, and the relative tightness of their ligaments, tendons and muscles during growth spurts. And because overuse injuries develop slowly and insidiously, unlike sprains or fractures, which happen all of a sudden, they often go undetected. The damage to a growing child's hard and soft tissues caused by an unreported or undetected overuse injury can be permanent. Evidence suggests that overuse injuries sustained in childhood may continue to cause problems in later life—arthritis, for instance.[30]

At Dr. Michel's practice in Boston, overuse injuries accounted for 20 percent of patients in 1989. In 2004 it was 70 percent.[31] Overuse injuries in children are increasing as these youths specialize in a single sport with year-round play. Athletes of any age who train seriously every day year-round engage in what sport sociologists call "positive deviance." This concept refers to "cases of conformity that are so intense, extensive, or extreme that they go beyond the conventional boundaries of behavior" (see chapter 5).

Dietary Dangers

Women and girls in certain sports (figure skating, gymnastics, tennis, swimming, diving, and distance running) are advantaged if they are slim. Thus, by choice or by coercion from parents or coaches, many severely limit their diets, sometimes causing anorexia nervosa (self-imposed starvation) and bulimia nervosa (cyclical binging and purging).[32] Bulimia nervosa particularly is found more often among athletes than nonathletes.[33]

World-class gymnast Christy Heinrich is an extreme example of a self-imposed eating disorder in an athlete.[34] In 1989 Christy was fifteen, standing four feet, eleven inches, and weighing ninety pounds.

A judge told her that she had to lose weight or she would never make the Olympic team. She knew that a small, lean, limber body was necessary (at the 1992 Olympics the average U.S. female gymnast weighed 83 pounds). A perfectionist, she took this advice seriously, increasing her training beyond the nine-hours-a-day regimen she was already following and severely restricting her diet. Food became her enemy. By the time she was eighteen, she weighed less than eighty pounds and became too weak to continue as a gymnast. She retired from the sport but could not stop the extreme dieting. After five years of virtual starvation, Christy died of multiple organ failure, weighing less than fifty pounds.

In some women's sports, such as gymnastics, figure skating, and diving, the athlete's appearance is a significant part of the judging. As a result, coaches insist on their athletes being thin. Bela Karolyi, the most famous women's gymnastics coach in the United States, is a fanatic about his gymnasts' weight. His 1992 Olympic squad members were limited to a thousand calories to fuel their bodies through their eight-hour-a-day workouts. Their food intake was monitored by assistant coaches and their belongings were searched for contraband food. "Karolyi draws the most criticism of any gymnastics coach for mistreating his athletes. Perhaps it's because he's the most famous coach and thus the easiest target. Or perhaps it's because his track record for producing gymnasts with eating disorders is stunning."[35]

For males, eating disorders are most prevalent among wrestlers and boxers, athletes who need to make a weight category to compete. The problem stems from the practice of competing at a weight level below one's natural weight. They may also lose weight to make the team, that is, they may not be able to beat their teammate at the 130-pound level or the 125-pound level, but they can defeat the 119 guy. If they can get down to 119 pounds, then they can wrestle in meets and get a letter. Otherwise, they stay on the sidelines.

To lose the necessary weight the athlete may take diuretics or laxatives. The athlete may also exercise in overheated rooms wearing rubber suits to lose weight through perspiration. In either case, the athlete's body is stressed by dehydration and the loss of important electrolytes and nutrients. On rare occasions an athlete has died from these excesses.

The Sexual Abuse of Girls

Athletes, male and female, are sometimes targets for sexual abuse from persons in authority, usually coaches. I shall focus on young girls, since they are victimized most frequently. This emphasis should not obscure the fact that adult women and some young male athletes are also sexually abused.[36] The social conditions that make female athletes vulnerable to sexual harassment and abuse are just as real for male athletes. These factors include the close bonds that form between coaches and athletes.[37]

In elite youth and high school sports, harassment by the coach might be tolerated more easily than in other social spheres, since the athletes accept the coach as the authority figure who gives orders that extend into the private sphere of their lives. This includes control over medical treatment, nutrition, injuries, social activities, use of alcohol and tobacco, and sexual behavior. Individual rights in athletes often take a backseat to the notion of "winning" and the "good of the team." Helen Lenskyj claims that "even the most assertive and independent women rarely question the coach's authority, nor do they challenge psychologically manipulative or abusive behavior on the part of coaches."[38] In many sports there is a lot of hands-on instruction, for example, in gymnastics and wrestling. Close physical contact between the coach and the athlete occurs during practice and is part of the sporting experience. However, this also creates possibilities for inappropriate touching, harassment, and abuse. This potential is intensified by the physical, technical, and social power that coaches have over athletes.[39]

Coaches, most of whom are men, have enormous power over athletes. The coaches decide who makes the team, who gets to play, who gets scholarships, and who gets to remain on the team. To say no to this all-powerful person places the athlete's career in jeopardy. Athletes have been socialized to obey their coaches, even if they disagree with their demands. Joan Ryan says that "the very traits that make young girls good gymnasts or figure skaters—obedience, reticence, pliability, naïveté—also make them prime targets for sexual abuse."[40]

The perceived and actual separation from "normal" life inside sport increases the reliance on support systems, especially coaches. Athletes spend most of their time with other athletes and coaches, practicing, eat-ing, and playing. Athletes do not have time to build relationships outside the sports sphere. Many athletes, some as young as ten, are separated from their parents, removing the parents as protectors and confidants. Their team becomes their surrogate family. A survivor of sexual abuse by a coach called his actions incest. "I consider it incest—that's what this is all about. Because of time spent, the demands, the friendship, the opportunity . . . they are giving you something no-one else can. They're brother, uncle, father . . . the child feels safe and will do anything. That's why it's incest."[41]

Another factor increasing the likelihood of sexual abuse (in this case, the abuse of young athletes) is that they are under a coach's control when they begin to mature sexually. The onset of puberty is a crucial time for a young athlete. Referring to males, sociologist Mike Messner says that "the athlete's relationship with his coach takes place during boyhood and young adulthood, when the young male's masculine iden-tity is being formed, when he is most insecure about his public status, about his relationships, his sexuality, his manhood."[42] The problem is even more acute for girls because they reach puberty at a younger age than boys. Their earlier sexual development makes them targets for sexual abuse at an earlier and more vulnerable age. Moreover, girls can achieve elite sports status much earlier, chronologically, than boys. Girls, for example, in swimming, ice skating, and gymnastics can be world-class at fourteen, whereas boys must wait until their late teens or early twenties to attain a similar rating. This means that young girl athletes, more so than young boys, are going to live away from home and be coached by someone with a top-notch reputation, making them vulnerable to a sexual predator.

A final variable leading to a higher risk of sexual abuse is an athlete's level of performance, the highest risk occurring when the athlete has the most at stake. Celia Brackenridge and Sandra Kirby's research re-veals that athletes who have reached a high standard of performance but are just below the elite level (the "stage of imminent achievement," SIA) are most vulnerable.[43] Novices can drop out or change coaches rather easily because they have invested less time, effort, money, and family sacrifice. Elite athletes have a proven record of success and may be less dependent on their coaches for continued achievement. These established athletes are also more likely to have high self-esteem and personal confidence, which provides them with the personal resources to operate independently of coaches. Athletes on the verge of stardom, however, are more likely than novices or elite athletes to be dependent on a coach. Brackenridge and Kirby claim that athletes whose SIA coincides with or precedes their age of sexual maturity are at greatest risk of sexual abuse in sport. This hypothesis, if true, means that prepubescent girls are the most likely victims of sexual abuse.

CONCLUSION

For many children, adult-organized sport is a positive experience, but for many it is not. Some children are pushed into sports too early. Adult-organized sports are often highly pressurized by overzealous parents and coaches. Play is transformed into work. Participation rates in adult-organized sports peak at age nine but before they become teenagers 7 in 10 will quit. They walk away for a number of reasons including the realization that they do not have the skills to compete or because of an injury. But more likely they disengage because the activity is not fun. They fear failure on the field and disappointing their parents who have invested so much in their success. The fault lies in the way sports for children have become organized, too adult-centered, and with the focus on a redefinition of fun in terms of the outcome (winning and becoming a better athlete), rather than on the process. Society, parents, and children would be better served if the children's sports were recentered—focusing on the interest of the children rather than the interests of adults.

NOTES

1. This first section and various parts of this chapter depend greatly on D. Stanley Eitzen and George H. Sage, *Sociology of North American Sport*, 8th ed. (Boulder, Colo.: Paradigm, 2009), chapter 4. George H. Sage is the

principal author of that chapter. Other sources used in this section are: Jay J. Coakley, *Sport in Society: Issues and Controversies*, 7th ed. (New York: McGraw-Hill, 2001), 118–24. See also Melissa Fay Greene, "Sandlot Summer: Hyperscheduled, Overachieving Children Learn How to Play," *New York Times Magazine*, November 28, 2004, pp. 40–44. For some ideas on how to fix children's sports, see Peter Cary, "Fixing Kids' Sports," *U.S. News & World Report*, June 7, 2004, pp. 44–53; and Peter Applebome, "What's to Come, Soccer Tryouts in the Cradle?" *New York Times*, October 17, 2004, p. 28YT.

2. Daniel Sanger, "5, 6, Pickup Sticks," *The Walrus* (December/January 2007), p. 64.

3. Tom Farrey, *Game On: The All-American Race to Make Champions of Our Children* (New York: ESPN Books, 2008), 115.

4. Bob Bigelow and Tom Moroney, *Just Let the Kids Play: How to Stop Other Adults From Ruining Your Child's Fun and Success in Sports* (Deerfield Beach, Fla.: HCI, 2001); Patricia A. Adler and Peter Adler, *Peer Power: Preadolescent Culture and Identity* (New Brunswick, N.J.: Rutgers University Press, 1998).

5. Eitzen and Sage, *Sociology of North American Sport*.

6. Farrey, *Game On*, 122.

7. Jay Coakley, *Sports in Society: Issues and Controversies*, 9th ed. (New York: McGraw-Hill, 2007), 136–37.

8. Timothy Williams and Cassi Feldman, "Anyone Up for Stickball? In a PlayStation World, Maybe Not," *New York Times*, July 1, 2007, pp. 25–26.

9. Coakley, *Sports in Society*, 137. See also, Adler and Adler, *Peer Power*.

10. Robert Lipsyte, "'Jock Culture' Permeates Life," *USA Today*, April 10, 2008, p. 11A.

11. David Light Shields, Brenda Light Bredemeier, Nicole M. LaVoi, and F. Clark Power, "The Sport Behavior of Youth, Parents, and Coaches: The Good, the Bad, and the Ugly," *Journal of Research in Character Education* 3.1 (2005): 43–59. See also Greg Toppo, "Image of Youth Sports Takes Another Hit," *USA Today*, September 15, 2006, p. 19C.

12. Farrey, *Game On*, 13.

13. Quoted in Marcus Kabel, "Small Fists, Big Brawls," *Chicago Tribune*, March 28, 2008, Section 1, p. 2.

14. Quoted in Douglas Robson, "Could This 5-Year-Old Be the Future of Tennis?" *USA Today*, July 30, 2007, p. 2A.

15. Tim Wendel, "When Smiles Leave the Game," *USA Today*, August 23, 2005, p. 13A. See also Patrick Welsh, "One-Sport Athletes: A Losing Proposition for Kids," *USA Today*, August 23, 2004, p. 11A.

16. Sage in Eitzen and Sage, *Sociology of North American Sport*, chapter 4.

17. Andy Staples, "Players: Too Young to Go Steady?" *Sports Illustrated*, May 19, 2008, pp. 14–15; Jack Carey, "Early Commitments Worry Coach Group," *USA Today*, May 8, 2008, 1C, 11C; Sean Gregory, "Courting Eighth-Graders," *Time*, October 8, 2007, pp. 57–58.

18. Reported in Matt Schuman, "Parents Need Self Control," *Greeley Tribune*, September 24, 2006, p. B9.

19. Greg Bach, "The Parents Association for Youth Sports," *Journal of Physical Education, Recreation, and Dance* 77.6 (2006): 16.

20. The following is from Mark Christensen, "Robo Quarterback," *California Magazine*, January 1988, pp. 69–77; Douglas S. Looney, "Bred to Be a Superstar," *Sports Illustrated*, February 22, 1988, pp. 56–58; Malcolm Moran, "Raising a Quarterback with a Game Plan," *New York Times*, August 24, 1990, pp. 11B–12B; and Denise Tom, "The Marinovich Plan Reaches Its Goal," *USA Today*, April 30, 1991, p. 9C.

21. Quoted in Tom, "Marinovich Plan."

22. Steve Elling, "What Price Success?" *Golf World* (January 21, 2005).

23. Luis Fernando Llosa and L. Jon Wertheim, "Sins of a Father," *Sports Illustrated*, January 21, 2008, pp. 30–34.

24. Larry Tye, "Injured at an Early Age," *Boston Globe*, September 30, 1997, 18A.

25. "All Hoops, No Chores," *USA Today*, June 2, 1997, p. 3C. See also Bruce Weber, "A Fierce Investment in Skates and Family Time," *New York Times*, January 16, 2005, pp. 1, 23.

26. The following is from Joan Ryan, *Little Girls in Pretty Boxes: The Making and Breaking of Elite Gymnasts and Figure Skaters* (New York: Warner Books, 1995), 109–20.

27. Ryan, *Little Girls*, 116.

28. Marilyn Elias, "Preteens Run Risk with Sports Overload," *USA Today*, October 23, 2001, p. 6D. See also David Noonan, "When Safety Is the Name of the Game," *Newsweek*, September 22, 2003, pp. 64–66.

29. Reported in Larry Tye, "Injured at an Early Age," *Boston Globe*, September 30, 1997, p. 18A; Laura Ungar, "Overuse Injuries on Rise in Youth Sports," *Fort Collins Coloradoan*, December 4, 2004, p. D2 (from Louisville, Kentucky, *Courier-Journal*).

30. Lyle J. Micheli, "Children and Sports," *Newsweek*, October 29, 1990, p. 12.

31. Mark Hyman, "Young Athletes, Big-League Pain," *Business Week*, June 7, 2004, p. 142.

32. For two sociological analyses of this phenomenon, see Diane E. Taub and Rose Ann Benson, "Weight Concerns, Weight Control Techniques, and Eating Disorders among Adolescent Competitive Swimmers: The Effect of Gender," *Sociology of Sport Journal* 9 (March 1992): 76–86; and David Johns, "Fasting and Feasting: Paradoxes of the Sport Ethic," *Sociology of Sport Journal* 15, no. 1 (1998): 41–63.

33. Jorunn Sungot-Borgen, "Eating Disorders," in *Women in Sport*, volume VIII of the *Encyclopaedia of Sports Medicine*, ed. Barbara L. Drinkwater (Oxford, U.K.: Blackwell Science, 2000), 364–76.

34. The following is from Ryan, *Little Girls*, 55–95. See also Jennifer Sey, *Chalked Up: Inside Elite Gymnastics' Merciless Coaching, Overzealous Parents, Eating Disorders, and Elusive Olympic Dreams* (New York: William Morrow, 2008).

35. Ryan, *Little Girls*, 72.

36. M. Ann Hall, "Review of *Crossing the Line*," *International Review for the Sociology of Sport* 32 (September 1997): 307–9. See also Merrill J. Melnick, "Male Athletes and Sexual Assault," *Journal of Health, Physical Education and Recreation* 63 (1992): 32–35.

37. The following is taken primarily from Celia H. Brackenridge, "Fair Play or Fair Game? Child Sexual Abuse in Sport Organizations," *International Review for the Sociology of Sport* 29 (1994): 287–99; Celia Brackenridge, "He Owned Me Basically: Women's Experience of Sexual Abuse in Sport," *International Review for the Sociology of Sport* 32 (June 1997): 115–30; and Celia Brackenridge and Sandra Kirby, "Playing Safe: Assessing the Risk of Sexual Abuse to Elite Child Athletes," *International Review for the Sociology of Sport* 32 (December 1997): 407–18; and Celia Brackenridge, "Sexual Harassment and Abuse," in *Women in Sport*, Volume VIII of the *Encyclopaedia of Sports Medicine*, ed. Barbara L. Drinkwater (Oxford, U.K.: Blackwell Science, 2000), 342–50.

38. Helen Lenskyj, "Unsafe at Home Base: Women's Experience of Sexual Harassment in University Sport and Physical Education," *Women in Sport and Physical Activity Journal* 1 (1992): 19–33.

39. Karin A. E. Volkwein et al., "Sexual Harassment in Sport: Perceptions and Experiences of American Female Student-Athletes," *International Review for the Sociology of Sport* 32 (September 1997): 285.

40. Ryan, *Little Girls*, 168–69.

41. Brackenridge, "He Owned Me," 118.

42. Michael A. Messner, *Power at Play: Sports and the Problem of Masculinity* (Boston: Beacon, 1992), 105.

43. Brackenridge and Kirby, "Playing Safe," 413–14.

AP/Wide World

SPORT IS EXPRESSIVE,
SPORT IS CONTROLLED

Fun is the essence of play.

—Johan Huizinga, sport scholar

*Our coaches are responsible for every aspect of the kids' lives—
academic, spiritual, social. We are their fathers away from home.*

—Urban Meyer, University of Florida football coach

*Players on a Rick Majerus-coached team are warned: You must
want it as much as he does. Lock your eyes on the man when he
speaks; glance away and he'll blow you to bits. If Coach calls your
name? Run—never walk—and stand in front of him, eyes wide, like
a puppy panting for a treat. And for God's sake don't take anything
he says personally.*

—S. L. Price, *Sports Illustrated*

PRELUDE

*At his first team meeting as the newly appointed head basketball coach
at the University of Texas, Rick Barnes set down the rules for the team,*

including no facial hair, no earrings, no hats in buildings, and no head-
phones on campus. Anyone who was late to a team meeting or workout
would cause the entire team to run laps. There would be mandatory
team breakfasts throughout the season every day, not just game day.[1]

The play element that characterizes all sport involves enjoyment,
self-expression, and creativity. Unorganized peer-centered play is
spontaneous, informal, and fun. But as sport becomes more organized,
these playful elements are replaced by rules, external decision making,
specialization, hierarchy, and nonsport concerns such as making money
and public relations. In short, as we move from the playground to Little
League, from Little League to school sports, and from school sports to
professional sports, the added layer of controls at each level removes the
fun, spontaneity, and joyous abandon that should be the foundation of
sports participation.[2]

Control is essential for social order. Without it, social organizations
(e.g., societies, communities, churches, prisons, hospitals, schools,
corporations, families, athletic teams, or sports leagues) would be
chaotic, fragmented, uncoordinated, unpredictable, and fragile. Sport
serves control functions for society, and social control is an integral
part of sport.

Social control is based on concepts such as social order, norms, and
deviance. Every human group attempts to achieve conformity to the
norms (the standards of right and wrong). If a social organization suc-
ceeds in controlling its members, then deviant behavior is minimized
and order is sustained. But attempts to achieve conformity in groups
often meet with noncompliance, resistance, or outright rebellion.[3] Social
control is never perfect, as evidenced, for example, by the boycott of the
1968 Olympics by many African Americans. Some black athletes who
participated did so but took the occasion to symbolize their solidarity
with the boycotters. Other black athletes, most notably boxer George
Foreman, opposed the boycott. These variations show that some athletes were part of the mainstream while others challenged the dominant
ideology. In this regard sport is a "dynamic social space where dominant
. . . ideologies are perpetuated as well as challenged and contested."[4]

All social groups have mechanisms to ensure conformity that can be
thought of in two dimensions: ideological control and direct interven-

tion. Ideological control manipulates the ideas and perceptions—the consciousness—of individuals so that they accept the ruling ideology and ignore or resist competing ideologies. It persuades members to follow the rules and to accept without question the existing distribution of power and rewards. Ideological social control works through the socialization of new members, or cultural control, because the individual is given authoritative definitions of what should and should not be done. To many group members there appears to be no choice. Leaders or their representatives also employ frontal attacks on competing ideologies or propaganda efforts in order to persuade the members of which actions are moral, who the enemies are, and why certain courses of action are required. Ideological control is more effective than overt social control measures—strictures on actual behavior—because individuals impose controls on themselves.[5] Through socialization people learn and internalize not only the rules of an organization but also the supporting ideology. When socialization works well, individuals are not forced to conform; they want to conform. As sociologist Peter Berger observed, "Most of the time we ourselves desire just that which society expects of us. We want to obey the rules."[6] But the efficiency of ideological control does not render useless direct social controls that reward those who conform and punish or neutralize those who deviate or rebel.

SPORT AS IDEOLOGICAL CONTROL

Sport, as an institution, is conservative. Sport promotes traditional values and societal arrangements and employs social control mechanisms to foster the status quo. Three representative areas in which it exercises this function are the transmission of societal values, traditional gender roles, and compulsory heterosexuality.

Sport and the Transmission of Values

In the United States, sport, through the influence of coaches, parents, and peers, transmits certain values—success in competition, hard work, perseverance, discipline, teamwork, and obedience to authority—to participants and observers. This is the explicit reason given for the existence of children's sports programs, such as Little League baseball, and the tremendous emphasis on sports in American schools.

Coaches commonly believe that they should not only teach sports skills but should also promote values. For example, when a Manhattanville College player, Toni Smith, looked away from the American flag during the National Anthem in protest to the war in Iraq, she was admonished by many. The highly successful women's basketball coach at the University of Connecticut, Geno Auriemma, said: "The flag is a symbol of what we stand for. Anybody who does [what Smith has], they have the right to do it, but to me it's disrespectful and . . . I would have that right not to have that person on the team."[7]

Coaches often place signs in locker rooms to inspire traits in their athletes such as hard work, perseverance, and teamwork. Sociologist Eldon Snyder provides some examples of these messages: "The will to win is the will to work." "By failing to prepare yourself you are preparing to fail." "Never be willing to be second best." "Winners never quit and quitters never win." "United we stand, divided we fall." "Win by as many points as possible."[8] Roy Williams, the highly successful University of North Carolina basketball coach, provides his players with a different inspirational quote each day during the season that they must memorize. Why does Coach Williams have his players spend time thinking about an aphorism instead of basketball fundamentals or game strategy?

Whether sport actually transmits these values is a good question. But organized sport clearly makes the effort. According to sociologist David Matza, "The substance of athletics contains within itself—in its rules, procedures, training, and sentiments—a paradigm of adult expectations for youth."[9]

Sport and Traditional Gender Roles

Sport in its organization, procedures, and operation serves to promote traditional gender roles, thus keeping order (order, however, is not always positive). Sport advances male hegemony in practice and ideology by legitimating a certain dominant version of social reality. From early childhood games to professional sports, the sports experience is "gendered." Boys are expected to participate in sports, to be aggressive, to be physically tough, to take risks, and to accept pain. Thus sport, especially aggressive physical contact sport, is expected for boys and men but not for girls and women. These expectations reproduce male domination in society.[10]

Lois Bryson has argued that sport reproduces patriarchal relations through four minimalizing processes for women: definition, direct control, ignoring, and trivialization.[11] "When we take a critical look at dominant sport forms in many societies around the world, we see that they often involve actions highlighting masculine virility, power, and toughness—the attributes associated with dominant ideas about masculinity in those societies."[12] Male standards are applied to female performance, ensuring female inferiority and even deviance. As sport sociologist Paul Willis has observed, "[The ideal description of sport] is a male description concerning males. Where women become at all visible, then the terms of reference change. There is a very important thread in popular consciousness which sees the very presence of women in sport as bizarre."[13]

Sports participation is expected for men. Sport is strongly associated with male identity and popularity. For women, however, the situation is entirely different. As Willis has stated, "Instead of confirming her identity, [sports] success can threaten her with a foreign male identity. . . . The female athlete lives through a severe contradiction. To succeed as an athlete can be to fail as a woman, because she has, in certain profound symbolic ways, become a man."[14] Superior women athletes are suspect because strength and athletic skill are accepted as "masculine" traits.

Women's sport is minimized when it is controlled by men. This is demonstrated in the gender composition of leadership positions in the International Olympic Committee, various international and national sports bodies, the National Collegiate Athletic Association (NCAA), and the administrative and coaching roles in schools and professional leagues.

Women in sport are minimized (and men maximized) when women's activities are ignored. The mass media in the United States have tended to overlook women's sports. When they are reported, the stories, photographs, and commentary tend to reinforce gender role stereotypes. Women's sports are also ignored when cities and schools disproportionately spend enormous amounts on men's sports. As writer Mariah Burton Nelson has noted:

> We live in a country in which the manly sports culture is so pervasive we may fail to recognize the symbolic messages we all receive about men, women, love, sex, and power. We need to take sports seriously—not the scores or the statistics, but the process. Not to focus on who wins, but on who's losing. Who loses when a community spends millions of dollars in tax revenue to construct a new stadium and only men get to play in it, and only men get to work there? Who loses when football and baseball so dominate the public discourse that they eclipse all mention of female volleyball players, gymnasts, basketball players, and swimmers?[15]

Women are also minimized when they are trivialized in sport. As noted earlier, the media framing of the female athlete reinforces gender stereotypes. Considering photographs of women and men athletes, scholar Margaret Carlisle Duncan[16] found that these images emphasized gender differences: (1) female athletes who are sexy and glamorous are most common; (2) female athletes are often photographed in sexual poses; (3) in the framing of photos, male athletes are more likely to be photographed in dominant positions and female athletes in submissive positions; (4) camera angles typically focus up to male athletes and focus down on female athletes; and (5) female athletes are more likely to be shown displaying emotions. As sociologist Michael A. Messner has argued, "The choices, the filtering, the entire mediation of the sporting event, is based upon invisible, taken-for-granted assumptions and values of dominant social groups, as such the presentation of the event tends to support corporate, white, and male-dominant ideologies."[17]

Another example of the trivialization of women's sports activities is the naming of their teams. A study comparing the unifying symbols of women's and men's teams found that more than half of colleges and universities in the United States employ names, mascots, and/or logos that demean and derogate women's teams.[18] As elaborated in chapter 3, some schools name their men's teams the Wildcats and their women's teams the Wildkittens. Or the men are the Rams and the women, the Lady Rams (an oxymoron if there ever was one). Thus the naming of women's teams tends to define women athletes and women's athletic programs as second-class and trivial.

The secondary treatment of women in sport that defines and characterizes them as inferior also defines them, by extension, as less capable than men in many other areas of life. Scholar Lois Bryson asserts that "each cultural message about sport is a dual one, celebrating the dominant at the same time as inferiorizing the 'other,'"[19] in this case, celebrating the masculine and inferiorizing the feminine.

Although this dominant ideology is perpetuated in many ways, it is also challenged and contested with some success in all institutional areas, including sport.[20] Pioneering women have broken down the "men-only" rules in such traditionally unlikely areas as automobile racing (Janet Guthrie became the first woman to race in the Indianapolis 500 in 1977; Danica Patrick became the first woman in history to win an Indy-style race in 2008), men's locker rooms (women sportswriters now routinely conduct interviews there), high school wrestling against boys, and refereeing men's games (in 1997 the NBA hired two women, Dee Kantner and Violet Palmer, as referees, the first women to officiate in a major, professional, all-male sports league). In 2002, we witnessed the first woman to referee in the NCAA's men's basketball championship tournament.

The traditional conception of femininity as passive and helpless is challenged today by the fit, athletic, and even muscular appearance of women athletes. Women now engage in pumping iron to sculpt their bodies toward a new standard of femininity that combines beauty with taut, developed muscles. Similarly, women are now rejecting traditional notions of femininity by pushing the limits in endurance events in running, cycling, swimming, and mountain climbing and by engaging freely in strength sports such as bodybuilding, weight lifting, and throwing weights.

Sport and Sexuality

Sport has been socially constructed as a masculine activity. Young boys are inducted into a fiercely heterosexual world of male toughness and competitiveness that embodies a fear of the effeminate and subordinates gay men.[21] In the United States, boys learn to play football and thereby develop both a social and a personal identity that is consistent with the hegemonic conception of masculinity.[22] This is the common pattern in other societies as well.[23] If boys in the United States do not meet these cultural expectations, they are called sissies. Once labeled, they typically are teased and excluded from peer group relationships and activities. Because they do not participate in "manly" sports, they are socially marginalized by their peers. Older boys and young men in the United States who do not fit the dominant behavior patterns of masculinity often face serious questions about their sexual orientation, with labels such as "fag," "gay," and "queer" being used to describe them.[24] A common motivational ploy by some coaches is to question a male athlete's heterosexuality (calling him a "pussy" or a "fag" or placing a tampon in his locker) if he does not play as aggressively as the coach demands. While coaching at Indiana, Bob Knight once stopped the videotape of a game to say to one of his players:

> Daryl, look at that. You don't even run back down the floor hard. That's all I need to know about you, Daryl. All you want to be out there is comfortable. You don't work, you don't sprint back. Look at that! You never push yourself. You know what you are Daryl? You are the worst f—pussy I've ever seen play basketball at this school. The absolute worst pussy ever. You have more goddamn ability than 95 percent of the players we've had here but you are a pussy from the top of your head to the bottom of your feet. An absolute f—pussy.[25]

Another example comes from basketball coach Rick Majerus. During a game in 1999 Majerus gathered his team around him during a timeout and zeroed in on struggling center Nate Althoff. "You've got none of these," Majerus growled, and reached over and lightly backhanded Athoff's groin, "you've got no nuts!"[26]

Sociologist Timothy Jon Curry's research on the male bonding in athletic locker rooms found that the talk there focused on affirmations of traditional masculinity, homophobia, and misogynistic slurs. Curry found that locker room talk by males was decidedly heterosexual and absolutely intolerant of homosexuality. Curry reasons that athletes do not want to be singled out as unmasculine in any way. Thus the "expression of dislike for femaleness or homosexuality demonstrates to oneself and others that one is separate from it and therefore must be masculine."[27] Needless to say, gay males are not welcome in the masculine sports world.

Female athletes, just as other women who enter traditional male do-mains, especially sports domains that require strength, endurance, and aggression, face the social control mechanism of slander concerning their sexuality. "Slander against female athletes usually takes the form of describing them as mannish, butch, muscle-bound, unpretty, unnatural, and otherwise unfeminine. It contains two related messages: one, that to be a female athlete is to be a lesbian (or at least in danger of becoming one), and two, that to be a lesbian is wrong."[28]

Women in sport, more than men, endure intense scrutiny about their sexual identity. A common fear among many men and women is that women in sport transgress gender lines, which disrupts the social order. "The lesbian label is used to define the boundaries of acceptable female behavior in a patriarchal culture: When a woman is called a lesbian, she knows she is out of bounds."[29] Sociologist Howard Nixon says when female athletes face accusations of lesbianism, they face two types of prejudice: "first, that being a lesbian is a bad thing and, second, that women's sport must be a bad thing for women because it is dominated by lesbians."[30]

Women (whether lesbian or not) sometimes face discrimination as they compete against men for coaching or sports administration jobs be-cause of the assumption of homosexuality. In 1991, Penn State basket-ball coach Rene Portland told the *New York Times* that she did not allow lesbians on her team (she was not fired or forced to change her policy by the authorities at Penn State, although she was asked to take a sensitiv-ity course).[31] Highly successful athletes (e.g., Martina Navratilova) have lost millions of dollars in endorsement money after acknowledging their homosexuality. The Ladies Professional Golf Association has faced alle-gations, epithets, and innuendo that its athletes were disproportionately lesbian, which has damaged women's professional golf through loss of sponsorship, television coverage, and fan support.

The result is that many lesbian athletes and coaches stay closeted. Some may act in an exaggeratedly "ladylike" way by using certain per-sonal effects (such as bows, ribbons, makeup, dresses, heels) and by talk-ing about eventually settling down and having children. Others develop a lesbian identity.[32] Still others resist and work with heterosexuals to overcome homophobia, heterosexism, and sexism in sport.[33] The larger consequence of homophobia in sport is that compulsory heterosexuality remains the norm. And, as with gender roles, the mechanisms of social control in sport have sustained "compulsory heterosexuality [as] part of a system of domination that perpetuates patriarchal relations and the wielding of power over other sexualities."[34]

DIRECT SOCIAL CONTROL IN SPORT

Athletes engaged in sport beyond the informal play stage are subject to various forms of social control aimed at shaping their behaviors. Control obviously comes from powerful sports organizations, which determine eligibility, scheduling, and rules for games. The NCAA sanctions schools and players for rules violations. The Olympic Committee decides what nations are eligible to compete, ruling, for example, that the Union of South Africa was banned from Olympic competition from 1964 to 1991 because of its racist policies.

In 1972 the U.S. Congress imposed its will on school sports by instituting Title IX to encourage gender equity in sports and other school programs. National leaders may also decide to prohibit their athletes from participating in an international event (e.g., the majority of Islamic nations prohibit their women from competing in the Olympics because participating violates Muslim rules for appropriate women's dress).

The gatekeeping function of sports organizations, although necessary, has been used historically to exclude or limit participation by athletes from certain social categories. The notion of "amateurism" was used, for example, by the affluent to exclude members of the working class from their athletic activities. "Amateurism" has also been used as an exploitative ideology, whereby colleges and universities use "amateur" athletes to generate considerable income for coaches, schools, leagues, the NCAA, and bowl/tournament organizers.[35] The highest paid college coaches, for instance, make as much as $4 million annually, while their athletes receive room, board, tuition, and books. African Americans were excluded from participation in mainstream U.S. college and professional leagues, with rare exceptions, from World War I until the years after World War II. This exclusion was a consequence of tradition, Jim Crow laws, institutional racism, and even explicit rules in the bylaws of certain sports (e.g., professional baseball, golf, and bowling).[36] Girls were excluded from Little League baseball until the "boys-only" clause was dropped as a result of a court case in the 1970s. Women were kept from competing in Olympic track-and-field events until 1928 by the men running the International Olympic Committee. Slowly and reluctantly, women's events have been added to the Olympics, with women finally allowed to run a marathon in the 1984 Olympics (overcoming the traditional belief that women were too fragile for endurance events). Women are still denied as ski jumpers, the argument being that the sport is too dangerous for women, but there is a grassroots effort to change this for the 2010 Winter Olympics in Vancouver.

Sports organizations attempt to control athletes' behavior on the field. These ruling bodies vary in their rules and enforcement zeal, but they all strive to control excessive violence, combat the use of banned substances to enhance performance, and oppose point shaving. With considerable variation, they also sanction against off-the-field behaviors by athletes, such as criminal acts, use of recreational drugs, and, most especially, gambling on sports events.

Each sports social organization includes authoritative positions that exert control over others. Coaches have the formal task of teaching and training athletes to maximize their athletic performance and devising game strategies that maximize the chances of winning. Most important, the coach-player relationship is an asymmetrical power relationship. Coaches decide who makes the team, who plays, and when they play. Coaches create the procedures for determining and enforcing team rules. They determine training schedules and sanction player behaviors that they deem detrimental to team goals.

Coach-centered power over athletes varies widely. A few coaches are open and democratic, allowing their athletes to make and enforce rules and involving them in strategy decisions. George Davis, for example, while coaching football at several California high schools and a junior college, employed a unique coaching system.[37] His players voted on who should be in the starting lineup, decided what positions they wanted to play, and established the guidelines for discipline. In other words, Davis's revolutionary system was democratic. Some of Coach Davis's critics were upset with this plan. They accused him of shirking responsibility,

promoting disunity, and aiding communist agitators. The irony is that
these evils were the presumed consequence of a democratic system. As
sociologists Howard Nixon and James Frey have commented:

> The adult doubts are ironic because George Davis was a genuine educa-
> tor who tried to translate the American Dream and the Dominant Sport
> Creed into reality for his athletes. The fact that his teams won [forty-five
> consecutive wins at one point] makes resistance to his approach even
> more curious. . . . Davis's willingness to give up some of his control to
> his players enabled him to teach a basic civics lesson about participatory
> democracy, and in doing so he did not have to give up winning. The pri-
> mary cost of his experiment was the backlash from community members
> and some athletes who apparently did not believe that adolescents could
> handle the responsibility of making team decisions or, perhaps, that de-
> mocracy belonged in sport.[38]

At the opposite extreme, some coaches are tyrants, demanding total
control over virtually all aspects of their players' lives. They have rules
about how to dress, when to go to bed, and what to eat. Most coaches
are either paternalistic or authoritarian in their methods. With few
exceptions, coaches impose their will on athletes. As we will see in
chapter 9, coaches often violate the privacy rights of athletes, deny their
individual rights, and, in extreme cases, subject athletes to oppression,
brutality, and terror. When Sark Arslanian was football coach at Colorado State University, he ruled that his players must wear a coat and tie
on road trips. When the players arrived to board the bus for the airport
for a game, he found that his star defensive back was not wearing a tie.
Coach Arslanian sent the player home. Why would a coach do this? Will
his action cause the player to play harder next time? Or is the issue one
of control—bending the players to the will of the coach? Coach Bob
Knight holds a practice (sometimes two practices) on Christmas Day.
Occasionally he does not inform his players when the next practice
will be, forcing them to stay near their phones (this was before cell
phones) until an assistant informs them—clearly a control technique.
Knight's basic coaching philosophy has been summarized as follows:
"His fundamental approach to motivation has never changed: fear is his
number one weapon. He believes that if the players are afraid of getting

screamed at or of landing in the doghouse, they will play better. And, if they fear him more than the opponent, they are likely to play better."[39]

Why are so many coaches demanding, inhumane, and autocratic? One possibility is that the coaching profession attracts inflexible and manipulative personalities, but empirical research does not support this contention. The key to understanding the tendency toward autocratic coaching behavior lies in the role of coach and the unique demands that coaches face. First, the limits on coaching behaviors are set by communities and societies. Within the United States, for example, there is wide approval for demanding, autocratic coaches. Most players accept their subordination to higher authority.[40] Ironically, a democratic society permits, even demands, undemocratic coaches.

A second and crucial reason for authoritarian coaches is the uniqueness of the coaching role. Coaches face distinctive pressures not present in other occupations. They are held totally accountable for game outcomes. The games are unpredictable and highly visible, and the outcomes are objectively measured. Coaches react to their pressured situations in three characteristic ways. First, they seek public support by demanding that their athletes behave according to community norms (in dress, demeanor, patriotism, and religiosity). Moreover, they generate community support by showing an absolute confidence in their methods and strategies. As coaches are fond of saying, "It's my way or the highway." The other tactic is to control as much as possible. Thus most coaches control on- and off-the-field behaviors, determine game strategy, and make all decisions during games.

Second, coaches themselves are subject to social control. Coaches are employed by clubs, schools, and professional teams. When their behaviors go too far, they are subject to sanctions by those who hold authority over them. Coaches engage in such outrageous behaviors as physical abuse of players, gambling, point shaving, drug and alcohol abuse, and insubordination. On rare occasions, coaches have been sanctioned because of the initiatives of aggrieved players who complained to authorities, threatened boycotts, and brought grievances to the civil courts. Although some coaches clearly get away with maltreating their players, on relatively rare occasions they do not. In 1993, Lou Campanelli lost his job as basketball coach at the University of California–Berkeley because players complained about the vulgar and personally degrading attacks that he directed against them. The athletic director, Robert Bockrath, said that Campanelli had crossed the line. Sportswriter Bryan Burwell commented on this unusually courageous act by the athletic director:

> Does it matter if [the coach] treats his players like indentured servants? It matters. Someone needs to point out to all these power-tripping task masters that there is a very distinct line between merely cursing at a player to scold or motivate and launching these pointless, humiliating, derogatory personal attacks that far too many coaches think is an acceptable practice. . . . The end doesn't justify the means. Times have changed. Athletes shouldn't have to deal with this abuse, and if the coach can't understand that, then there ought to be more administrators with the guts to make them get IT.[41]

Social control is not limited to the powerful, supervising and managing those below them in a social organization. Most significantly, social control emerges from interactions among peers within the informal social order. Sociological research from such diverse settings as workplaces and urban street corners has found that social norms, sanctions, and roles emerge in informal interaction, resulting in social order. This social phenomenon has also been observed in sport settings. Regulars participate as individuals with others whom they see during the activity but exchange few words with. Sociologist Howard Nixon found, for example, that the regular participants in swimming constructed and maintained social order in that setting.[42] This order involved an informal code of behavior, enforcement of rules, and role differentiation. Social control mechanisms used by the participants included nonverbal cues, polite verbal prods, and even aggressive retaliation.

Sociologist Loic Wacquant's ethnographic study of a boxing gym[43] located in a South Chicago ghetto portrays the informal but elaborate social order maintained by the participants:

> The first thing trainers always stress is what you are not supposed to do in the gym. Stoneland's coach-in-second offers the following compressed enumeration of the gym's don'ts: "Cursin' Smokin' Loud talkin.' Disrespect for the women, disrespect for the coaches, disrespect for each other. No animosity, no bragging." To which could be added a host of

smaller, often implicit rules forming a tightly-woven web of restrictions that converge to pacify behavior in the gym: It is forbidden to bring food or drinks in the club, to talk during training, to rest leaning on the sides of tables, to alter the sequence of drills (for instance), to start a session by skipping rope instead of loosening up and shadow-boxing. It is mandatory to wear a jockstrap under one's towel when coming out of the shower and dry clothes when out of the gym. There is no using the equipment in an unconventional fashion, throwing punches against objects, sparring if one is not fully equipped for it, or worse, starting or even simply faking a fight outside of the ring. . . . Most of the implicit "internal regulations" of the club are visible only in the conduct and demeanor of the regulars who have progressively internalized them, and they are brought to explicit attention only when violated. Those who do not manage to assimilate this unwritten code of conduct are promptly dismissed or advised . . . to transfer to another gym.[44]

Children at play also exert control over each other. Peers may mock behaviors that go beyond their norms, such as boys not being aggressive or girls who are tomboys. Thus behaviors are channeled in approved ways and gender is socially constructed.[45] Male locker rooms, as I have noted, constitute a sports setting in which the informal norms promote aggression, homophobia, and sexism. Peer group dynamics encourage such talk, since avoiding it calls an individual's masculinity into question.[46]

Ethnographic studies of sport subcultures (e.g., bodybuilders, surfers, climbers, gymnasts, skateboarders, snowboarders) reveal that new members engage in the deliberate act of identity construction. They adopt the attitudes, style of dress, speech patterns, and behaviors of the established members of the subculture.[47] In short, the behavior of these neophyte members is controlled even before they become full members in the subculture through a process called "anticipatory socialization."

CONCLUSION

I emphasize in this book the centrality of social control in sport. Observers of this ubiquitous phenomenon can interpret it in two contradictory ways. One interpretation of social control is that it has positive functions, leading to consensus and cooperation among members, everyone pulling together for a common goal, and stability in the social organization. The opposite view is that the status quo is not necessarily good for all members of the group. From this perspective, certain categories benefit while others do not from the normal ways in which the group is structured. The irony is that the power of social control is so great and so thoroughly constructed into the culture of sport that many who are oppressed do not recognize their oppression.

NOTES

1. "Texas Coach Lays Down the Law," *Rocky Mountain News*, April 14, 1998, p. 16C.

2. My thanks to George Sage for highlighting this paradox in his review of the manuscript.

3. John Walton, *Sociology and Critical Inquiry: The Work, Tradition, and Purpose*, 2nd ed. (Belmont, Calif.: Wadsworth, 1990), 343–61.

4. Michael A. Messner, "Sports and Male Domination: The Female Athlete as Contested Ideological Terrain," *Sociology of Sport Journal* 5 (September 1988): 198.

5. Randall Collins, *Sociological Insight: An Introduction to Non-Obvious Sociology*, 2nd ed. (New York: Oxford University Press, 1992), 63–85.

6. Peter L. Berger, *Invitation to Sociology: A Humanistic Perspective* (Garden City, N.Y.: Doubleday-Anchor, 1963), 93.

7. Quoted in *USA Today*, February 27, 2003, p. 2C.

8. Eldon E. Snyder, "Athletic Dressing Room Slogans and Folklore," *International Review of Sport Sociology* 7 (1972): 89–102.

9. David Matza, "Position and Behavior Patterns of Youth," in *Handbook of Modern Sociology*, ed. Robert E. L. Faris (Chicago: Rand McNally, 1964), 207.

10. Michael A. Messner, *Taking the Field: Women, Men, and Sports* (Minneapolis: University of Minnesota Press, 2002).

11. Lois Bryson, "Sport and the Maintenance of Masculine Hegemony," *Women's Studies International Forum* 10 (1987): 349–60.

12. Jay J. Coakley, *Sport in Society: Issues and Controversies*, 8th ed. (New York: McGraw-Hill, 2004), 266.

13. Paul Willis, "Women in Sport Ideology," in *Sport, Culture and Ideology*, ed. Jennifer Hargreaves (London: Routledge and Kegan Paul, 1982), 121.

14. Willis, "Women in Sport Ideology," 123.

15. Mariah Burton Nelson, *The Stronger Women Get, the More Men Love Football: Sexism and the American Culture of Sports* (New York: Harcourt Brace, 1994), 8.

16. Margaret Carlisle Duncan, "Sports Photographs and Sexual Difference: Images of Women and Men in the 1984 and 1988 Olympic Games," *Sociology of Sport Journal* 7 (March 1990): 22–43.

17. Messner, "Sports and Male Domination," 204–5.

18. D. Stanley Eitzen and Maxine Baca Zinn, "The De-athleticization of Women: The Naming and Gender Marking of Collegiate Sport Teams," *Sociology of Sport Journal* 6 (1989): 362–70.

19. Bryson, "Sport," 349–60.

20. Messner, "Sports and Male Domination."

21. Jennifer Hargreaves, *Sporting Females: Critical Issues in the History and Sociology of Women's Sport* (London: Routledge, 1994); see also Douglas E. Foley, "The Great American Football Ritual: Reproducing Race, Class, and Gender Inequality," *Sociology of Sport Journal* 7 (June 1990): 111–35; Michael A. Messner and Donald F. Sabo, eds., *Sport, Men, and the Gender Order: Critical Feminist Perspectives* (Champaign, Ill.: Human Kinetics, 1990); and Brian Pronger, *The Arena of Masculinity: Sports, Homosexuality, and the Meaning of Sex* (London: GMP Publishers, 1990).

22. Donald F. Sabo, "The Football Coach as Officiant in Patriarchal Society: Conformity and Resistance in the Social Reproduction of Masculinity" (paper presented at the annual meeting of the North American Society for the Sociology of Sport, Edmonton, Alberta, November 1987).

23. Lois Bryson, "Challenges to Male Hegemony in Sport," in *Sport, Men, and the Gender Order: Critical Feminist Perspectives*, ed. Michael A. Messner and Donald F. Sabo (Champaign, Ill.: Human Kinetics, 1990), 175.

24. Jay J. Coakley, *Sport in Society: Issues and Controversies*, 7th ed. (New York: McGraw-Hill, 2001), 234–35.

25. Quoted in John Feinstein, *A Season on the Brink: A Year with Bob Knight and the Indiana Hoosiers* (New York: Macmillan, 1986), 7.

26. S. L. Price, "The Life and Times of Rick Majerus," *Sports Illustrated*, January 21, 2008, p. 56.

27. Timothy Jon Curry, "Fraternal Bonding in the Locker Room: A Profeminist Analysis of Talk about Competition and Women," *Sociology of Sport Journal* 8 (June 1991): 119–35.

28. Gail Whitaker, "Social Control Mechanisms: Ties That Bind—and Chafe," *Perspectives* (1982): 83.

29. Howard L. Nixon, *Sport in a Changing World* (Boulder, Colo.: Paradigm, 2008), 100.

30. Pat Griffin, "Changing the Game: Homophobia, Sexism, and Lesbians in Sport," *Quest* 44.2 (1992): 252.

31. Dylan B. Tomlinson, "Fear and Loathing," *Denver Post*, April 28, 1998, p. 10D.

32. Birgit Palzkill, "Between Gymshoes and High-Heels: The Development of a Lesbian Identity and Existence in Top Class Sport," *International Review for the Sociology of Sport* 25.3 (1990): 221–34.

33. Griffin, "Changing the Game."

34. Hargreaves, *Sporting Females*, 261.

35. See D. Stanley Eitzen, "The Sociology of Amateur Sport: An Overview," *International Review for the Sociology of Sport* 24.2 (1989): 95–105; Walter Byers with Charles Hammer, *Unsportsmanlike Conduct: Exploiting College Athletes* (Ann Arbor: University of Michigan Press, 1995); and Bruce Kidd, "Sport, Amateur," in *The Blackwell Encyclopedia of Sociology*, vol. IX, ed. George Ritzer (Malden, Mass.: Blackwell, 2007), 4656–58.

36. Ocania Chalk, *Pioneers of Black Sport* (New York: Dodd, Mead, 1975).

37. Described in Neil Amdur, *The Fifth Down: Democracy and the Football Revolution* (New York: Delta, 1972).

38. Howard L. Nixon II and James H. Frey, *A Sociology of Sport* (Belmont, Calif.: Wadsworth, 1996), 132–33. See also Nixon, *Sport in a Changing World*, 201–3; and D. Stanley Eitzen and George H. Sage, *Sociology of North American Sport*, 8th ed. (Boulder, Colo.: Paradigm, 2009), chapter 5.

39. Feinstein, *Season on the Brink*, 86.

40. Robert Hughes and Jay Coakley, "Positive Deviance among Athletes: The Implications of Overconformity to the Sport Ethic," *Sociology of Sport Journal* 8 (December 1991): 307–25.

41. Bryan Burwell, "Cal Lesson: Coaches Better Not Cross Line," *USA Today*, February 19, 1993, p. 3C.

42. Howard L. Nixon II, "Social Order in a Leisure Setting: The Case of Recreational Swimmers in a Pool," *Sociology of Sport Journal* 3 (December 1986): 320–32.

43. Loic J. D. Wacquant, "The Logic of Boxing in Black Chicago: Toward a Sociology of Pugilism," *Sociology of Sport Journal* 9 (September 1992): 221–54.

44. Wacquant, "Logic of Boxing," 235–36.

45. See Barrie Thorne, *Gender Play: Girls and Boys in School* (New Brunswick, N.J.: Rutgers University Press, 1993); and Monica A. Kunesh, Cynthia

A. Hasbrook, and Rebecca Lewthwaite, "Physical Activity Socialization: Peer Interactions and Affective Responses among a Sample of Sixth Grade Girls," *Sociology of Sport Journal* 9 (December 1992): 385–96.

46. Curry, "Fraternal Bonding."

47. Peter Donnelly and Kevin Young, "The Construction and Confirmation of Identity in Sport Subcultures," *Sociology of Sport Journal* 5 (September 1988): 223–40; Joy Crissey Honea, "Sport, Alternative," in *The Blackwell Encyclopedia of Sociology*, vol. IX, ed. George Ritzer (Malden, Mass.: Blackwell, 2007) 4653–56.

MYTH: SPORTS ARE PLAYED ON A LEVEL PLAYING FIELD

Sports is about competition. And you can't compete by keeping out talent of any color or any sex.

—Diane Pucin, *Los Angeles Times* sportswriter

A danger is that the perceived level playing field of sport can serve an ideological function by leading people to assume that western societies in particular have achieved a meritocracy that transcends the structural correlates of a racialized social order.

—Ben Carrington, sports scholar

A . . . characteristic of modern sports is equality in two senses of that complex concept: (1) everyone should, theoretically, have an opportunity to compete; (2) the conditions of competitions should be the same for all contestants.

—Allen Guttmann, sports historian

In big-time college basketball there is an upstairs and a downstairs. There are Dukes and there are Butlers.

—Robert Lipsyte, *New York Times* sportswriter

Sport is an institutional realm in which men construct and affirm their separation from, and domination over, women.

—Michael A. Messner, sociologist

Hope springs eternal in March for all 30 major league teams. Or does it? Recent history indicates there is little hope unless you are in the top half of baseball's revenue producers.

—Matt Cimento, *USA Today* sportswriter

A widely held belief is that sport is fair. That is, physical ability, skill, strategy, and energy (and occasionally luck) determine the winners rather than arbitrary notions based on social class, race, gender, or other ascribed characteristics. Under these conditions, athletes and teams are winners because of their achievements, not who they are and where they come from. And, of course, sport does work this way some of the time. But there are many instances where other variables make sport unfair. Some examples:

- Typically, in sports determined by judging (such as ice skating, diving, gymnastics), the contestants appearing later in the contest are scored easier than those who competed early. This occurs because to score an early contestant high does not leave any room for higher marks by later contestants who might perform better.
- Historically, African Americans were excluded from white-dominated professional leagues and intercollegiate sports.
- Women athletes and coaches in Division I sports programs don't have the same economic resources as male athletes and coaches.
- Exclusion from sports participation on the basis of sex has deprived women of equality. In the Olympics, for example, women have not been allowed to participate in certain events historically (distance races), and even today women are not allowed to participate in the ski jump.
- The children of the affluent are advantaged in sport over their less advantaged peers in several ways. First, they either attend private schools or public schools in wealthy districts. Wealthy districts provide more sports opportunities, more coaches, and better facilities

and equipment than do the poorer districts. Second, these children can afford the costs of attending sports camps and participation in traveling club leagues. Third, they have access to coaches and facilities at private clubs that are important to the successful performance in individual sports (golf, tennis, gymnastics, swimming). And, fourth, success in some sports, most especially ice skating, requires many years of training at a cost of as much as $60,000 a year (coaching, ice time, travel, costumes).

INEQUALITY IN SPORTS

This chapter focuses on four examples of uneven playing fields in sport: (1) racial inequities; (2) gender inequities; (3) the rich getting richer in big-time college sport; and (4) the rich getting richer in major league baseball.

Racial Inequities

Is the playing field level for racial minorities? Does race restrict, or is it irrelevant? If sport offers social mobility for minorities, it should help bring the races together so that minorities are found throughout the social structure, not disproportionately at the bottom. The answers to these questions, however, are not clear-cut, since a case can be made for both sides.

The case for the affirmative begins with history. There are opportunities now for African Americans in sport that were not present until after World War II. In the first half of the twentieth century, African Americans were absent, with few exceptions, from intercollegiate and professional sports, except for all-black colleges and all-black leagues. This raises the interesting question: Should baseball records from the all-white era (prior to 1947) have asterisks, since blacks were not allowed to compete?[1]

Professional baseball, basketball, and football integrated in the late 1940s and early 1950s. The last major college conference to integrate was the Southeastern Conference (SEC) in 1966, and it was the last conference to have an African American head football coach (Sylvester Croom at Mississippi State, hired in 2004). The year 1966 is significant because of a watershed event—an all-black starting lineup for Texas Western (now the University of Texas–El Paso) upset the all-white University of Kentucky team for the NCAA men's basketball championship. Then fast-forward to 2001 at the SEC tournament championship basketball game, where Kentucky faced Mississippi. Both head coaches, all three officials, and most of the players in that game were African Americans. Another sign of progress is that in 2006 75 percent of the players in professional basketball (the NBA) were African Americans, as were 66 percent of professional football players and 8 percent of those in major league baseball (Latinos made up 29 percent of baseball players). In big-time college basketball and football, about 60 percent of the players are African Americans. Clearly, sport is an open system in which ability, rather than race, is important.

But that is only part of the story. There are still limits placed on African Americans and other racial minorities. Minority players are rarely found in certain sports (golf, tennis, bowling, skiing, ice skating, polo, auto racing) where barriers to full minority participation remain. Before 1990, for example, the U.S. Golf Association (USGA) and the Professional Golf Association (PGA) regularly played their golf tournaments at country clubs that did not allow minorities as members. When the various governing bodies in golf adopted antidiscrimination guidelines for their host clubs, eleven country clubs with tournaments refused to integrate. Since then, four of them have come into compliance, but seven clubs continue to discriminate openly. Moreover, many of those that did integrate did so by admitting a token African American athlete to silence the protesters.

In team sports, racial minorities are underrepresented in central leadership and thinking positions and are overrepresented in physical, reactive positions. This form of discrimination, known as "stacking," is one of the best-documented forms of discrimination in both U.S. college (e.g., men's football and women's volleyball) and professional ranks (football, baseball) and in other societies as well (Canadian football, British soccer, and Australian rugby).[2] In football, whites are much more likely to play on offense than defense and are found disproportionately at center, guard, and quarterback. Blacks are found disproportionately on defense, at wide receiver, and running back. In baseball, blacks are underrepresented at pitcher and catcher and overrepresented in the outfield. Are these differences in racial composition by position accidental or based on actual performance criteria, or are the decisions made by athletes, coaches, scouts, and general managers based on racial stereotypes?

Racial minorities do not have the same opportunities as whites when their playing careers are finished. This is reflected in media positions, where blacks and Latinos are rarely found in radio and television broadcasting, even more rarely as play-by-play announcers, and very infrequently as sportswriters or officials. And racial minorities seldom hold positions of authority in sport—head coaches, athletic directors, general managers, and owners.

African Americans are also underrepresented among assistant coaches, and then they tend to be assigned the less prestigious roles. In football, African American assistant coaches are typically assigned to coach receivers, running backs, and defensive backs, positions dominated by blacks. Rarely are they offensive or defensive coordinators, the most important coaching positions after head coach. In major league baseball, minorities coaching the baselines overwhelmingly coach first base, where the responsibilities are much less important than at third base. This is significant because the third base coach is the most important on-the-field coach. When managing jobs open up, third base coaches have the best experience for moving to the top job.

The paucity of minorities in positions of leadership (coaches and administrators) in professional and college sports could be the result of two forms of discrimination. Overt discrimination occurs when owners ignore competent blacks because of their prejudices or because they fear the negative reaction of fans to blacks in leadership positions. In this regard, *Sports Illustrated* has editorialized: "Though 68% of NFL players are African American, NFL owners, an all-white club, have given short shrift to well qualified [African American] candidates [for head coaching positions]. . . . What really has to change is the close-mindedness of owners and general managers, who have long been practicing a pernicious form of racism."[3]

The other type of discrimination is more subtle. It takes two forms. First, blacks may not be considered for coaching positions because they did not, as a result of stacking, play at high interactive positions requiring leadership and decision making. We know that major league managers, for example, tend to have played as catchers or infielders. African Americans, because of stacking, have been in the outfield and therefore do not possess the requisite infield experience that tradition-ally provides access to a manager position. The situation is similar in football, where research has shown that most coaches played at the central positions of quarterback, offensive center, guard, or linebacker during their playing days. Since blacks rarely play these positions, they are more likely to be excluded from head coaching responsibili-ties. The second subtle form of discrimination addresses the question: Who is doing the hiring? The people that select head coaches are overwhelmingly white. Among the Division I-A schools, 95 percent of the presidents are white, as are 93 percent of the athletic directors, 91 percent of the faculty athletic representatives, and 100 percent of the league commissioners. These data suggest, says Richard Lapchick, head of the Institute for Diversity and Ethics in Sport at the University of Central Florida, that the "old boys" network continues to operate in sport:

> Consider the hiring process in Division IA football—it is quick, quiet, and exclusive, and university affirmative action guidelines are rarely followed. . . . Many African American coaches are waiting in the wings, ready to lead Division IA programs, but when significantly more than 90 percent of our campus leaders are white, chances are they will seek who they know. History shows that in the 'old boys' network, white men are likely to hire people who look like them.[4]

At the conclusion of the 2007 football season, there were only seven minority head coaches (5.8 percent) among the 119 Division I-A schools, yet 55 percent of the players were black. In 2006 when 21 I-A schools had vacancies, only two minority coaches were hired.

Writing about American society and the changes that have occurred since Jackie Robinson broke through baseball's color line in 1947, Roger Angell says, which applies to all sports:

> This same pattern of minority impotence may be in force all across un-stable corporate America, where African American or Latino C.E.O.s and

board members are also hard to find, but pointing this out should be of no comfort to baseball. Nor should it be taken as disparaging what was accomplished by Jackie Robinson's courage and class; if anything, it tells us something about the size and the lumpish Jabba-the-Hutt immobility of racial prejudice in this country. What we can say is that baseball has changed, but not nearly enough; in too many ways, . . . [racial prejudice is] still the national pastime.[5]

Gender Inequities

Until the 1970s, high school, college, and professional sports in the United States were, with few exceptions, male activities. The barriers were breached finally by court cases (for example, a legal decision to open Little League baseball to girls) and by federal legislation (Title IX in 1972). With these changes, sports opportunities for girls and women have increased greatly.

However, prejudices and discrimination are not altered by courts and legislation, and culturally conditioned responses to gender ideology are ubiquitous and resistant to sudden changes. Therefore, laws may force compliance in equality of opportunity for females in the world of sport, but inequities in sport continue, albeit in more subtle and insidious forms, as has been the case with racism.[6]

Major gender inequities remain, despite the tremendous gains generated by Title IX. An assessment of the situation at the collegiate level in 2006 and 2007 discloses the following disparities by gender:[7]

- Viewed as a whole, only 17.7 percent of head coaches of men's and women's teams are women. Fewer than 2 percent of coaching positions in men's programs are held by women, and most of those are coaches of combined men's and women's teams in cross-country, tennis, and swimming.
- Men outnumber women (57.6 percent to 42.4 percent) as coaches of women's teams.
- Only 18.6 percent of women's intercollegiate programs are administered by women. 14.5 percent of women's athletic programs lack any female administrator at any level.

- At the Division I-A level, women hold less than 8 percent of athletic director positions. There are more female college presidents of Division I-A schools than there are female athletic directors.
- The higher the level of competition and the better paying the positions, the more likely men will be head coaches and top administrators of women's teams and programs.
- African American women, facing the double jeopardy of minority race and gender, are underrepresented among coaches and administrators.
- Women's collegiate sports are controlled by the NCAA, a male-dominated organization.
- In 2007, while female students comprise 57 percent of college student populations, female athletes received only 43 percent of participation opportunities. Despite being a majority of college students, women received only 45 percent of the athletic scholarships.
- In 2007 Division IA, head coaches for women's teams received an average salary of $850,400 while head coaches for men's teams average $1,783,100, a difference of $932,700.
- It is not uncommon for a school with a big-time football program to spend twice as much on its football team as it spent on all women's sports.

At the professional level, women have many fewer opportunities than men, and the monetary rewards are considerably less (with the exceptions of ice skating and women's tennis). In professional basketball, for example, there are more teams for men within the United States and abroad. Moreover, the pay is highly skewed, with top men receiving in excess of $20 million a year, while only a few women superstars approach $100,000. The women's professional basketball league is the WNBA, operating under the auspices of the NBA. In 2007, women with four or more years of experience in the WNBA received $49,134, and a maximum salary was $93,000 (with few endorsement opportunities). Compare this with the average player salary in excess of $5 million in the NBA, with the highest paid, Shaquille O'Neal, making $20 million in salary and another $15 million in endorsements. The prize money for PGA tournaments (for male professional golfers) is about five times more than for women professionals playing in the LPGA (the L stands for La-dies, by the way, which connotes elegance, a decidedly unathletic trait). Very few women have been able to make it in automobile racing. Most significant, while men have the chance for careers as relatively well-paid professional athletes in a number of sports, women do not have these opportunities in sports such as baseball, hockey, and football.

For ancillary positions in sport, women again have many fewer op-portunities than men. Some examples of positions where women are disproportionately underrepresented include team physicians, head trainers, referees and umpires, radio and television announcers, and sports information directors.

Historically, the International Olympic Committee (IOC) has re-stricted the number and type of women's sports that were part of the Olympic Games. For example, there were no women athletes at the 1896 games, and only 14 percent of the athletes in the 1968 summer games were women. By 2000 women had gained in participation but were still only 38 percent of the athletes at the games in Sydney (there were 168 men's events, 120 women's events, and twelve events in which women and men competed). The gender composition of the IOC was exclusively male until the 1980s, and now only about 10 percent of this powerful administrative body are women. Between 1990 and 1996, forty of the forty-two new appointments went to men.[8] The U.S. Olympic Committee is better represented by women, but they were still a de-cided minority.

The data show that women in sport are second-class citizens. Women have fewer sports participation and career opportunities, fewer re-sources devoted to their programs, and they are given less media at-tention than men. Added to this is the discrediting of women athletes by trivializing or marginalizing their accomplishments (such as with nonathletic team names, as noted in chapter 3), and focusing on their sexiness or the possibility of their deviant sexuality (the whisper charge of lesbianism). Sport sociologist Mary Jo Kane puts it this way:

> Sport is one of the most powerful institutions in this culture, because of its status and economic and political clout. There's a great deal at stake in sports participation, and the group that has monopolized sport doesn't

want to give that up. They know that the best way to maintain control is to trivialize or marginalize [women's] accomplishments. . . . After all, if females are great athletes, then it's harder to say as a society that they shouldn't get press coverage, money, scholarships. But if they are portrayed as people who do sports in their spare time, or as merely pretty girls, it's much easier to deny them access and to maintain the status quo. . . . [The University of Minnesota's Tucker Center for Research on Girls and Women in Sport] 1998 research found that because of the notion that sport belongs to men, there remain deep-seated and persistent barriers to girls in sport: gender stereotyping, sexism, and homophobia.[9]

The Rich Get Richer: The Case of Big-Time College Sport

In intercollegiate athletics, success begets success. That is, the best high school athletes tend to gravitate toward the dominant athletic programs because they will be on television more, they will play before larger and more enthusiastic crowds, and they will likely be playing for championships. The recruiting classes for basketball programs, following the victory of the national championship, provide ample proof of this claim. So, too, with football players. Most top recruits say that they considered Bowl Championship Series (BCS) schools (the ones who are eligible for the biggest bowl games) first.[10] Attracting the best athletes, in turn, increases the likelihood of winning, which brings in more money to the athletic department, which, in turn, is spent on larger recruiting budgets, building better facilities, and publicity, all of which increase the allure of these programs for the most talented recruits. This cycle perpetuates advantage, making it difficult for teams without winning traditions and leaving those schools in mediocre conferences at a distinct disadvantage. There are several dimensions to this cycle of advantage that makes the already successful likely to retain their superiority.

There is a huge disparity in athletic budgets among Division I schools. At one extreme, Ohio State had an athletic budget of $109.3 million in 2007, and the University of Texas had a $106 million budget. At the other extreme, there are Division I schools with athletic budgets of less than $10 million. Even within a conference, there are huge gaps. In the Big 12, for example, Texas had an athletic budget twice that of Kansas, and almost four times that of Baylor. Moreover, while the Big Ten splits television revenues evenly among the member schools, the Big 12 splits half evenly and distributes the other half based on the number of television appearances each school makes. This, of course, makes the rich in that conference—Texas, Oklahoma, and Nebraska—richer. To change this rule requires nine votes (75 percent), and the wealthy schools vote to keep the system unfair.[11] Are the Big 12 teams playing on a level playing field? I think not.

The discrepancy is greatest when the imbalance in monies received by each conference of Division I schools is considered. Each conference receives money from bowl appearances, NCAA basketball appearances, and television contracts. This money is then distributed (minus administrative costs) to the member schools. Some big-money conferences such as the Southeastern (SEC), the Big Ten, and the Big 12, have revenues exceeding $100 million. At the other extreme, ten Division I-A conferences have total revenues of less than $2 million.

Money is critical in creating and sustaining winning programs. Money builds bigger stadiums and field houses, with expensive skyboxes. Money builds state-of-the-art weight rooms with saunas and spas to attract recruits. Money buys better equipment. The elite schools spend about $90,000 per athlete annually (Ohio State, for example, spends $110,000 on each of 980 athletes, which is triple the amount the university spends per undergraduate on education).[12]

Winning programs attract money. Corporations pay handsomely to have their logos displayed in the arenas. Shoe/equipment companies provide subsidies, amounting to several million dollars annually, to be the exclusive supplier. Nike, for example, has arrangements with about 200 college athletic departments, offering cash and equipment ranging from $4 million annually to the successful programs and just free shoes to the least successful. Royalties from the sale of merchandise generates millions to the elite schools (near the top, the University of Michigan has received an average of $4.38 million annually over the past ten years in royalties from such sales). Proud supporters attend games, buy season tickets, pay for the right to purchase tickets, contribute to the athletic programs, and subsidize athletic scholarships. Penn State, for example, collected $8.8 million from its football seating plan, which rewarded boosters based on the size of their contributions. It raised another $5 million in endowments and gifts for the athletic department. Schools like Michigan, Tennessee, and Penn State attract over 100,000 spectators to each home football game, and other schools with elite programs (for example, Nebraska, Florida, Florida State, and Texas) sell out at 80,000 or more per game. Similarly, schools such as Syracuse, Tennessee, and North Carolina sell out their field houses for men's basketball games with 20,000-plus fans. Other Division I men's basketball programs struggle for fans (and money), with attendance averaging less than 2,000 per home game. While the elite programs flourish, the majority of Division I athletic programs grapple with financial losses. And the financial gap widens.

To reduce losses, the "have-nots" typically schedule games with elite teams. These games are always played at the elite schools, where the "have-nots" typically are pummeled, but they get a large payoff (Penn State, which made more than $3 million on the game, paid Toledo $350,000 to play a football game, an amount that represented about one-third of its annual football revenue and more than double the take for one of its home games). Similarly, schools like Troy State and Middle Tennessee State schedule such football powers as Nebraska, Florida State, and Ohio State. Morris Brown, a new Division I member in 2001, played twenty-two basketball games away from home at Clemson, Tulsa, Mississippi, Oregon, Iowa State, and Marquette. Traveling some 17,000 miles, they took in $287,000 and went 6–23 as sacrificial lambs, winning only four games against Division I opponents. Even with this economic boost of playing against the heavyweights, Morris Brown's athletic department had revenues of $1.9 million but spent $3.5 million for a deficit of $1.6 million.[13]

Big-time college sport is structured to make the rich richer by the payouts for participation in bowl games and the NCAA basketball tournament. I will concentrate here on the bowl games. Who gets invited to a bowl game seems fair enough since the selection appears to be based on performance. One hundred and nineteen Division I-A teams play their seasons, monitored by coaches, writers, computers for the BCS bowls, and the bowl committees for the lesser bowls. However, the process is not fair and clearly aids the rich in getting richer.

Beginning in 1998, the BCS (in lieu of a championship tournament, as is the case in basketball) consists of four bowl games (Sugar, Orange, Fiesta, and Rose), with one designated as the national championship on a rotating basis. The decision as to which teams are selected is determined by a format combining human polls with computer-generated data on strength of schedule and other variables. But this process is skewed in favor of the elite teams. In a deal between the television networks and the top six conferences, plus Notre Dame, it was determined that the champion in each of the six power conferences would be guaranteed a slot in one of the high-paying bowls. The remaining two slots are open, but the chances are high that they, too, will be filled by schools from the power conferences. Thus there is the possibility but no guarantee that two schools will be chosen from the remaining fifty-seven schools in Division I-A from the second- and third-tier conferences. Since 2004, the University of Utah, Boise State, and Hawaii have been the only non-BCS conference schools to be selected for one of the high-payout games. Since each team in a BCS bowl receives $17 million, this means that the power conferences and their member schools, and an occasional non-BCS school, share at least $136 million annually (minus expenses). Adding to this skewed arrangement, the guarantee of the conference champion from the favored six conferences being included in the big bowl games leaves more deserving teams out.

Moreover, many teams playing in the lesser bowl games actually lose money. Many of the lesser bowls have payouts per team of around $750,000, with a low of $300,000 in 2008, not the $17 million that each team receives for being in a BCS bowl. Furthermore, to accept a bowl bid means, for many bowls, guaranteeing that the school will sell a certain number of tickets. This often results in a bowl team losing money.

Another dimension of the "unequal playing field" in college sports is the manner in which teams are selected to participate in the non-BCS bowls. Team records count less than ticket sales and television appeal in the decision. Thus, in the 2002 bowl season, Hawaii with a 9–3 record was not invited while thirty-one teams with records worse than 9–3 played in bowl games. In that year, the Gator Bowl was obligated by contract to select the Big East's runner-up but invoked an escape clause to invite third-place Virginia Tech instead. "Bowl officials said bluntly that economics made the difference: Virginia Tech played there last year and sold 18,000 tickets. Syracuse, which finished second in the conference, sold only 7,000 tickets when it last played there in 1996."[14] In other words, money talks louder than performance.

The financial payoffs for wins in the NCAA men's basketball tournament is another way that the "rich get richer." The system works this way.[15] The money a team earns from the tournament is determined by the number of games it plays. Each game played is considered a "unit," and the value of each unit was just under $200,000 in 2008. The maximum number of units a school can earn is five (there is no credit given for the championship game). In addition, each league gets credit for the units earned by each of its teams. In the 2008 tournament, for example, the eventual champion—Kansas (full disclosure, KU is my alma mater) earned about $1 million for its five units, while the Big 12 received credit for KU's five units, plus six league teams earned another 16 units. So Kansas, a consistent power in men's basketball earned $1 million plus a twelfth of the value of the combined league units. The six power conferences received 28 of the 34 at-large berths in the 2008 tournament, with the Big East qualifying eight teams. Some leagues, of course, received, at most, one unit for playing a game. Hence, the financial gap widens between the successful and the relatively unsuccessful.

The conclusion, then, is obvious: the system in Division I sports is structured to ensure that the rich will become richer and the poor poorer.

The Rich Get Richer: The Case of Major League Baseball

Major league baseball teams have revenues from the league's television deals, ticket sales, rentals of expensive luxury boxes, advertising, and the sale of broadcasting rights to local radio and television outlets. The money from the league's television deals is shared, as are ticket sales (not luxury boxes), and to a lesser extent there is some sharing of a team's net local broadcasting revenues among the other teams. The remainder is retained by each team. This arrangement provides an enormous advantage to the large market teams (those in bigger cities with larger fan bases and lucrative cable-television income, such as the New York Yankees, the Boston Red Sox, the Los Angeles Dodgers, and the New York Mets). In the 2007 season, the average revenue of a major league team was $183 million. At the top the New York Yankees had revenue of $327 million, while at the bottom the Florida Marlins generated only $128 million.[16] Illustrating the gap, Alex Rodriguez of the Yankees, the highest paid player in baseball at $28 million, made $6.2 million more than the entire 33-man opening-day roster of the Florida Marlins.

This imbalance diminishes the competitive balance in the league. The high-revenue clubs are able to pay enormous salaries for marquee players whose contracts at low-revenue clubs have expired. For example, in 2008 the Yankees' player payroll was $209.1 million compared to the lowly Florida Marlins, whose $21.8 million payroll is $187.3 million less than that of the Yankees. In 1990 this payroll gap between the richest and poorest teams was only about $13 million.[17]

To counter the advantage of the high-revenue teams, Major League Baseball has instituted a revenue-sharing strategy, whereby the richer teams pay into a pool that is divided among the poorer teams In 2006 more than $300 million was redistributed in this manner. The problem, as noted by Michael Lewis, is that the "teams receiving payments have come to use them as a primary source of income—rather than to build winning teams."[18]

As a consequence, there is little hope of going to the World Series if the franchise is in the bottom half in revenue.

Two facts underscore this: (1) Since revenue sharing began in 1998, at least one team from each of the big four markets—New York, Los Angeles, Chicago, and Boston, has appeared in every World Series except 2006. (2) Over the past twenty years, teams with relatively small payrolls have won their divisions less than 10 percent of the time. [19]

Revenue sharing appears to be fair, but the team owners with local media properties can deflate their incomes and thus reduce their revenue-sharing payments. For example, Yankees owner George Steinbrenner controls 60 percent of YES, the Yankees' exclusive cable channel, which brings in an estimated $200 million from cable operators and advertising. The bulk of this money stays in YES and with its shareholders and is not presented as income for the Yankees.[20]

The National Football League (NFL), in contrast to Major League Baseball, shares much of its wealth among its thirty-two teams. The television package and its NFL merchandise are shared equally. Gate receipts are split 60/40 in favor of the home team, but that does not include revenues from skyboxes, parking, and concessions. Other equalizing methods in the NFL are mixing a free-agency system with a stringent cap on team payrolls, the weakest teams pick earliest in the college draft, and the poorer the performance in the previous year, the softer the schedule.

In an editorial, the *New York Times* compared the unequal arrangement in baseball with the more equitable situation in professional football. "[Major League Baseball] represents the triumph of raw, laissez-faire capitalism, with rich, successful teams getting richer and more successful by the year. The N.F.L., in sharp contrast, is a socialist society that incessantly strives for parity."[21] An editorial in the *Boston Globe* made these interesting comparisons between the two leagues, resulting from their differing approaches:[22]

- From 1995 to 2001 only seven different teams have played in the World Series. In those same years, twelve different teams have played in the Super Bowl.
- While only one of the seven World Series participants from 1995–2001 came from a metropolitan area of under 3 million, six of the twelve teams that have played in the Super Bowl during that period came from metropolitan areas of under 3 million.

Nicholas Dawidoff, editor of *Baseball: A Literary Anthology*, laments what has happened to baseball:

In a national pastime laden with symbolism, the rituals of the new baseball season have long served as an annual re-enactment of the most basic American premise—that at the beginning, anything is possible for everyone. Yet when this year's season begins tomorrow, that democratic sense of possibility will be diminished. In recent years, winning has come too predictably to the teams with the biggest payrolls. . . . As a professional game played by men sized and shaped like average citizens, baseball has always seemed to represent the virtues of honest competition and fair play. It is enormously alienating to most fans—for whom baseball is an escape from the prosaic matters like wages and budgets—that it has become impossible to talk about the sport without talking about money.[24]

I have made the case in this chapter that sport is sometimes structured to be unfair—that sport does not always take place on a level playing field. In each of these illustrations (racial and gender inequities, and the rich getting richer in big-time college sport and major league baseball), structural changes could correct the imbalances. The entrenched benefactors of the status quo, however, are reluctant to give up their advantages and level the playing field, making a mockery of the notion that success in sport is based strictly on performance.

NOTES

1. DeWayne Wickham, "The Asterisks Should Start in the Pre-Blacks Baseball Era," *USA Today*, November 20, 2007, p. 11A.

2. For a survey of the research, see D. Stanley Eitzen and George H. Sage, *Sociology of North American Sport*, 8th ed. (Boulder, Colo.: Paradigm, 2009), chapter 13.

3. "The NFL's Numbers Problem," *Sports Illustrated*, March 31, 1997, pp. 29–30.

4. Institute for Diversity and Ethics in Sport, "Lack of Diversity Among Campus, Conference Leaders at Division I-A Schools May Contribute to Lack of Diversity in Head Football Coaching Positions," press release, November 17, 2004.

5. Roger Angell, "Box Score: Has Baseball Fulfilled Jackie Robinson's Promise?" *New Yorker*, April 14, 1997, p. 6.

6. Eitzen and Sage, *Sociology of North American Sport*, 310.

7. R. Vivian Acosta and Linda J. Carpenter, "Women in Intercollegiate Sport: A Longitudinal Study—Twenty-Nine Year Update: 1977–2006" (West Brookfield, Mass.: Carpenter/Acosta, 2006). Donna Lopiano, "The State of

Women's Sports 2006," East Meadow, NY: Women's Sports Foundation, 2006; Donna Lopiano, "Pay Inequity in Athletics," East Meadow, NY: Women's Sports Foundation, 2007.

8. Jay J. Coakley, *Sport in Society: Issues & Controversies*, 8th ed. (New York: McGraw-Hill, 2004).

9. Mary Jo Kane, "Can Women Save Sports? An Interview by Lynette Lamb," *Utne Reader* 97 (January/February 2000): 57.

10. Steve Wieberg, "Most Top Recruits Say BCS Schools Considered First," *USA Today*, January 22, 2004, p. 6C.

11. Joe Walljasper, "A Half-Dozen Questions for Big 12 Commission," *Columbia Tribune*, May 20, 2007. D. Stanley Eitzen, "Sport, College," in *The Blackwell Encyclopedia of Sociology*, vol. IX, ed. George Ritzer (Malden, Mass.: Blackwell, 2007), 4655–68.

12. Jon Weinbach, "Inside College Sports' Biggest Money Machine," *Wall Street Journal*, October 19, 2007.

13. Grant Wahl and George Dohrmann, "Welcome to the Big Time," *Sports Illustrated*, November 19, 2001, pp. 143–51.

14. "Bowl Winners, Sinners," *USA Today*, December 31, 2001, p. 10A.

15. Fred Mann, "Final Four Worth a Million to KU," *Wichita Eagle*, April 4, 2008, p. 1A.

16. "Team Valuations," *Forbes*, May 5, 2008, p. 93.

17. "Baseball Salaries," *USA Today*, April 2, 2008, pp. 1C, 4C–5C; Hal Bodley, "Yankees Keep Checkbook Wide Open," *USA Today*, April 10, 2003, p. 1C.

18. Michael Lewis, "Baseball's Losing Formula," *New York Times*, November 3, 2007, p. A31.

19. Lewis, "Baseball's Losing Formula," A31.

20. Michael K. Ozanian, with Cecily J. Fluke, "Inside Pitch," *Forbes*, April 28, 2003, pp. 64–66.

21. "Socialism Triumphs on the Gridiron," *New York Times*, December 30, 2000, online: www.nytimes.com/2000/12/30/opinion/30SAT3.html.

22. "What Baseball Could Learn from Football," *Boston Globe*, December 12, 2001.

24. Nicholas Dawidoff, "Buying Up Baseball's Possibilities," *New York Times*, March 30, 2002, online: nytimes.com/2002/03/30/opinion/30DAWI.html.

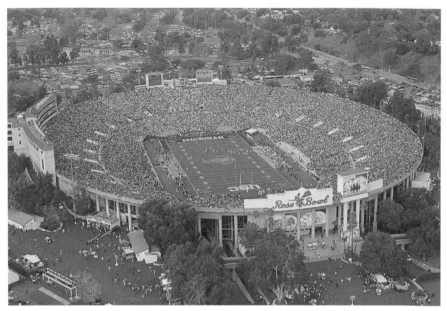

Long Photography/AP/Wide World

THE CONTRADICTIONS
OF BIG-TIME COLLEGE SPORTS

The business of college sports is not a necessary evil. Rather it is a proper part of the overall enterprise.

—Myles Brand, president of the NCAA

It's a dirty business, big-time college sports. The best way to watch is with blinders and to pretend what you're seeing smells like school spirit.

—Mike Littwin, *Rocky Mountain News* sportswriter

Mega college athletics . . . prospers because for the most part we (our faculty, our staff, our alumni, our trustees) want it. We could easily change it, if most of us wanted to change it. All protestations to the contrary, we . . . do not want to change it.

—John V. Lombardi, president of the
Louisiana State University System

Awhile back, after Duke was eliminated from the NCAA Division I men's basketball tournament, its highly successful and esteemed coach, Mike Krzyzewski, made an emotional speech. Coach K, as he is affectionately known, extolled the virtues of big-time college sport—

the camaraderie, the shared sacrifice, the commitment to excellence, collective responsibility, and integrity. He said, "All this stuff where people talk about college sports and things as bad, you have no idea. I want to whack everybody who says that. College sports are great. They're O.K. when you yell at each other, when you hug each other, when you live."[1]

I love sports. As sportswriter John Feinstein says, "As in life, [sport] is really about competition and teamwork and succeeding—or failing—after a worthy struggle."[2] College sport intensifies those feelings for me. Although I truly love college sport, I believe that big-time college sport compromises the values of higher education. I am one of those critics that Coach K wants to "whack." Coach K acknowledges that there are abuses in college sports—cheating and other unethical practices. In his view, these are behaviors by bad people "who have lost sight of the true purpose of college sport and let the pursuit of winning override the pursuit of teaching." I do not question Coach K's genuine affection for his players or his sincerity about the glories of big-time college sport. I do question his perception and analysis. Coach K takes an individualistic perspective, which means that he does not see—and this is the crucial sociological point—the wrongs that occur because of the way big-time college sport is organized.

Is big-time college sport[3] compatible with higher education? Clearly, it has entertainment value, unites supporters of a given school, provides free publicity for the schools, gives good athletes from economically disadvantaged backgrounds the chance for a college education, and serves as a training ground for the relatively few future professional athletes. But does big-time college sport complement or promote the educational goals of colleges and universities? Put another way, are the athletic programs at big-time schools consistent with the educational mission of U.S. colleges and universities? To answer this question, I shall, as is my sociological inclination, examine the dark side of big-time college sport as well as the "big picture."

A brief survey of the history of college sport shows that aspects of commercialization, sham students, and "tramp" athletes were there at the start. In 1852 the first intercollegiate sports contest occurred as the crews from Harvard and Yale raced against each other. The expenses of both teams were funded by the Boston, Concord, and Montreal Railroad, which saw the event as a commercial venture. In 1867 the first college football game was played, between Princeton and Rutgers, with several players taking the field who could have been ruled academically ineligible. Later, some schools used players who had no connection to their institutions. These early contests, for the most part, were organized by students. Faculties, administrators, friends of the school, and alumni were not involved. Alas, the students soon lost their control over their sports. Leagues were formed and a national organization, later called the National Collegiate Athletic Association (NCAA), was organized in 1905 to standardize rules and address problems associated with college sport (questions concerning the eligibility of athletes, the high rate of injuries, cheating, and the like).

The popularity of college sport was rather localized during the first half of the twentieth century. There were occasional scandals that involved cheating in recruitment and gambling. Around 1970 the advent of televised athletics transformed college sport. Television focused on a few schools and funneled ever greater amounts of money to them. This was the true beginning of big-time college sports, which became hugely popular, national in scope, and increasingly commercial. With the new source of funds flowing into a few schools, university athletic departments became quasi-separate entities, some boosters wielded extraordinary influence over athletic departments, and players were often abused and exploited—a far cry from the beginning of intercollegiate sport.

What was once a student-run activity has been transformed, and now students have virtually no voice in athletic policies, control being vested in coaches, boosters, school administrators, leagues, national organizations, corporations, and television. In the process, college sport changed from an activity primarily for the participants to full-scale commercial entertainment with large monetary payouts. This transformation of intercollegiate sport saw scandals increase in number and gravity. These scandals stem from intense pressure to win and to succeed financially. Again I ask, is the current state of big-time college sport appropriate to institutions of higher learning?

EDUCATION AND BIG-TIME COLLEGE SPORT

Ironically, athletes who are recruited for reasons other than their cognitive abilities receive more than $1 billion in full or partial athletic scholarships. Many schools award more merit-based scholarship money to athletes than to all other scholarship students combined.[4] Penn State, for example, spends twice as much on athletic scholarships as it does on academic aid for its top students. During one year in the 1990s, Duke University awarded $4 million to its 550 student-athletes, and only $400,000 in academic merit grants for its 5,900 other undergraduates.[5] Not only do schools spend more scholarship money on athletes than on scholars, but many of these athletic scholarships are given to athletes who have little chance of making it academically or even to those who do not care about receiving a college education. One egregious example from the past involves North Carolina State. Whereas the average SAT score for the student body was 1030 at the time, the school admitted a basketball player, Chris Washburn, who had an SAT of 470 and an IQ of 86. Especially telling about this example is that over one hundred universities offered Chris Washburn a full scholarship. Under current NCAA rules, Chris Washburn would not receive a scholarship and would not even be eligible to play. Now there is a sliding scale to determine initial eligibility. The lower the grade-point average, the higher the SAT score must be, plus the athlete has to earn at least a C in fourteen core high school courses. Nevertheless, athletes who are marginal students continue to be admitted. Football and men's basketball players in big-time sports programs are more than six times as likely as other students to receive special treatment in the admissions process; that is, they are admitted below the standard requirements for their universities. This is true also for elite schools such as Williams College where sport is not big-time. James L. Shulman and William G. Bowen, in their book *The Game of Life*, analyzed data from 90,000 students from the classes of 1951, 1976, 1989, and to a lesser extent in 1999 at thirty highly selective liberal arts colleges and Ivy League universities and found that recruited male athletes had a 48 percent better chance of being admitted to school than typical applicants, meaning that they enter these colleges with considerably lower SAT scores and high school grades, on average, than their nonathletic classmates. As a result, among those studied who entered in the fall of 1989, 58 percent of the recruited male athletes were in the bottom third of their class at graduation, as were 72 percent of the male athletes in the high-profile sports of football, basketball, and ice hockey and 39 percent of female athletes.[6] The same tendency to admit athletes who are below academic standards has even been found at the Air Force Academy. The class of 2001 admitted 277 freshman cadets (21 percent) who were below the academy's grade standards. Of these 277 waivers, 165 went to sports recruits. A study by the *Colorado Springs Gazette* found that the athletes who got into the academy with academic waivers were less likely to graduate, less likely to become pilots, less likely to move into critical high-tech jobs, and less likely to rise to the service's top echelons.[7]

Many argue that special admissions criteria should be targeted to assist underprivileged minority students. This is a legitimate argument because many young people live in a "third world" of grinding poverty, violent neighborhoods, inadequately financed schools, and few successful role models. However, I argue that these exceptions for admission should be granted to those who have the potential for academic success, not, as is the case now, for athletic success.[8] Although affirmative action is frowned on by many as favoritism, there is a comprehensive, well-financed, and widely supported form of affirmative action for athletes, especially African American athletes. Coaches, scouts, and sports recruiters nurture disadvantaged athletes, identifying talented athletes and finding ways to enhance their talents. No similar infrastructure exists to coach minority youngsters with nonathletic talents.

What is troubling about this imbalance is not that athletes are undeserving or that helping them is wrong. The problem is that an opportunity to provide an education for academically talented minorities is missed. Their talents are not developed, which limits them and society. African Americans are underrepresented as physicians, lawyers, and other professionals in the United States. On the other hand, African Americans are overrepresented as professional athletes. They make up 75 percent of the players in professional basketball and 66 percent in professional football. Some argue that the disproportionately high number of African Americans in professional sport is an appropriate rationale for giving them scholarships to college—going to college allows them to hone their skills for a professional sports career. But only a small proportion of college athletes make it at the professional level. More than 17,600 young men play Division I-A football and basketball, and each year only 150 to 200 (about 1 percent) reach the professional leagues, and even fewer last more than a year. When schools overrecruit minorities for their athletic skills and underrecruit minorities for their academic skills, they contradict the fundamental purpose of education in a democratic society. Moreover, recruiting African Americans for their physical skills reinforces the negative stereotype that African Americans are endowed with special physical attributes but lack the necessary mental aptitude.

College athletes in big-time programs are recruited to be part of a commercial entertainment organization that has nothing to do with the educational mission of schools. As president of the University of Chicago, Robert Hutchins dropped the football program, saying, "A college racing stable makes as much sense as college football. The jockey could carry the college colors; the students could cheer; the alumni could bet; and the horse wouldn't have to pass a history test."[9] Murray Sperber, former Indiana professor, makes a similar point:

> Athletes are the only group of students recruited for entertainment—not academic—purposes, and they are the only students who go through school on grants based not on educational aptitude, but on their talent and potential as commercial entertainers.
>
> If colleges searched for and gave scholarships to up-and-coming rock stars so that they could entertain the university community and earn money for their schools through concerts and tours, educational authorities and the public would call this "a perversion of academic values." Yet every year, American institutions of higher education hand out over a hundred thousand full or partial scholarships, worth at least $500 million [now $1 billion], for reasons similar to the hypothetical grants to rock performers.[10]

The Education of Athletes

The education of inadequately prepared athletes is a daunting task. As we have seen, many athletes are admitted to their schools even though they are below the minimum standards. As a result, athletes in big-time programs are more than two hundred points behind the average student on the SAT. How do the schools keep their inadequately prepared athletes eligible? The athletic departments hire tutors for their athletes. Typically, there are mandatory study sessions for freshmen and for nonfreshmen whose grades are in jeopardy. That's the good news. The bad news is that the athletic role, in the eyes of many coaches and athletes, supersedes the student role. A statement by the late Paul "Bear" Bryant, legendary football coach at the University of Alabama, illustrates a fundamental contradiction that big-time sport brings to academe: "I used to go along with the idea that football players on scholarship were 'student-athletes,' which is what the NCAA calls them. Meaning a student first, an athlete second. We were kidding ourselves, trying to make it more palatable to the academicians. We don't have to say that and we shouldn't. At the level we play, the boy is really an athlete first and a student second."[11]

Coaches who concur with this sentiment, coupled with the pressure to win, tend to diminish the student role by counseling their students to take easy courses, to choose easy majors, and to sign up for courses from cooperative faculty members who are willing to give athletes "special" considerations in the classroom. Or they may steer them toward correspondence courses with few or no requirements. They also use a loophole in the current rules, which states that a student-athlete must be making adequate progress toward a degree. To get around this rule, the athlete is counseled to change majors, thus starting the "progress toward a degree" all over again as well as avoiding the hardest courses in a major, such as statistics. To accentuate the athlete role, the coaches demand incredible amounts of time (practices, meetings, travel, studying videotape and playbooks). Athletes are required to lift weights and engage in other forms of conditioning as well as "informal" practices during the off-season, including summers.[12] The NCAA has attempted to control the excesses of these demands but has met with little success.

In addition to the time constraints of big-time college sport, the athletes must also cope with physical exhaustion, mental fatigue, media attention, and demanding coaches. Athletes in these commercialized, professionalized programs have trouble reconciling the roles associated with their dual status of athlete and student. This problem is especially acute for those who were poorly prepared for higher education. Academically challenged athletes, research has shown, are most likely to take easy courses, cheat on exams, hire surrogate test-takers, take phantom courses, and otherwise do the minimum required. A study of one basketball program by sociologists Patricia and Peter Adler found that the pressures of big-time sport and academic demands resulted in the gradual disengagement of the athletes from their academic roles.[13]

The researchers found that most athletes entered the university feeling idealistic about the academic side of their college performance. This idealism lasted about one year and was replaced by disappointment and a growing cynicism as they realized how difficult it was to keep up with their schoolwork. The athletic role came to dominate all facets of their existence. The athletes received greater positive reinforcement for their athletic performance than for their academic performance. They became increasingly isolated from the student body as a result of segregated living arrangements, and their racial and socioeconomic differences isolated them culturally from the rest of the students. They were even isolated socially from other students by their physical size, which many found intimidating. They interacted primarily with other athletes, and these peers tended to put down academics. First-year athletes took courses from "sympathetic" professors, but this changed as they moved through the university curriculum. The athletes were unprepared for escalating academic expectations. The typical response of these athletes was distancing themselves from the student role, also known as role distancing. The Adlers say that for these athletes, "it was better not to try than to try and not succeed."[14] This attitude was reinforced by the peer subculture. Thus the structure of big-time programs works to maximize the athlete role and minimize the academic role—clearly opposite the goals of higher education.

Poor preparation for college and depreciation of the student role result in a lower graduation rate for big-time college athletes compared to their nonathlete peers, tracking them six years after entering college. Using this measure, some categories of athletes exceed nonathletes in graduate rates: women, whites, and athletes in non-revenue-producing sports. Those below the student body rate are male athletes, African American athletes (women and men), athletes in football and men's basketball, and football players in the major football conferences. Focusing on football and men's basketball in the big-time programs, the data for the classes entering in 2000 reveal graduation rates in 2006 for the top-tier schools:[15]

- Of the top twenty-five ranked football teams, sixteen were below the average for the sport. Texas, the defending champion, had a graduation rate of 40 percent.

- While three schools (Navy, Boston College, and Notre Dame) in Division I-A had rates at 95 percent or better for their football teams, three (San Jose State, Florida Atlantic, and the University of Arizona) were below 40 percent.
- For basketball, seventeen schools had 100 percent graduation rates. Three schools, however (New Mexico, Florida A&M, and the University of Georgia), had rates below 10 percent.
- Twelve Division I-A schools had sub-50 percent graduation rates in both football and basketball, including the University of Arizona, the University of California-Berkeley, Louisiana State University, and the Universities of Georgia, Minnesota, and Texas.

Consider two caveats when interpreting these data. First, be wary of official statistics supplied by the NCAA that compare athletes' graduation rates with the student body, because they are lumping all athletes together, washing out in part the relatively low grades of male athletes and athletes in revenue-producing sports. And, second, comparing athletes, many of whom come from economically disadvantaged backgrounds, with the more privileged nonathletes in the student body yields distorted information.

In every study, African Americans, when compared to their white counterparts, are less prepared for college. They enter as marginal students and, in general, leave that way. Sociologist Harry Edwards, an African American, has argued that the black "dumb jock" is a social creation. "Dumb jocks are not born; they are systematically created."[16] This social construction results from several factors. First, African American student-athletes must contend with two negative labels: the dumb athlete caricature and the dumb black stereotype. This double negative tends to result in a self-fulfilling prophecy as professors, fellow students, and the athletes themselves assume low academic performance.

Moreover, as soon as African American youngsters are labeled as potential athletic superstars, many teachers, administrators, and parents lower their academic demands, believing that athletic stardom will be the ticket out of the ghetto. In junior high school and high school, little is demanded of them academically. The reduced academic expectations continue in college (or in community college if they do not qualify for a higher-level college). With professors who "give" grades, occasional altered transcripts, surrogate test-takers, and phantom courses, there is, as Harry Edwards has said, "little wonder that so many black scholarship student-athletes manage to go through four years of college enrollment virtually unscathed by education."[17]

The inescapable conclusion is that providing a free education to athletes, while expecting more from them as athletes than as students, as well as creating a situation that moves them away from academic pursuits, is contrary to the lofty goals of higher education.

COLLEGE SPORT AS BIG BUSINESS

Big-time college sport is organized in such a way that separating the business aspects from the play on the field is impossible. The intrusion of money into collegiate sport is evident in the following representative examples:[18]

- College sports is a more than $5 billion business.
- At a cost of $6 billion, CBS has an eleven-year agreement to televise the NCAA men's basketball championship tournament.
- The Coca-Cola Company has an 11-year, $500 million contract with the NCAA giving it the exclusive right to advertise and promote its products at the 86 championships in 22 sports sponsored by the NCAA.
- The NCAA receives an average of $545 million annually through 2013 from CBS for the rights to televise the Final Four men's basketball tournament.
- ABC purchased the TV rights to the Rose Bowl with an eight-year deal worth about $300 million for ten games, beginning after the 2006 game. ESPN and ABC renewed their deal to carry Atlantic Coast Conference football for seven years, at $270 million.
- The University of Minnesota sold the naming rights to its football stadium to TCF Bank for $35 million.
- The nation's largest athletic department, Ohio State, had a budget in 2007–2008 of $109.3 million, followed by the University of Texas at $106 million.

- In 2005, T. Boone Pickens donated $165 million to the Oklahoma State athletic department. Nike chairman Philip H. Knight gave $100 million to the University of Oregon athletic department.
- Schools sell licensing rights for the right to use their logos on clothes, beer mugs, and other items. In the year following winning the national football championship, Texas received licensing royalties of $8.2 million.
- Thirty-three Division I-A universities have live mascots. It cost $3 million for the 15,000 sq. ft. home of Louisiana State University's Mike the Tiger.
- The winning team in the title game for the men's basketball championship has the right to purchase the court used in the Final Four. After Florida won in 2007, the university purchased the floor for $70,000 and sold 1,026 1 ft. × 2 ft. pieces of the floor for $199 each ($204,174).
- The average salary for major-college football coaches topped $1 million at the end of 2007. Nick Saban at Alabama had a $4 million contract, and four coaches exceeded $3 million. In addition to Saban's $4 million a year, there are $700,000 in incentives, as well as perks such as two cars, a skybox, country club membership, and personal use of a private plane.
- Twenty basketball coaches exceeded $1 million a year not including benefits, perks, and incentives. The highest paid—Rick Pitino of Louisville—makes about $4 million.

The facts illustrated here have serious implications for institutions of higher education. First, they demonstrate clearly that college athletic programs are not amateur athletics (we will return to this point later in the chapter). Second, the system creates economic imperatives that lead college administrators, athletic directors, and coaches to make business decisions that supersede educational considerations. Tulane law professor Gary Roberts argues that this emphasis results in what he calls an "athletic arms race" among the schools:

The careers of key policy-makers [in sport] depend on the program's ability to produce and sell an entertainment product that will be attractive to consumers only if it spends enough money to be consistently competitive with other institutions that are constantly increasing their expenditures. So the desperate pressure to generate increasingly large amounts of revenue inevitably leads to business, not academic decisions.

What else could explain why schools have special admits for the most unprepared students, go to all great lengths to keep them eligible, schedule as many games as allowed and play them at absurd times of the week and night to accommodate television? Division I programs are, first and foremost, market-driven revenue producers, and their professed commitment to academics and the welfare of the student-athlete must be accommodated within and compromised by the limits that each institution's minimum-revenue requirements dictate.[19]

Thus, to make money, an athletic department must spend money on, for example, increasing the recruiting budget, hiring more fundraisers, improving practice facilities, adding new seating in the stadiums and arenas (especially skyboxes), purchasing the latest equipment, and building expensive new sports annexes with state-of-the-art locker rooms, weight rooms, training rooms, meeting rooms, and offices for the coaches and athletic administrators.

Nevertheless, except for a few schools, athletic programs lose money. Andrew Zimbalist, an economist, puts it this way:

The most successful programs (perhaps a dozen top schools, such as Michigan, Notre Dame, Florida, Washington, Alabama, Nebraska, Oklahoma, and Tennessee) are generating real surpluses year after year. Another group of programs (perhaps two to three dozen schools) generates an occasional surplus when their teams perform well in postseason tournaments. [The remaining big-time schools lose money.] Division I-A schools, which support the high expenses of football scholarships, large facilities, recruiting, travel, etc., but have not enjoyed on-field success, can lose large sums of money.[20]

These deficits would be much greater, however, if the accounting procedures were more appropriate. That is, the football teams play in stadiums paid for by taxpayers, contributors, and, more typically, bonds being paid off by students at no expense to the athletic departments. Moreover, a large proportion of student fees are automatically turned over to the athletic departments, as are subsidies from state legislatures and school administrators to pay for the athletes' scholarships. Using the University of Colorado as an example, the athletic budget is supplemented by over $3 million from mandatory student fees and money provided by the president's office. These student fees and university subsidies artificially inflate athletic department income. At Colorado State University, more than one-third of the budget comes from within the university—university support and student fees.

These subsidies also show how universities make business decisions concerning athletics that override educational considerations. In 1996, Tulane's governing board announced that it would increase its subsidy to the athletic department sixfold, from $550,000 to $3.4 million. This action by the board occurred just as it approved trimming $8.5 million from the university's budget while raising the tuition by 4 percent, freezing most faculty and staff salaries for one year, cutting fifty staff positions, and reducing funds for undergraduate student financial aid and graduate student stipends.[21] Clearly, in this situation monies are being transferred from the educational function of the universities to the entertainment function—a questionable transfer of wealth to say the least.

Successful programs (mostly in football) do not generate donations to the university. A study by economist Robert H. Frank found that, "Alumni donations and applications for admission sometimes rise in the wake of conspicuously successful seasons at a small number of institutions. But such increases are likely to be small and transitory . . . and there is not a shred of evidence to suggest that cuts in spending on athletics would reduce either donations by alumni or applications."[22]

Big-time programs generate significant donations from booster clubs and fans ($1.2 billion in 2006–2007). Most of these monies go for capital expenditures. But this sports fund-raising success comes at a cost—while the athletic departments benefit, the overall giving to the universities has remained flat. In effect, the more the athletic program gets, the less there is to support the academic programs.[23]

There are several reasons for the red ink generated by big-time athletic departments. I have already mentioned the continuing perception that programs must be upgraded with costly improvements to stay even with or ahead of competitors. Another reason is that employees in athletic departments tend to be better paid than other university employees. Travel budgets for the teams and recruiters are generous. A common practice, for example, is for the football team and coaches to stay in a local hotel the night before home games. Deficits are also generated by the costs associated with perks lavished on influential alumni, boosters, and legislators. At Wake Forest, for example, "contributors giving at least $55,000 a year fly free on teams' charter flights, are wined and dined, and get private 'chalk talks' from coaches before games. 'We don't skimp on these people,' says Cook Griffin, executive director of the Deacon Club, Wake's athletics fund-raising arm. 'You can't spend too much on them.'"[24]

Another consequence of an athletic department's quest for money is that decision making tends to leave the university and flow toward the sources of revenue. Television money dictates schedules. Booster organizations that supply funds may influence the hiring and firing of coaches. Who has the power when a football coach makes over eight times more money than the university president and when the coach has a powerful constituency outside the university? On numerous occasions, public opinion, governors, and boards of regents have sided with the coach when the university president and a popular coach clashed. For example, John DiBiaggio resigned as president of Michigan State University when its board of trustees twice circumvented his authority, extending the contract of the head football coach and then making that coach, George Perles, interim director of athletics. The point of these examples is that the athletic "tail" is wagging the university "dog." As Murray Sperber says, these practices "undermine one of the fundamental tenets of colleges and universities—their independence."[25]

Still another consequence of the athletic money chase is that students are, for the most part, left out. The irony is that students, who typically help the athletic department through their fees (which total more than $1 million annually at most big-time programs), have no influence over how their money is spent. Of all the categories of contributors to athletics, only students are left out of the power equation. Over 25,000 students at the University of Colorado give more than $1.2 million annually to the athletic budget with their student fees. Twenty-five boosters gave $40,000 each (a total of $1 million) to help the football coach buy an expensive home. Which group do you suppose has more influence over athletic department policy?

Students are also left out in the distribution of the relatively scarce seats available in the arenas of successful teams. These seats go to big-spending boosters, depriving some students of the chance to watch their teams play. The University of Louisville, for example, allots 10 percent of seats at basketball games to students. The University of Arizona holds a lottery to choose the students who may attend basketball games. The situation worsens during tournament time, when schools are allotted relatively few tickets. These scarce tickets, typically, are given to the greatest benefactors of the athletic department rather than to the students. This common practice raises a serious question: Should not school sports be primarily for the enjoyment of students?

Winning begets money, which increases the pressure to win, which, when the pressure becomes too great, may result in cheating. Cheating takes several forms. Most common is the offer of special inducements outside the rules by coaches and/or boosters to lure athletes to the school and to keep them there. Cheating may also involve unethical means to ensure the scholastic eligibility of the athletes. According to an exposé by *Sports Illustrated*, test fraud on the SAT examination is common, promoted by recruiters, high school coaches, middlemen, agents, and college coaches.[26] Scandals also involve altering transcripts, taking fraudulent courses from diploma mills, using surrogate test-takers, and the like. In one celebrated case, a federal jury indicted Baylor University's head basketball coach and three of his assistants, two junior college coaches, and two junior college administrators on charges of violating federal mail fraud, wire fraud, and conspiracy statutes. In effect, Baylor had faxed a term paper to a junior college player it was recruiting so that the player could use that paper in an English composition class he was taking at Westark Community College. Moreover, another Baylor recruit was instructed to take a correspondence course on the Old Testament from Southeastern College of the Assemblies of God because the Baylor coaches had a copy of the final exam for this course and others.[27] Finally, an athlete wanting to enroll at Baylor was provided with a fraudulent transcript by two administrators at his school, Shelton State Community College.[28]

There are many examples of scandal in big-time programs. In most instances, school administrators, students, and supporters do not demand that guilty coaches be fired for their transgressions—if they win.

As *Sports Illustrated* writer John Underwood has characterized the situation, "We've told them that it doesn't matter how clean they keep their programs. It doesn't matter what percentage of their athletes graduate or take a useful place in society. It doesn't even matter how well the coaches teach their sports. All that matters are the flashing scoreboard lights."[29]

The pursuit of money has prostituted the university, demeaning the education of the athletes and fostering immorality. In this milieu, winning and the money that is generated by winning are paramount. Thus the evil that results is not due to the malevolent personalities of coaches but to a perverse system. In this regard Philip Taubman says:

> [Big-time college sport] has become a big business, completely disconnected from the fundamental purposes of academic institutions. The goal of college ball is no longer for young men to test and strengthen their bodies, to learn about teamwork, and to have a good time. All that matters is winning, moving up in the national rankings, and grabbing a bigger share of the TV dollar. . . . To achieve these aims, schools and coaches not only bend and break the National Collegiate Athletic Association (NCAA) rules governing college football but, far more destructively, violate the intellectual integrity and principles of the American university system.[30]

Finally, there are always schools that seek to be in the big-time category, despite the problems associated with big-time college sports, including the long odds against financial success. This desire creates major fiscal problems for them. They must upgrade their facilities. They have to launch special fundraising campaigns that may siphon money that might otherwise be donated to the academic side of the university. They need increased subsidies from the university administration. They need to take more money from student fees. They may also seek subsidies from various levels of government. As an example, *Sports Illustrated* noted that "in Birmingham, where 25 percent of the population lives in poverty and 11 percent has less than an eighth-grade education, the city council has voted to give the University of Alabama at Birmingham $2.2 million in public funds to start a Division I-A football program."[31]

These schools typically schedule away games with established powers for big payouts. On the surface, this is a win-win situation for the two schools. The big-time school adds a win to its record, fills the arena, and keeps its place in the polls while the school on the make gets money to float its program. The downside for the would-be big-time school is that it might be humiliated on the field, and some of its players might be injured by the superior team. Surely this practice of deliberately scheduling mismatches for money is a form of prostitution.

THE DOMINANCE OF MALE ELITE SPORT

Title IX, which Congress passed in 1972, mandated gender equity in school sports programs. Women's intercollegiate sports programs have made tremendous strides toward that goal in the intervening years. In 1970, two years before Title IX, there were only 2.5 women's teams per school for a total of about 16,000 female athletes nationally. In 2006 there were 8.45 teams per school for a total of more than 170,000 female athletes. In 1971 only about 2 percent of the athletic budget went to women, whereas in 2006 it was 38 percent. Athletic scholarships for women were virtually unknown in 1972, whereas in 2006 women athletes received 45 percent of the athletic scholarship money that was distributed.[32] These increases in a generation represent the good news concerning gender equity in collegiate sport. The bad news, as elaborated in chapter 8, is that on every budgetary dimension, men's programs receive more resources than women's programs.

Clearly, gender equity is not part of big-time college sports programs. To move from its current imbalance, athletic administrations have three choices: spend more on women's sports, reduce or eliminate nonrevenue men's sports, or constrict football. If recent history is a guide, athletic departments will continue to add low-cost women's sports such as soccer and crew and cut low-profile men's sports such as wrestling, gymnastics, and baseball. Adding women's sports increases their participation, but it does not move them much closer to gender parity in scholarships or in other forms of economic assistance. Cutting men's programs is unfair to men because it reduces their participation and opportunities in the so-called minor sports. College sport, it seems to me, should enhance opportunities for participation, not limit them. Athletic departments achieve high male participation, but they do this with disproportionate participation opportunities for men in football.

Division I-A programs are allowed to have eighty-five scholarship play-ers, and squads include as many as 130 players. Thus football is a huge drain on the athletic budget and forms the basis for gender inequality in college athletics.

The rationale advanced to justify this unequal largesse to one sport is that football underwrites women's sport. This is a myth. Only about one-third of Division I-A football programs make a profit; one-third of them run an annual deficit that averages more than $1 million. The truth is that at most schools students pay for football through mandatory student fees and university subsidies.

Another myth is that football has already been cut to the bone. The NCAA a few years back did institute some cost-cutting reforms for football, such as reducing the number of scholarships to eighty-five and limiting the number of coaches. But some incredibly spendthrift practices remain, such as quartering entire squads in off-campus hotels on the night before home games, buying out the lucrative contracts of coaches no longer in favor and replacing them with even more expensive coaches, and building ever more palatial football annexes and arenas.

The law requires that women receive the same opportunities to play sports as men. Football, "the overfed sacred cow of college sports," stands in the way of gender equity, however. Football does bring in more money than any other sport and generates a profit for relatively few schools. Football and men's basketball do bring in the deals from shoe and apparel companies that provide a good share of the equipment for athletes in all sports, but only at the most successful programs. But with football considered sacred, men's so-called minor sports have been cut and women's sports underfunded. The answer, I believe, is to re-duce the outlay for football without reducing the quality of the product. This can be easily achieved by reducing football squads to sixty schol-arship athletes (the pros have squads of forty-five without sacrificing quality). This reduction in numbers decreases the cost of scholarships, equipment, training supplies, and the like. Accompanying this reduction would be a proportionate decrease in the number of coaches. Does a football team really need an interior offensive line coach or an outside linebacker coach? Such a plan cannot be enacted unilaterally and must be accomplished by the NCAA. This plan can also bring more balance to big-time football, as it would prevent the major powers from stockpiling talented benchwarmers.

Another solution to the gender equity bind is for women's sports to generate more revenue. Women's sports programs are at a disadvantage in producing significant revenues for several reasons:

1. Men's intercollegiate sport had a hundred-year head start in building tradition and fan support.
2. It takes money to make money, and women's sports programs have not been given anything approaching parity in resource allocation.
3. Women's sports are relatively ignored by university sports publicity and promotion staff, local and national newspapers, magazines, and television.
4. Women's sports continue to be trivialized by the schools in the naming of their teams (e.g., Wildkittens), as well as by the emphasis on the looks and nonathletic side of women athletes rather than their performance.

Granted, some of these obstacles to gender equity are changing slowly, with more television time being devoted to women's play, better promotions by the athletic departments, and the success of U.S. women athletes in international competition. Some women's basketball programs are profitable (Connecticut and Tennessee are quite profitable, as are a handful of other schools). But with success, women's budgets increase just as men's do. The highest paid women's basketball coach—Pat Summit of Tennessee—makes $1.125 million annually (two other coaches of women's teams—Geno Auriemma at Connecticut and Gail Goestenkors at Texas—exceed $1 million).

The problem with women's programs focusing on revenue is that in time they are likely to replicate all of the problems that money has brought to men's collegiate programs. Women's programs need more money, but at what point will money taint the women's game?

Finally, with regard to gender, universities must address the following question: Is it appropriate for a college or university to deny women the opportunities that it provides men? Shouldn't our daughters have the same opportunities that our sons have in all aspects of higher education? Women represent slightly more than half of the undergraduates in U.S. higher education. They receive half of all master's degrees. Should they be second-class participants in any aspect of the university's activities? The present unequal state of affairs in sport is not inevitable. Choices made in the past have given men an advantage in university sports. As Duke law professor John Weistart puts it, "Just as the existing tensions between genders in sport are the product of choice, they can be unchosen."[33] University administrators could implement true gender equity if they wished. Why do they continue to drag their collective feet on gender equity?

BIG-TIME COLLEGE SPORTS AS A PLANTATION

Many young people dream of playing football or basketball for a university with a big-time program. They want to be part of the pageantry, glory, excitement of intense competition, shared sacrifice, commitment to excellence, bonding with teammates, and to be the object of adoring fans. Not incidentally, they would also receive an all-expenses-paid college education, which, if a professional sports career does not work out, will open other lucrative career opportunities. Many observers of big-time college sports accept this idealized version, but just how glamorous is participation in athletics at this level? Are the athletes as privileged as they appear?

There is a dark side to big-time college sports for the participants. To show this, I will use the metaphor of big-time college sports as a plantation system.[34] I admit that such a metaphor is overdrawn. Big-time college sports is not the same as the brutalizing, inhumane, degrading, and repressive institution of slavery found in the antebellum South. Nevertheless, there are significant parallels with slavery that highlight the serious problems plaguing collegiate athletes. Thus the plantation/slavery metaphor is useful to understand the reality of the college sports world.

There is an organization—the NCAA—that preserves the plantation system, making and enforcing the rules to protect the interests of the individual plantation owners. The plantations are the universities with big-time programs. The overseers are the coaches who extract the labor from the workers. The workers are owned by the plantation and, much like the slaves of the antebellum South, produce the riches for their masters while receiving a meager return on the plantation's profits.

Many observers of big-time college sports, most certainly the coaches and players, would argue vehemently with this assertion that the athletes are slaves in a plantation environment. After all, they not only choose to participate, they want desperately to be a part of big-time sports. Moreover, they have special privileges that separate them from other students (much like what house slaves received, when compared to field slaves of the Old South), such as more and better food, special housing, favorable handling in registration for classes, and, sometimes, generous treatment by the criminal justice system when they cross the line. Also, the athletes, unlike slaves, can leave the program if they wish.

If participation is voluntary and the athletes want to be a part of the system, what is the problem? My argument that these athletes are slaves in a plantation system, whether they realize it or not, involves several dimensions: The athletes (slaves) are exploited economically, making millions for their masters, but provided only with a subsistence wage of room, board, tuition, and books; they are controlled with restricted freedoms; they are subject to physical and mental abuse by overseers; and the master-slave relationship is accepted as legitimate.

Financial Exploitation

We have seen that big-time college sports is a multi-billion-dollar industry (about $5 billion annually). The NCAA and the successful schools in the biggest conferences have huge budgets, fueled by 90,000 to 110,000 people attending a single football game at $60 or more a ticket. In 2008 at least 50 coaches made at least $1 million. At least a dozen pulled down $2 million or more, and five made more than $3 million. Obviously, big-time athletic programs are commercial enterprises. The irony is that, while sports events generate millions for each school, the workers are not paid. Economist Andrew Zimbalist has written that "Big-time intercollegiate athletics is a unique industry. No other industry in the United States manages not to pay its principal producers a

wage or a salary."[35] The universities and the NCAA claim that their athletes in big-time sports programs are amateurs and, despite the money
generated, the NCAA and its member schools are amateur organizations promoting an educational mission. This amateur status is vitally
important to the plantation owners in two regards. First, by not paying
the athletes what they are worth, the schools' expenses are minimized.
Second, since athletic departments and the NCAA are considered part
of the educational mission, they do not pay taxes on their millions from
television, sponsorships, licensing, the sale of skyboxes and season
tickets, and gate receipts. Moreover, contributions by individuals and
corporations to athletic departments are tax-deductible.

To keep these programs "amateur," the NCAA has devised a number
of rules that eliminate all economic benefits to the athletes: (1) they
may receive only educational benefits (room, board, tuition, and books);
(2) they cannot sign with an agent and retain eligibility; (3) they cannot
do commercials; (4) they cannot receive meals, clothing, transportation,
or other gifts from individuals other than family members; and (5) their
relatives cannot receive gifts of travel to attend games or other forms of
remuneration.

These rules reek with injustice. Athletes can make money for others,
but not for themselves. Their coaches have agents, as may students engaged in other extracurricular activities, but the athletes cannot. Athletes
are forbidden to engage in advertising, but their coaches are permitted
to endorse products for generous compensation. Corporate advertisements are displayed in the arenas where they play, but with no payoff to
athletes. The shoes and equipment worn by the athletes bear very visible
corporate logos, for which the schools are compensated handsomely.
The athletes make public appearances for their schools and their photographs are used to publicize the athletic department and sell tickets,
but they cannot benefit. The schools sell memorabilia and paraphernalia
that incorporate the athletes' likenesses, yet only the schools pocket the
royalties. The athletes cannot receive gifts, but coaches and other athletic
department personnel receive the free use of automobiles, country club
memberships, housing subsidies, and so forth.

Most significantly, coaches receive huge deals from shoe companies
(for example, Duke basketball coach Mike Krzyzewski has a fifteen-year
deal with Adidas, including a $1,000,000 bonus plus $375,000 annu-

ally), while the players are limited to wearing only that corporation's shoes and apparel. An open market operates when it comes to revenue for coaches, resulting in huge pay packages for the top names, but not so for star players. When a coach is fired or resigns, he often receives a "golden parachute," which sometimes is in the multi-million-dollar category, while players who leave the program early receive nothing but vilification for being disloyal. When a team is invited to a bowl game, it means an extra month of practice for the athletes, while coaches receive generous bonuses. A university entourage of administrators and their spouses accompany the team to the bowl game with all expenses paid, while the parents and spouses of athletes must pay their own way.

Restricted Freedoms

Slaves, by definition, are not free. The slaves of the antebellum era did not have the right to assemble or petition. They did not have the right to speak out nor did they have freedom of movement. Those conditions characterize today's college athletes as well. The NCAA, schools, and coaches restrict the freedom of athletes in many ways. By NCAA fiat, once athletes sign a contract to play for a school, they are bound to that institution. They make a four-year commitment to that college, yet the school makes only a one-year commitment to them. If an athlete wishes to play for another big-time school, he is ineligible for one year (two years if his former coach refuses to release the athlete from his contract). Yet, if a coach wants to get rid of an athlete, the school is merely bound to provide the scholarship for the remainder of that school year. Coaches, on the other hand, can break their contracts and immediately coach at another school. Economist Richard Sheehan illustrates how unfair this rule is for athletes, when they are compared to nonathlete students: "Suppose you accept a scholarship from Harvard to study under a Nobel laureate who then takes a position at Yale. Are you under any obligation to attend Harvard and not attempt to matriculate at Yale? This NCAA regulation, like many others, gives schools options and gives athletes nothing."[36]

The right to privacy is invaded routinely when it comes to college athletes. They—but not their coaches, teachers, or administrators—are subject to mandatory drug testing. Personnel from the athletic department watch athletes in their dorms and locker rooms, either in person or on closed-circuit television, for "deviant behaviors." Bed checks are not uncommon. Sometimes, there are "spies" who watch and report on the behaviors of athletes in local bars and other places of amusement.

Freedom of choice is violated when athletes are red-shirted (held from play for a year) without their consent. Athletes may have little or no choice in what position they play. They may be told to gain or lose weight, with penalties for noncompliance. Similarly, there are "voluntary" practices in the off-season that athletes must attend or incur the wrath of their coaches. Coaches may demand mandatory study halls and determine what courses the athletes will take and what their majors will be.

A number of coaches insist that their athletes avoid political protest. Some paternalistic coaches prohibit their athletes from associating with individuals or groups that they feel will have a negative influence on their players. Certain coaches demand dress codes and may even organize leisure-time activities that everyone must attend. Former University of Colorado basketball coach Ricardo Patton, for example, included among his mandatory team activities touring a prison, attending church services, sleeping as a group on cots in the gym for a week, and practicing at six in the morning. During slavery, the masters imposed their religious beliefs on their slaves. In today's sports world, team chaplains, chapel services, Bible study, and team prayers are commonplace. Coach Patton concluded each practice with the players holding hands in a circle while he or an athlete he called upon led the team in prayer. Patton claimed that participation was voluntary. Sportswriter Mike Littwin of the Denver *Rocky Mountain News* argues that the practice is anything but voluntary: "According to the argument, players, whose playing time and scholarship are dependent upon the coach's whim, are free to pray or not to pray with him. Here's what I believe: Anyone who thinks that when the coach says it's time to pray that it's somehow voluntary ought to pray for more wisdom. It is inherently coercive. It's about as voluntary as when the coach tells you to run laps. You're not the coach for 60 minutes of practice and then not the coach once you kneel on the floor."[37]

Physical and Mental Abuse

Although by no means a universal practice of coaches, instances of physical and mental cruelty toward players occur all too frequently.

University of South Carolina football coach Lou Holtz, for example, has used intimidation, humiliation, and even physical aggression on his players. When Holtz was at Notre Dame, one of his players, Chet Lacheta, made several mistakes in practice. In Lacheta's words: "[Holtz] started yelling at me. He said that I was a coward. He said that I should find a different sport to play and that I shouldn't come back in the fall. He was pretty rough. . . . First he grabbed my face mask and shook it. Then he spit on me."[38]

In addition to verbal and physical abuse, coaches use various means to control their athletes, such as having midnight practices after the team returns from a disappointing loss. Coach Bob Knight, while he was at Indiana, scheduled some holiday practices, without telling the players when to report for the next one. Consequently, they had to wait by their phones to hear from the manager about the practice schedule.[39] If not, they would incur the wrath of their autocratic boss. My point is that just as the owners of slaves were allowed to brutalize their chattel, so, too, are powerful coaches.

The Slave Mentality

Historians George Fredrickson and Christopher Lasch have stated that the real horror of slavery was that many of the slaves "mentally identified with the system that bound and confined them."[40] This is an especially troubling aspect of the plantation system that is found in big-time college sports. Jerry Farber's description of students in his classic 1960s critique of higher education, *The Student as Nigger*, aptly describes athletes as well: "They're pathetically eager to be pushed around. They're like those old greyheaded house niggers you can still find in the South who don't see what all the fuss is about because Mr. Charlie 'treats us real good.'"[41]

Sports sociologist George H. Sage provides some of the reasons why athletes rarely resist these authoritarian and unjust regimes:

A question may be raised about the lack of protest from intercollegiate athletes about the prevailing conditions under which they labor. In one way, it can be expected that the athletes would not find anything to question: they have been thoroughly conditioned by many years of organized sports involvement to obey athletic authorities. Indeed, most college athletes are faithful servants and spokespersons for the system of college sport. They tend to take the existing order for granted, not questioning the status quo because they are preoccupied with their own jobs or making the team and perhaps gaining national recognition. As a group, athletes tend to be politically passive and apathetic, resigned to domination from above because, at least partly, the institutional structure of athletics is essentially hostile to independence of mind. Hence, athletes are willing victims whose self-worth and self-esteem have largely become synonymous with their athletic prowess. Their main impulse is to mind their own business while striving to be successful as athletes.[42]

Another reason for the docility and submissiveness of athletes is that they are politically disenfranchised. Those who challenge the athletic power structure risk losing their scholarships and eligibility. Athletes who have a grievance are on their own. They have no union and no arbitration board. The coaches, athletic directors, and, ultimately, the NCAA have power over them as long as they are scholarship athletes. Their sole option is to leave the plantation. If they do quit, they are often viewed by others as the problem. After all, most accept the system. Those who quit are seen not as victims but as losers. So powerful is the socialization of athletes that even those who quit are likely to turn their anger inward, regarding themselves as the problem.

DEVIANT ATHLETES

A final and especially disturbing issue concerning big-time college sport is that the athletes in these programs are disproportionately involved in assaults, rapes, robberies, and other crimes. In the late 1980s, for example, over a thirty-two-month interval, there were twenty incidents involving University of Colorado athletes that resulted in criminal charges. Arizona State in one year had fourteen of its football and men's basketball players involved in arrests, charges, plea bargains, probation, or jail time. The *Los Angeles Times* reported that in 1995 some 220 college athletes faced criminal proceedings.[43] In 1995 *Sports Illustrated*

wrote an open letter to the president of the University of Miami arguing that he should eliminate the football program to salvage his school's
reputation. Included in that letter was a rationale for doing so:

> During the past decade your school enrolled and suited up at least one
> player who had scored a 200 on his verbal SAT—the number you get for
> spelling your name correctly. An on-campus disturbance, involving some
> 40 members of the football team, required 14 squad cars and a police dog
> to quell. Fifty-seven players were implicated in a financial scandal that
> the feds call "perhaps the largest centralized fraud upon the federal Pell
> Grant program ever committed." And among numerous cases of improper
> payments to players from agents was one in which the nondelivery of a
> promised installment led a Hurricane player to barge into the agent's of-
> fice and put a gun to his head. The illegal acts with which your Hurricanes
> have been charged run the gamut from disorderly conduct and shoplift-
> ing to drunken driving, burglary, arson, assault and sexual battery. . . . No
> fewer than one of every seven scholarship players on last season's team
> has been arrested while enrolled at your university.[44]

Two large studies reveal the extent of deviant athletes. A study of
reported violence against women (battering and sexual assaults) at
thirty Division I schools over a three-year period found that male student-athletes, who composed 3.3 percent of the total male population,
nevertheless represented 19 percent of sexual assault perpetrators and
35 percent of domestic violence perpetrators.[45] A 1990 national survey
of 13,000 students found that male athletes were three and a half times
more likely than nonathlete males to admit to having committed date
rape.[46] More recently, athletes at several universities, most notably, the
University of Colorado, were accused of rape at unofficial sex and alcohol parties for potential recruits.[47] A common practice is to use women
in their recruiting process. Sometimes it's hiring strippers for their
entertainment. Or there is the institutionalized hosting of athletes by
attractive coeds. For example, Texas has its Angels, Alabama its Bama
Belles, and the University of Maryland its Black-eyed Susans. These
women schmooze prospective recruits, show them the campus, and go
with them to parties. While, theoretically, these women are not there for
sex, some recruits may find it hard to see where the lines are drawn. A

former Bama Belle said that "one high-profile recruit tried to lure her to his hotel room, saying, 'The girls at Kentucky and Georgia did it.'"[48]

Although only a small percentage of student-athletes actually engage in criminal acts, college athletes are, nevertheless, disproportionately involved in deviance. There are a number of reasons for this, but I shall focus on two that have special relevance. First, many big-time programs recruit players who were in trouble before college. For example, five big-time college programs tried to recruit New York City high school star Richie Parker despite his felony conviction for sexual abuse. Cleveland State gave a scholarship to basketball player Roy Williams even though he had been convicted of murder as a teenager in California. While he was at Cleveland State, he was arrested for rape. The University of Cincinnati basketball program offered scholarships to three athletes who had criminal problems before college. Clearly, some coaches are willing to add a criminal element to their player mix if they believe it will increase their chances of success on the field. Second chances and redemption have their place, but should a university's scarce scholarship dollars go to convicted felons just because they are big, strong, and fast?

Second, many athletes come from deprived economic backgrounds. They are on scholarship but nevertheless lack money for clothes, food, and entertainment. These athletes are well aware that the school, the administrators, the coaches, and seemingly everyone else connected to the athletic program make money from their athletic performance. Logically, it seems to many of them that they deserve a piece of the action. So they may take money from an agent, use the athletic department's long-distance telephone credit card, accept money under the table from a booster or assistant coach, shoplift, or steal a laptop from a dorm room.

Whatever the reason for the disproportionate criminality among college athletes, universities ought to do some soul searching regarding their possible complicity in such deviance. The evidence is that the problem athletes are male and are involved with the revenue-producing sports of football and basketball. This clearly raises serious questions about the extra subsidies that are given to these programs, the evaluation of athletes to be given scholarships, and the monitoring of athletes when they are on campus.

CONTRADICTIONS

Big-time college sport confronts us with a fundamental dilemma. Positively, college football and basketball offer entertainment, spectacle, excitement, festival, and excellence. Negatively, the commercial entertainment function of big-time college sport has severely compromised academia. Educational goals have been superseded by the quest for big money. Because winning programs receive huge revenues from television, gate receipts, bowl and tournament appearances, boosters, and even legislatures, many sports programs are guided by a win-at-any-cost philosophy.

The enormous pressures to win result sometimes in scandalous behaviors. Sometimes there are illegal payments to athletes. Education is mocked by recruiting athletes unprepared for college studies, by altering transcripts, by using surrogate test-takers, by providing phantom courses, and by not moving the athletes toward graduation. William Reed of *Sports Illustrated* made the following comment about college basketball, but it is relevant to college football as well:

> Every fan knows that underneath its shiny veneer of color, fun and excitement, college basketball is a sewer full of rats. Lift the manhole cover on the street of gold, and the odor will knock you down. . . . The misdeeds allegedly committed by college basketball programs today are the same stuff that has plagued the game for decades—buying players, cheating in academics, shaving points, etc. And the NCAA is powerless to stop it. Make a statement by coming down hard on a Kentucky or a Maryland, and what happens? Nothing, really. The filth merely oozes from another crack.[49]

To this ugly mix can be added problems associated with the exploitation of athletes, gender inequality, and the maintenance of a male-segregated athletic subculture that, when compared to its nonathletic counterpart, tends to be more anti-intellectual, sexist, aggressive, and criminal. How can any university defend and promote this hypocritical, scandal-laden activity?

Several contradictions further delineate the dilemma that big-time college sport presents.[50] The overarching contradiction is that we have organized a commercial entertainment activity within an educational environment, and in the process we have compromised educational goals. Ernest L. Boyer, former president of the Carnegie Foundation for the Advancement for Teaching, puts it this way: "I believe that the college sports system is one of the most corrupting and destructive influences on higher education. It is obscene, and there is no way to put an educational gloss on this enterprise."[51] In short, as currently structured, big-time sport is not compatible with education.

A fundamental problem is that athletes are recruited as students. Yet demanding coaches, as well as the athletic subculture, work against the student role. At the heart of this contradiction is the fact that institutions of higher learning allow the enrollment and subsidization of ill-prepared and uninterested students solely for the purpose of winning games, enhancing the visibility of the university, and producing revenue. Sometimes these universities recruit known thugs for the same purposes.

The third contradiction is that although big-time sports are revenue producing, for most schools they actually drain money away from academics. This occurs when scholarship money is diverted from students with cognitive abilities to students with athletic abilities, and when athletic budgets are supplemented with generous sums from student fees and subsidies from the academic budgets.

The fourth contradiction is that although the marketing/sales side of big-time sport is big business, the production side is an amateur extracurricular activity in which athletes are "paid" only with an "education."[52] Meanwhile, individuals and organizations make huge amounts of money. For example, basketball star Jameer Nelson brought an estimated $2 million to his school during his four years (in ticket revenues, the sale of merchandise, fundraising, tournament and television appearances).[53] Should he be paid just in room, board, tuition, and books? Similarly, Michael Beesley, when confronted with the decision as to whether to remain at Kansas State for his sophomore year, a deal worth about $16,000, or should he enter the NBA draft where he was projected to receive a salary of $5.5 million plus endorsement deals, he made the obvious choice of becoming a paid professional. A final contradiction involves the issue of whether or not participation in sport is educational. University administrators often advance this as a rationale for college sport. But such administrators are caught in a contradiction because most of them willingly accept the present maldistribution of resources, scholarships, and opportunities for women's sport. Sociologist Allen Sack argues:

> If one accepts the notion that student-athletes are the prime beneficiaries of college sport, how in the world can women's programs receive less financial support than men's? If sport is educational, what possible academic justification can there be for denying this aspect of education for women? Wouldn't the denial of equal athletic opportunities be tantamount to saying that men should have more microscopes, laboratory facilities and library privileges than women?[54]

And, I would add, if sport is a useful, educational activity, why limit these benefits to the athletic elite? Why should the best athletic facilities be reserved for their exclusive use? Why are we limited to one team in each sport, rather than several teams based on differences in size and skill? If sport is justifiable as an educational experience, why limit the number of men's so-called minor sports? Should they not be expanded to meet the wishes of the student body? In my view, participation in sport is good and we should maximize it instead of limiting its benefits to the few.

ALTERNATIVES

How are we to respond to these dilemmas? Do we ignore them and maintain the shame and the sham of the status quo? Or do we seek true reform? Can the corporate and corrupted sports programs at our major universities be changed to redress the wrongs that make a mockery of academe's educational goals? Can these wrongs be eliminated while the high level of achievement by the athletes and the excitement generated by college sports spectacles are maintained?

I offer two scenarios, one based on what I wish would happen and one based on what is more likely to happen. Let me begin by outlining what I wish would happen. I would like to see a significant reform effort led by college presidents that would clean up college sports programs so that they are consonant with the educational objectives of the institutions they represent. In that spirit, I propose a three-pronged attack, beginning with changes in the administration of sport.

Athletic departments must not be self-contained corporate entities that are separate from the university, as is so often the case. They must be under the direct control of university presidents. Presidents must set up independent impartial review boards or other mechanisms to monitor athletic programs for illegalities such as the use of illicit drugs, dehumanizing behaviors by coaches, recruiting violations, and other unethical acts. Most crucially, college sports programs must be monitored and sanctioned externally when warranted. The NCAA is not the proper external agent, since it has a fundamental conflict of interest. That organization is too dependent on sport-generated television money and tournament revenues to be an impartial investigator and jury. An independent educational body, such as the North Central Accrediting Association (ironically, also with the acronym NCAA), must oversee all aspects of universities, including the sports sphere, to assess whether educational goals are being met. Any school not meeting such goals in regard to athletics would lose accreditation, just as it would if the library was inadequate or too few professors held doctorates. Also, federal district attorneys and the courts should become involved in the investigation and prosecution of crimes by schools because big-time sports are involved in interstate commerce.

Coaches must be part of the academic community, thus gaining reasonable job security and being recognized as teachers. This means that coaches must be part of the tenure system as are other educators. As educators with special responsibilities, their salaries would be similar to academic administrators. Their outside income must be sharply curtailed. In particular, they should not be allowed to participate in commercial ventures as coaches (e.g., advertising, shoe contracts) or to receive the free use of automobiles. And they should not be permitted to participate in "sweetheart" business deals with boosters.

The performance of coaches should be evaluated on a number of criteria. It would be naive to suggest that winning is unimportant. Winning is important, but it is just one criterion for being a successful coach. Other factors should include teaching skills, the humane treatment of players, and, most critically, the proportion of athletes who graduate in six years. The number of scholarships available for the new recruits should be contingent on the graduation rate of previous athletes in the program.

The second point of attack involves the education of athletes. Academic institutions worthy of that label must make a commitment to their athletes as students. This requires, first, that only those students who have the potential to compete as students be admitted. Athletes must meet the minimum requirements demanded of all students for admission: no special admissions and no special curricula for athletes. Academically marginal student-athletes must be the recipients of an extraordinary effort by the university to raise their skills through remedial classes and tutorials so that they can achieve academic success. Second, no freshman eligibility; freshmen may practice but are prohibited from playing in intercollegiate contests. This requirement has symbolic value because it shows athletes and the academic community that school performance is the ultimate priority of the institution. Most important, this requirement allows incoming athletes time to adjust to the demanding and competitive academic environment before taking on the pressures of big-time sports participation. Third, the schools must insist that student-athletes make satisfactory progress toward a degree. Fourth, the time demands on athletes must be reduced: No spring practice and no fall practice before classes start. Abolish mandatory off-season workouts. Reduce the number of football and basketball games. Start basketball games after the second semester begins. Lower the in-season demands on athletes (practice, weight training, film sessions, meetings, and travel) to manageable limits.

Finally, establish a comprehensive athletes' bill of rights to ensure a nonexploitive context. At a minimum, it should include:

- The right to transfer schools. Athletes who do should be eligible to play the next school year.
- The right to a four-year scholarship. Those athletes who compete for three years should be given an open-ended scholarship guaranteeing that they will receive aid as long as it takes to graduate.
- The rights that other college students have, such as freedom of speech, protections from the physical and mental abuse of authorities, privacy rights, and the fair redress of grievances. There should be an impartial committee on each campus, separate from the athletic department, which monitors the behavior of coaches

and the rules imposed by them on athletes to ensure that individual rights are guaranteed.

• The right to consult with agents concerning sports career choices.
• The right to make money from endorsements, speeches, and appearances. Walter Byers, former executive director of the NCAA, under whose reign many of these abuses abounded, has stated that athletes deserve the same access to the free market as coaches and just as other students exploit their special talents, whether they are musicians playing on weekends or journalism students working for local newspapers.[55]

The final plank of my reform package has to do with finances. Money from student fees should be funneled exclusively to women's sports and to minor men's sports to achieve greater equity. Lower the expenditures for football by limiting scholarships and squads to sixty, reducing the number of coaches and eliminating hotel stays by the squad and coaches the night before home games. In addition, stop the athletic arms race by placing limits on the amount that can be spent on weight rooms, locker rooms, and the like. Finally, pay athletes in the revenue-producing sports fair compensation for the revenues they generate. Clearly, college athletes are not amateurs, but just as clearly, they are not well-paid professionals either. Athletes should receive a monthly stipend for living expenses, paid insurance, and paid trips home during holidays and for family emergencies. Their parents should be given two paid trips annually to see their children play.

The problem with the plan that I have just outlined is that it will never be implemented. The presidents of the universities involved in big-time college sport are too weak or too meek or too unwilling to change. If history is a guide, they will push the NCAA (National Collegiate Athletic Association) to make cosmetic changes, but they will balk at meaningful structural changes and will continue to look the other way while athletic programs do what they have to do to win. Moreover, the NCAA will not promote changing the present system because it is compromised by a massive conflict of interest.

Another alternative, some version of which will eventually emerge, will take the hypocrisy out of big-time college sports by separating them from academia. The public wants big-time college sport. Corporations want big-time college sport. Television and cable networks want big-time college sport. These demands will result, I suspect, in the money from television and bowl/tournament appearances going to fewer and fewer teams. The best athletes will gravitate to those relatively few teams because of the media exposure, which they believe will translate into greater opportunities for a professional career. This will lead to a bifurcation of the schools into a two-tiered system. At the big-time level, there will be an elite composed of, say, sixty-four premier schools, divided into eight conferences and an overarching administrative organization. These schools will have sports programs explicitly designed and packaged commercially as part of a mega-entertainment industry. They will have a monopoly of the national television revenue. They will be partially subsidized by the professional leagues because they provide a developmental program for future professional players. Players will be professionals, recruited as entertainers with contracts, salaries, bonuses, and insurance. They will not be required to register as students, although this would be an option and, if chosen, funded. No more rules concerning academic eligibility. No more empty rhetoric about the ideals of amateurism. No more talk of making big-time sport compatible with the educational mission of universities. This plan removes the hypocrisy present in current programs but, of course, if implemented it mocks the purpose of the university.

The dilemma is this: We like (I like) big-time college sport—the festival, the pageantry, the exuberance, the excitement, and the excellence. But are we then willing to accept the hypocrisy that goes with it? I long for a more pristine sports system for our schools such as the one that exists at the NCAA Division III level or among the NAIA-level schools. Here the athletic programs are in harmony with what college sport, in my view, should be. That is, athletic scholarships would be partial and based on academic potential. Schedules and recruiting would be regional in scope. There would be a full complement of minor sports for men and the absolute implementation of Title IX, financed by student fees and discretionary funds from the administration, as well as from legislatures. I like this part of the scenario. Here college sport is in balance with other activities and academics; participation opportunities are maximized. This would truly eliminate the sham and the shame from college sports. If academic institutions really stand for educational values, they would move to this lower level of sports programming. In doing so, they would leave the professional level to the professional leagues, which would fund minor league systems that are outside the school system.

NOTES

1. Mike Krzyzewski, "Despite Loss, Krzyzewski Lauds His Team," *New York Times*, March 28, 1993, sec. 8, p. 9.

2. John Feinstein, "Why the Ryder Cup Makes Legs Shake," *USA Today*, September 25, 1997, p. 15A.

3. Big-time college sport refers exclusively to men's football in the 119 Division I-A football schools and the 313 men's basketball programs in NCAA Division I.

4. Douglas Lederman, "Athletic Merit vs. Academic Merit," *Chronicle of Higher Education*, March 30, 1994, pp. 37A–38A.

5. Gilbert M. Gaul and Frank Fitzpatrick, "Rise of Athletic Empires," *Philadelphia Inquirer*, September 10, 2000, p. 1A; and Andrew Zimbalist, *Unpaid Professionals: Commercialism and Conflict in Big-Time College Sports* (Princeton, N.J.: Princeton University Press, 1999), 12.

6. James L. Shulman and William G. Bowen, *The Game of Life: College Sports and Educational Values* (Princeton, N.J.: Princeton University Press, 2001); and James L. Shulman and William G. Bowen, "Playing Their Way In," *New York Times*, February 12, 2001, online: www.nytimes.com/2001/02/22/opinion/22BOWE.htm. See also, Justin Ewers, "Running Numbers," *U.S. News & World Report*, September 22, 2003, p. 27.

7. Reported in Associated Press, "Paper Says Air Force Lowering Academic Standards for Athletes," February 4, 2002.

8. Frank Deford, "Who's Entitled? Athletes Don't Deserve Preferential Treatment," *Sports Illustrated*, December 11, 2002.

9. Quoted in Richard G. Sheehan, *Keeping Score: The Economics of Big-Time Sports* (South Bend, Ind.: Diamond Communications, 1996), 261.

10. Murray Sperber, *College Sports Inc.: The Athletic Department vs. the University* (New York: Holt, 1990), 1–2.

11. Paul W. Bryant and John Underwood, *Bear: The Hard Life and Good Times of Alabama's Coach Bryant* (Boston: Little, Brown, 1974), 325.

12. Natalie Meisler, "College Football Has Almost Become a Year-Round Sport," *Denver Post*, June 11, 2007.

13. Patricia A. Adler and Peter Adler, *Backboards and Blackboards: College Athletics and Role Engulfment* (New York: Columbia University Press, 1991).

14. Adler and Adler, *Backboards and Blackboards*, 247.

15. Steve Wieberg, "Grad Rates Show Improvement in Most Sports," *USA Today*, September 28, 2006, p. 8C.

16. Harry Edwards, "The Black 'Dumb Jock': An American Sports Tragedy," *College Board Review* (Spring 1984): 8.

17. Edwards, "The Black 'Dumb Jock,'" 9.

18. D. Stanley Eitzen and George H. Sage, *Sociology of North American Sport*, 8th ed. (Boulder, Colo.: Paradigm, 2009), 113–14.

19. Gary R. Roberts, "Financial Incentives Wrong for College Athletics," *NCAA News*, November 4, 1991, p. 4.

20. Zimbalist, *Unpaid Professionals*, 164; See also Andrew Zimbalist, *The Bottom Line: Observations and Arguments on the Sports Business* (Philadelphia: Temple University Press, 2006), 230–32, 255–56.

21. Debra E. Blum, "Faculty Is Furious over Six-Fold Budget Increase for Athletics," *Chronicle of Higher Education*, February 16, 1996, p. 40A.

22. Cited in Jack Carey, "Study: Athletic Success Doesn't Pay Off in Donations," *USA Today*, September 8, 2004, p. 3C. See also Jennifer Jacobson, "Winning Sports Teams Have Little Effect on Colleges," *Chronicle of Higher Education*, September 17, 2004, p. A35.

23. Jeffrey L. Stimson and Dennis R. Howard, "Athletic Success and Private Giving to Athletic and Academic Programs at NCAA Institutions, *Journal of Sport Management* 21 (April 2007); Brad Wolverton, "Growth in Sports Gifts May Mean Fewer Academic Donations," *Chronicle of Higher Education*, October 5, 2007, p. A1, A34.

24. Wolverton, "Growth in Sports Gifts," p. A34.

25. Sperber, *College Sports Inc.*, 65.

26. Don Yaeger and Alexander Wolff, "Troubling Questions," *Sports Illustrated*, July 7, 1997, pp. 70–79.

27. For an exposé on how a Bible college, Southeastern College, was used by various colleges and junior colleges for bogus academic credits, see Alexander Wolff and Don Yaeger, "Credit Risk," *Sports Illustrated*, August 7, 1995, pp. 47–55.

28. Jack McCallum, "Paper Trail," *Sports Illustrated*, November 28, 1994, pp. 45–48. See also Wolff and Yaeger, "Credit Risk," 46–55.

29. John Underwood, "A Game Plan for America," *Sports Illustrated*, February 23, 1981, p. 81.

30. Philip Taubman, "Oklahoma Football: A Powerhouse That Barry Built," *Esquire* 90 (December 1978): 91.

31. *Sports Illustrated*, December 12, 1994, p. 18. For the costs at the University of South Florida, see Michael Sokolove, "Football Is a Sucker's Game," *New York Times Magazine*, December 22, 2002, pp. 36–41, 64, 68–71.

32. R. Vivian Acosta and Linda J. Carpenter, "Women in Intercollegiate Sport: A Longitudinal Study—Twenty-Nine Year Update: 1977–2006" (West Brookfield, Mass.: Carpenter/Acosta, 2006). Donna Lopiano, "The State of Women's Sports 2006," Women's Sports Foundation, 2006.

33. John C. Weistart, "Can Gender Equity Find a Place in Commercialized College Sports?" *Duke Journal of Gender Law and Policy* 3 (Spring 1996): 264.

34. This section is taken from D. Stanley Eitzen, "Slaves of Big-Time College Sports," *USA Today: The Magazine of the American Scene* 120 (September 2000): 26–30. For a similar analysis focusing on black athletes, see Billy Hawkins, *The New Plantation: The Internal Colonization of Black Student Athletes* (Winterville, Ga.: Sadiki Publishing, 2000). For two books using this metaphor at the professional sports level, see: William C. Rhoden, *Forty Million Dollar Slaves* (New York: Crown, 2006); and Anthony E. Prior, *The Slave Side of Sunday* (Los Angeles: Stone Hold Books, 2006).

35. Zimbalist, *Unpaid Professionals*, 6.

36. Sheehan, *Keeping Score*, 292–93.

37. Quoted in Eitzen, "Slaves of Big-Time College Sports," 29.

38. Quoted in Don Yaeger and Douglas S. Looney, *Under the Tarnished Dome: How Notre Dame Betrayed Its Ideals for Football Glory* (New York: Simon & Schuster, 1999), 22–23.

39. John Feinstein, *Season on the Brink: A Year with Bob Knight and the Indiana Hoosiers* (New York: Macmillan, 1986).

40. Quoted in Eitzen, "Slaves of Big-Time College Sports," 29.

41. Jerry Farber, *The Student as Nigger* (New York: Pocket Books, 1970), 93.

42. George H. Sage, *Power and Ideology in American Sport*, 2nd ed. (Champaign, Ill.: Human Kinetics, 1998), 248.

43. Reported in Jeffrey R. Benedict, "Colleges Must Act Decisively When Scholarship Athletes Run Afoul of the Law," *Chronicle of Higher Education*, May 6, 1997, pp. 6B–7B.

44. Alexander Wolff, "Broken Beyond Repair: An Open Letter to the President of Miami Urges Him to Dismantle His Vaunted Football Program to Salvage His School's Reputation," *Sports Illustrated*, June 12, 1995, p. 22.

45. Todd W. Crosset et al., "Male Student-Athletes and Violence against Women," *Violence against Women* 2 (June 1996): 163–79.

46. Reported in Tim Larimer, "Asking for Trouble: Under Pressure to Produce Winners, Some Coaches Turn to Risky Recruits," *Sporting News*, December 16, 1991, pp. 9–12.

47. Todd Crosset, "Capturing Racism: An Analysis of Racial Projects within the Lisa Simpson vs. University of Colorado Football Case," *International Journal of the History of Sport* 24 (February 2007): 172–96.

48. Kelly King, "Doing the Legwork," *Sports Illustrated*, January 27, 2003, p. 31.

49. William F. Reed, "Absolutely Incredible!" *Sports Illustrated*, March 26, 1990, p. 66.

50. This section depends on D. Stanley Eitzen, "College Sport," *Blackwell Encyclopedia of Sport* (Malden, Ma.: Blackwell, 2006), 4665–68.

51. Quoted in Michael Goodwin, "When the Cash Register Is the Scoreboard," *New York Times*, June 8, 1986, pp. 27–28.

52. Kelly Whiteside, "College Athletes Want a Cut of the Action," *USA Today*, September 1, 2004, p. 3C.

53. Steve Wieberg, "$2 Million: A Star Player's Value," *USA Today*, March 17, 2004, pp. 1C–2C.

54. Allen L. Sack, "College Sports Must Choose: Amateur or Pro?" *New York Times*, May 3, 1981, p. 2S.

55. Walter Byers, *Unsportsmanlike Conduct: Exploiting College Athletes* (Ann Arbor: University of Michigan Press, 1995), 13.

Mike Powell/Getty Images

10

THE PATH TO SUCCESS?
MYTH AND REALITY

Sports are a detriment to blacks, not a positive. You have a society now where every black kid in the country thinks the only way he can be successful is through athletics.

—Charles Barkley, former NBA star and an African American

Compared with much of the world, the United States is a society that allows social mobility. It is possible for poor children and penniless immigrants to become prosperous or even wealthy adults, based on some combination of hard work, educational attainment, skills/talents, and luck. Upward mobility within the system of social stratification is not only permitted but is also part of the American creed that everyone should aspire to a higher social position. Americans, moreover, firmly believe that the United States is a "meritocratic" society in which social status is determined by achievement.

This belief, however, is largely a myth. Income statistics show that by far most children in this country remain in the social class of their parents. If there is movement, it tends to be slight. Traditionally, this mobility was more likely to be up than down, but Greg Duncan's research has found that the degree of social mobility has slowed in recent decades. This he attributes to the shrinkage of the middle class and to the extremes of wealth and poverty that have become more intransigent.[1]

Moreover, research by Duncan and Timothy Smeeding concluded that in the United States the poor are more likely to stay poor and the affluent are more likely to stay affluent.[2] Actually, according to economist Miles Corak, the United States is less mobile than other wealthy nations: "The U.S. and Britain appear to stand out as the least mobile societies among the rich countries studied. France and Germany are somewhat more mobile than the United States: Canada and the Nordic countries are much more so."[3] Although blatant forms of racism and sexism are less relevant today than in the past, race and gender issues continue to hinder the upward mobility of racial minorities and women. White males have higher pay and higher-status jobs than women and racial minorities even when their parents have similar status. To belabor the point, in 2005, the median net worth of the average African American family was $5,166—less than one-tenth of the average white family's wealth of $67,000.[4]

To summarize, sociological and economic research leads to several conclusions about social mobility in the United States:[5]

- Few children of white-collar workers become blue-collar workers.
- Most mobility moves are slight.
- Occupational inheritance is highest for children of professions (physicians, lawyers, professors).
- The opportunities for the children of nonprofessionals to become professionals are very small.
- While the long-term trend in social mobility has been upward, since the 1970s this trend has reversed.
- Social mobility is the least likely at the extremes of wealth and poverty.
- While there are many individual exceptions, the overall trend by race/ethnicity is that the gap in wealth/income between African Americans and Latinos and the more privileged whites has remained about the same.
- While there are more and more exceptions, barriers still remain for full equality for women.

SPORT AS AN AVENUE OF SOCIAL MOBILITY

Typically, Americans believe that sport is a path to upward social mobility. Poor boys (rarely girls) from rural and urban areas, whether white or black, sometimes skyrocket to fame and fortune through success in sports. The financial rewards can be astounding, such as the high pay that some racial minority athletes have received in recent years. In 2007, eight of the top ten in salary and endorsement income were African Americans and Latinos, with Tiger Woods leading the way at $111.9 million. LaBron James, only three years removed from high school, was ranked sixth at $30.8 million, with $25 million coming from endorsements. The highest paid woman athlete was Michelle Wie at $20.2 million. Over 96 percent of that total came from endorsements.[6]

High salaries and endorsement contracts are not the only financial opportunities provided by sport. The road to success in football, basketball, and some other sports virtually requires the athletes to attend college. Thus sports participation has the effect of encouraging athletes to attain more education and increasing the opportunities for success outside the sports world for those who do not find positions as players. Higher education also widens athletes' opportunities after a professional career.

Several studies indicate that after graduation, male college athletes are more upwardly mobile than their nonathletic peers.[7] There are at least three possible reasons for this. First, athletic participation may lead to various forms of "occupational sponsorship." The male college athlete, especially in big-time sport, is a popular hero and therefore is more likely to date and marry a woman of higher socioeconomic status and may acquire a father-in-law who can provide him with benefits in the business world much greater than those available to the average nonathlete male. Another form of sponsorship may come from well-placed alumni who offer former athletes positions in their businesses after graduation. This may be done to help the firm's public relations, or it may be part of a payoff in the recruiting wars that some alumni are willing to underwrite.

A second reason for athletes' better outcomes is that the selection process for many jobs requires the applicant to be "well-rounded," meaning that a premium is placed on participation in extracurricular activities in addition to classes taken and grade-point averages.

Finally, participation in highly competitive sports situations may lead to the development of attitudes and behavior patterns highly valued in the larger occupational world. If attributes such as leadership, human relations skills, teamwork, good work habits, and a well-developed competitive drive are acquired in sports, they may ensure that athletes will succeed in other endeavors. Considerable debate surrounds the question, does sports participation build character? Or is it that only certain kinds of personalities survive the sports experience (see chapter 4)? There may be a self-fulfilling prophecy at work here, however. Employers who assume that athletes possess these valued character traits will make hiring and advancement decisions accordingly, giving former athletes the advantage. Yet a closer look at the situations that actually exist shows that for the vast majority, these benefits are fleeting at best.

MYTHS ABOUT SOCIAL MOBILITY THROUGH SPORT

The belief that sport is a social mobility escalator is built on a succession of myths, including (1) sport provides a free college education; (2) sport leads to a college degree; (3) a professional sports career is possible; (4) sport is a way out of poverty, especially for racial minorities; (5) Title IX has created many opportunities for upward mobility through sport for women; and (6) a professional sports career provides security for life.

Myth 1: Sport Provides a Free College Education

Outstanding high school athletes get college scholarships. These athletic scholarships are especially helpful to poor youth who otherwise would not be able to attend college because of the high costs. But, in reality, very few high school athletes actually receive full-ride scholarships. Football provides the easiest route to a college scholarship because Division I-A colleges each have eighty-five football scholarships, but even this avenue is exceedingly narrow. In 1999–2000, there were 286,683 high school football seniors, and only 3,824 received scholarships at Division I-A schools.[8] A common assumption is that full athletic scholarships are plentiful. However, the data show otherwise:

> According to NCAA data, there were 5.75 million undergraduate students in NCAA institutions in 2003. Of these, about 132,758 students (58 percent) had some form of athletic aid, but most received partial scholarships. Only an estimated 17,561 athletes (4.7 percent of all NCAA athletes) received full scholarships (tuition, room, books, meals).[9]

As low as the chances are for men, women athletes have even less chance to receive an athletic scholarship. Although women make up about 57 percent of all college students, they receive only 45 percent of the athletic scholarships (see chapter 8). Another reality debunking the notion that sport is an easy avenue to a free college education is that the chances of a full-ride scholarship for a male athlete in a so-called minor sport (swimming, tennis, golf, gymnastics, cross-country, wrestling) are virtually nil. At most, such an athlete can hope for a partial scholarship, since these sports are underfunded and stand to be eliminated at many schools.

Myth 2: Sport Leads to a College Degree

College graduates exceed high school graduates in lifetime earnings by hundreds of thousands of dollars. Since most high school and college athletes never play at the professional level, the attainment of a college degree is a crucial determinant of upward mobility through sport. The problem is that relatively few athletes in the big-time revenue-producing sports, compared to their nonathlete peers, actually receive college degrees. As shown in chapter 9 this is especially the case for African Americans, who are much less likely to graduate than white athletes in the revenue-producing sports. Even more damning, there are NCAA Division I schools that have graduation rates of less than 10 percent for their African American basketball players.

There are a number of barriers to graduation for athletes. The demands on their time and energy are enormous, even in the off-season. To cope with these pressures and to maintain eligibility, many athletes take easy courses that do not lead to graduation. This strategy either delays graduation or makes it an unrealistic goal.

Another barrier to graduation for many college athletes is that they are recruited for athletic prowess rather than academic ability in the first place. The data show that football players in big-time programs are, on average, more than two hundred points behind their nonathlete classmates. Even at a rigorous academic school such as Duke, its football players have an average SAT of 1140, considerably below the average of 1400 for nonathletes at that school.[10] Poorly prepared students are the most likely to take easy courses, cheat on exams, hire surrogate test-takers, and otherwise do the minimum required. In other words, although they are in school, they are not receiving an education that will be an asset when they leave school.

A third barrier to graduation for some college athletes is their attitude, as they may not take advantage of their scholarships to obtain a quality education and graduate. This is especially the case for those who perceive their college experience only as preparation for a professional career in sport. Study for them is important only to maintain their eligibility. The goal of a professional career is unrealistic for all but the superstars. And the superstars who do make it at the professional level probably do not graduate from college (only 42 of the 750 active major league baseball players had college degrees in 2004[11]), and only about 10 percent of the players in the National Basketball Association had college degrees,[12] nor do they go back to finish their degrees when their professional careers are over. Even a successful professional athletic career is limited to a few years, and not many professional athletes are able to translate their success in the pros to success in postathletic careers. Such a problem is especially true for African Americans, who often face employment discrimination in the wider society.

Myth 3: A Professional Sports Career Is Possible

A survey by the Center for the Study of Sport in Society found that two-thirds of African American males between the ages of thirteen and eighteen believe that they can earn a living playing professional sports (more than double the proportion of young white males who hold such beliefs). Moreover, African American parents were four times more likely than white parents to believe that their children are destined for careers as professional athletes.[13]

If these young athletes do play as professionals, the economic rewards are excellent, especially in basketball and baseball. In 2006 the average annual salary for professional basketball was $5.215 million. In baseball the average salary was $2.7 million. The average salaries for the National Hockey League and National Football League were $1.46 million and $1.4 million, respectively. These numbers are inflated by the use of averages, which are skewed by the salaries of the superstars. Use of the median (in which half the players make more and half make less) reveals, for example, that the median salary in baseball is more than

$1 million under the average. Regardless of the measure, however, the financial benefits of a professional sports career are great.

The dream of financial success through a professional sports career is just that, a dream, however, for all but an infinitesimal number. The career opportunities are few. Sociologist Wilbert M. Leonard has calculated that the odds that an American man between the ages of fifteen and thirty-nine will be a professional athlete in the four major team sports are about 20,000 to 1. For all African American men, the odds of playing in the NFL or the NBA are 10,000 to 1 and 20,000 to 1, respectively.[14] In baseball, about 120,000 players are eligible each year for the free-agent draft (high school seniors, college seniors, collegians over twenty-one, junior college players, and foreign players). Only about 1,200 (1 percent) are actually drafted, and most of them will never make it to the major leagues. Indeed, only 10 percent of the players who sign a professional baseball contract ever play in the major leagues for at least one day.[15]

The same rigorous winnowing process occurs in football. About 15,000 players are eligible for the NFL draft each year. Of them, 336 are drafted and about 160 actually make the final roster. About forty new players are added to the rosters in the NBA, and sixty rookies make it into the NHL each year. In tennis, about a hundred men and an equal number of women make enough money to cover expenses.

Myth 4: Sport Is a Way Out of Poverty, Especially for Racial Minorities

Sport appears to be an important avenue out of poverty for African Americans. The major professional sports are dominated numerically by African Americans. Although they constitute only 12 percent of the population, African Americans make up about 75 percent of the players in professional basketball, about 67 percent in professional football, and 10 percent in professional baseball (Latinos account for about 29 percent of professional baseball players, and Asians about 1 percent). Moreover, as noted earlier in this essay, African Americans dominate the list of the highest moneymakers in sport (salaries, endorsements). These facts are nevertheless illusory.

Although African Americans dominate professional basketball, football, and, to a lesser extent, baseball, they are rarely found in other

sports, such as hockey, automobile racing, tennis, golf, bowling, and skiing. Moreover, African Americans are severely underrepresented in positions of authority in sport—head coaches, referees, athletic directors,
scouts, general managers, and owners. Writing about the reason for this
racial imbalance in hiring, white sports columnist Bob Kravitz remarks
that "something here stinks, and it stinks a lot like racism."[16]

Although African American males have better odds of making it as
professional athletes than whites, their odds remain exceedingly slim. Of
the 40,000 or so African American boys who play high school basketball
in a given year, only thirty-five will make the NBA and only seven will be
starters. Referring to the low odds for young African Americans, Harry
Edwards, an African American sociologist specializing in the sociology
of sport, said with a bit of hyperbole: "Statistically, you have a better
chance of getting hit by a meteorite in the next 10 years than getting
work as an athlete."[17] These low odds are for African American males.
The chances for African American females are virtually nonexistent (except for the one fledgling women's professional basketball league).

Despite these discouraging facts, the myth is alive for poor youth:
Two-thirds of young African American boys believe they can be professional athletes. Their parents too accept this belief. The film *Hoop
Dreams* and Darcy Frey's book *The Last Shot: City Streets, Basketball
Dreams* document the emphasis that young African American men
place on sport as a way up and the disappointment that they experience.[18] For many of them, sport represents their only hope of escape
from a life of crime, poverty, and despair. They latch on to the dream of
athletic success partly because they have few opportunities for middle-
class success. They spend many hours per day developing their speed,
strength, jumping height, or "moves," to the virtual exclusion of abilities
that have a greater likelihood of paying off in upward mobility, such as
reading comprehension, mathematical reasoning, communication skills,
and computer literacy. Sociologist Jay Coakley puts it this way:

> My best guess is that fewer than 6,000 African Americans, or about 1 in
> 6,600, are making a good living as professional athletes. Data from the
> U.S. Department of Labor indicates that, in 2004, 18,640 African Ameri-
> can men and women were classified as "athletes, coaches, umpires, and
> related workers." In that same year, 50,630 African Americans were phy-

sicians and surgeons, 44,840 were lawyers, and 69,388 were college and university teachers. Therefore, there were thirty-six times more African Americans working in these three prestigious professions than African American athletes in top-level professional sports; and nine times more African American doctors, lawyers, and college teachers than African Americans working in all sports. Furthermore, physicians, lawyers, and college teachers have greater lifetime earnings than most athletes whose playing careers, on average, last less than five years and whose salaries outside the top pro leagues rarely exceed $50,000.[19]

This futile pursuit of sports stardom has serious consequences for individual African Americans as well as for the African American community. First and foremost, they spend their time learning skills that are worthless in the job market. Harry Edwards posits that by spending their energies and talents on athletic skills, young African Americans are not pursuing occupations that would help them meet their political and material needs. Thus their belief in the "sports-as-a-way-up" myth causes them to remain dependent on whites and white institutions.[20] Salim Muwakkil, an African American political analyst, argues:

> If African-Americans are to exploit the socio-economic options opened by varied civil rights struggles more fully, blacks must reduce the disproportionate allure of sports in their communities. Black leadership must contextualize athletic success by promoting other avenues to social status, intensifying the struggle for access to those avenues and better educating youth about those potholes on the road to the stadium.[21]

John Hoberman also challenges the assumption that sport has progressive consequences.[22] The success of African Americans in the highly visible sports gives white America a false sense of black progress and interracial harmony. But the social progress of African Americans in general has little relationship to the apparent integration that they have achieved on the country's playing fields: "The illusory sense of racial harmony on countless playing fields across America masks the true depth of the racial conflict that survives in one and the same society. In this sense, the material gains of a Michael Jordan or a Tiger Woods impede the process of social change. For every black Superstar, there are thousands of blacks behind bars."[23]

Hoberman also contends that the numerical superiority of African Americans in sport, coupled with their disproportionate underrepresentation in other professions, reinforces the racist ideology that African Americans are physically superior to whites but are inferior to them intellectually. In short, sport harms African Americans by serving up imagery and metaphors that reinforce racism and the racial divisions that continue to plague U.S. society.

I do not mean to say that talented African Americans should not seek a career in professional sport. Professional sport is a legitimate career with the potential for exceptional monetary rewards. What is harmful, to reiterate, is that the odds of success are so slim, rendering extraordinary, sustained effort futile and misguided for the vast majority. If this effort were directed at areas having better odds of success, then upward mobility would occur for many more. The late African American tennis star Arthur Ashe argued that "we have been on the same roads—sports and entertainment—too long. We need to pull over, fill up at the library and speed away to Congress, and the Supreme Court, the unions, and the business world."[24]

Myth 5: Title IX Has Created Many Opportunities for Upward Mobility through Sport for Women

Since Title IX was passed in 1972, requiring schools receiving federal funds to provide equal opportunities for women and men, sports participation by and scholarships for women in college have increased dramatically (see chapter 9). Upward mobility from sport is another matter for women. Women have fewer opportunities than men in professional team sports. Beach volleyball is a possibility for a very few, but again the rewards are minimal. There is one professional women's basketball league, but the pay is very low compared to what men make. Another option for women is to play in professional leagues in Europe, Australia, and Asia, but again the pay is relatively low.

Women have more opportunities as professionals in individual sports such as tennis, golf, ice skating, skiing, bowling, cycling, pool, and track. Ironically, the sports with the greatest monetary rewards for women are those of the middle and upper classes (tennis, golf, and ice skating). These sports are expensive, and they require considerable individual coaching as well as access to private facilities. In short, sport does not offer poor women, even in a very limited way, the potential for upward mobility. Speaking of African Americans in this regard, Harry Edwards has observed, "We must also consider that to the extent that sport provides an escape route from the ghetto at all, it does so only for black males."[25]

Opportunities in sport apart from the athlete role are more limited for women than for men. Ironically, with the passage of Title IX, which increased the participation rates of women so dramatically, there has been a decline in the number and proportion of women as coaches and athletic administrators. In addition to the glaring pay gap that exists between coaches of men's teams and coaches of women's teams, men who coach women's teams have higher salaries than women coaching women's teams. Women also have fewer opportunities than men as athletic trainers, officials, sports journalists, and other adjunct positions.

Myth 6: A Professional Sports Career Provides Security for Life

Even among those who attain a career in professional sport, fame and fortune are in short supply. Of course, some athletes make an income from salaries and endorsements that, if invested wisely, provides financial security for life. Some highly paid athletes, however, do not invest wisely. An investigative report by *U.S. News & World Report* found a number of professional athletes who had lost more than $1 million to fraud. Some present and former professional football players who lost money to the same alleged swindler: Simeon Rice lost $2.4 million, Eric Dickerson lost $1.8 million, Sean Gilbert lost $350,000, and Shannon Sharpe lost $300,000.[26] More important, many professional athletes make relatively low salaries. While average salaries are enormous, many major league baseball players receive at or near the minimum of $300,000. For those who do not make the big leagues (there is room for only 750), playing in the minor leagues is anything but lucrative. Second-year players in the Colorado Rockies minor league system at the Triple-A level (the highest minor league level) receive $2,150 a month. Those at the Single-A level receive $1,200 a month.[27] Athletes in minor league professional basketball and hockey also receive low salaries. Professional football does not even have a minor league program (other than the colleges).

Moreover, the average length of a professional career in a team sport is about five years (and only three and one-half years for professional football players). Marginal athletes in individual sports, such as golf, tennis, boxing, and bowling, struggle financially. They must cover their travel expenses, health insurance, equipment, and the like with no guaranteed paycheck. And that brief sports career diverts the young athletes from developing other career skills and experiences that would benefit them throughout life.

A career as a professional athlete is short, even for those who extend their playing days beyond the average. Athletes leave sport involuntarily when they are injured or when they are replaced by more talented athletes. They leave voluntarily when age slows them down so much that they cannot continue to compete successfully.

Ex-professional athletes leave sport, on average, when they are in their late twenties or early thirties, at a time when their nonathlete peers have begun to establish themselves in occupations leading toward retirement in forty years or so. What are the ex-professional athletes to do with their remaining productive years?

Exiting a sports career can be relatively smooth or it can be difficult. Some athletes plan ahead, preparing themselves for other careers in sport (coaching, scouting, administering) or for a nonsport occupation. Others do not prepare themselves for this abrupt change. They graduate from college but do not spend the off-seasons apprenticing nonsport jobs. Exiting the athlete role is difficult for many because they lose (1) what they have focused on for most of their lives; (2) the primary source of their personal identity; (3) their physical prowess; (4) adulation bordering on worship from others; (5) the money and the perquisites of fame; (6) the camaraderie with teammates; (7) the intense "highs" of competition; and (8) status (for most ex-athletes). As a result of these losses, many ex-professional athletes have trouble adjusting to life after sport.[28] A study by the NFL Players Association found that emotional difficulties, divorce, and financial strain were common problems for retired athletes.[29]

For most, the real world is a big step down. Big-time pro athletes are pampered like royalty. They fly first class while hired hands pay the bills and tote the luggage. High-powered executives and heads of state fawn over them. "You begin to feel like Louis XIV," says Wilbert McClure, a two-time Golden Gloves boxing champion who is now a psychologist and counselor to basketball players. Step off the pedestal and everything changes. McClure likens it to "being dipped into hell."[30]

Often retirement occurs because the athlete has "failed," that is, is demoted to nonstarter, is let go by management, or no longer meets the qualifications, such as not making the cut in tournament after tournament in golf. These once successful athletes now face marginality, degradation, and the stigma of failure.[31]An athlete has some potential for a sport-related career after his or her playing days are over, such as coaching, managing, scouting, sportscasting, public relations, and administration. For all but superstars, however, the opportunities are severely limited. Racial minorities and women rarely attain such careers.

In summary, the evidence supports the contention that sports participation has limited potential as a social mobility escalator. The allure in its potential, however, remains strong, and this has at least two negative consequences. First, ghetto youngsters who devote their lives to the pursuit of athletic stardom are, except for the fortunate few, doomed to failure in sport and in the real world as well, since sports skills are essentially irrelevant to occupational placement and advancement. The second negative consequence is more subtle but is very important. Sport contributes to the ideology that legitimizes social inequalities and promotes the myth that all it takes to succeed is extraordinary effort. Sport sociologist George H. Sage makes this point forcefully:

> Because sport is by nature meritocratic—that is, superior performance brings status and rewards—it provides convincing symbolic support for hegemonic [the dominant] ideology—that ambitious, dedicated, hardworking individuals, regardless of social origin, can achieve success and ascend in the social hierarchy, obtaining high status and material rewards, while those who don't move upward simply didn't work hard enough. Because the rags-to-riches athletes are so visible, the social mobility theme is maintained. This reflects the opportunity structure of society in general—the success of a few reproduces the belief in social mobility among the many.[32]

NOTES

1. Greg J. Duncan, "Slow Motion: Earnings Mobility of Young Workers in the 1970s and 1980s" (paper presented at the annual meeting of the Midwest Sociological Society, Chicago, 1996).

2. Cited in Martin N. Marger, *Social Inequality*, 2nd ed. (New York: McGraw-Hill, 2002), 159.

3. Cited in David Wessel, "As Rich-Poor Gap Widens in the U.S., Class Mobility Stalls," *Wall Street Journal*, May 13, 2005, online: www.mindfully .org/Reform/2005/Rich-Poor-Gap13may05.htm.

4. Reported in Monisha Bansal, "'State of Black America' Lamented by Urban League," Cybercast News Service, March 29, 2006.

5. D. Stanley Eitzen, Maxine Baca Zinn, and Kelly Eitzen Smith, *In Conflict and Order: Understanding Society*, 12th ed. (Boston: Allyn and Bacon, 2009), chapter 10.

6. The 50 Highest Paid American Athletes," *Business*, June 1, 2007.

7. John W. Loy Jr., "The Study of Sport and Social Mobility," *International Review of Sport Sociology* 7 (1972): 5–23; Allen L. Sack and Robert Thiel, "College Football and Social Mobility: A Case of Notre Dame Football Players," *Sociology of Education* 52 (January 1979): 60–66; and Douglas Lederman, "Students Who Competed in College Sports Fare Better in Job Market Than Those Who Didn't, Report Says," *Chronicle of Higher Education*, September 26, 1990, pp. 47A–48A.

8. Data from the National Federation of High School Associations and the NCAA, reported in Darrell Blair, "College Recruiting," *Coloradoan* (Fort Collins), February 3, 2000, pp. 1D, 6D.

9. Jay Coakley, *Sports in Society: Issues and Controversies*, 9th ed. (New York: McGraw-Hill, 2007), 354–55.

10. Ben Wildavsky, "Graduation Blues," *U.S. News & World Report*, March 18, 2002, p. 69.

11. *Business Week*, "The Stat," July 12, 2004, p. 14.

12. Andrew Zimbalist, *Unpaid Professionals* (Princeton, N.J.: Princeton University Press, 1999), 36.

13. Cited in John Simons, "Improbable Dreams: African Americans Are a Dominant Presence in Professional Sports. Do Blacks Suffer as a Result?" *U.S. News & World Report*, March 24, 1997, pp. 46–52.

14. W. M. Leonard II, "The Odds of Transiting from One Level of Sports Participation to Another," *Sociology of Sport Journal* 13.3 (1996): 288–99. 15. *NCAA News*, October 21, 1991, p. 16.

16. Bob Kravitz, "NFL Hiring Practices Look Like Racism," *Rocky Mountain News*, January 21, 1998, p. 3N.

17. Harry Edwards, quoted in Bob Oates, "The Great American Tease: Sport as a Way Out of the Ghetto," *New York Times*, June 8, 1979, p. 32A.

18. *Hoop Dreams*, film documentary directed by Steve James (1994); Darcy Frey, *The Last Shot: City Streets, Basketball Dreams* (Boston: Houghton Mifflin, 1994).

19. Coakley, *Sport in Society*, 348.

20. Harry Edwards, "The Black Athletes: 20th Century Gladiators for White Americans," *Psychology Today* 7 (November 1973): 43–52.

21. Salim Muwakkil, "Which Team Are You On?" *In These Times*, May 3, 1998, p. 16.

22. John Hoberman, *Darwin's Athletes: How Sport Has Damaged Black America and Preserved the Myth of Race* (Boston: Houghton Mifflin, 1997).

23. Jim Nadell, review of *Darwin's Athletes: How Sport Has Damaged Black America and Preserved the Myth of Race*, by John Hoberman, Z *Magazine* 10 (December 1997): 54.

24. Arthur Ashe, "Send Your Children to the Libraries," *New York Times*, February 6, 1977, p. 2S.

25. Edwards, "Black Athletes," 47.

26. Edward T. Pound and Douglas Pasternak, "Money Players," *U.S. News & World Report*, February 11, 2002, pp. 30–36.

27. Troy E. Renck, "For Richer or Poorer: Pro Baseball Not Always a Home Run," *Denver Post*, March 10, 2002, pp. 1C, 13C.

28. Jo Anne Tremaine Drahota and D. Stanley Eitzen, "The Role Exit of Professional Athletes," *Sociology of Sport Journal* 15 (September 1998): 263–78; Jo Anne Tremaine Drahota, "The Role Exit of Professional Athletes" (Ph.D. diss., Colorado State University, 1996); and Michael A. Messner, *Power at Play* (Boston: Beacon, 1992).

29. Reported in a five-part series by Brian Hewitt, *Chicago Sun-Times*, September 19–22, 1993. See also Curtis Bunn, "Some Pro Athletes Fumble Marriage," *Denver Post*, January 14, 2002, p. 11D.

30. Andrea Rothman and Stephanie Anderson Forest, "The Thrill of Victory, the Agony of Retirement," *Business Week*, June 3, 1991, pp. 54–55.

31. Donald W. Ball, "Failure in Sport," *American Sociological Review* 41 (1976): 726–39. See also Donald S. Harris and D. Stanley Eitzen, "The Consequences of Failure in Sport," *Urban Life* 7 (1978): 177–88; and Drahota and Eitzen, "The Role Exit of Professional Athletes."

32. George H. Sage, *Power and Ideology in American Sport: A Critical Perspective* (Champaign, Ill.: Human Kinetics, 1990), 41.

11

PROFESSIONAL SPORTS FRANCHISES: PUBLIC TEAMS, PRIVATE BUSINESSES

Christopher Columbus would have made an appropriate club owner. He didn't know where he was going. He didn't know where he was when he got there. He treated people like slaves. And he did it with other people's money.

—Woodrow Paige, *Denver Post* sportswriter

The players change teams, the teams move from city to city. The only thing that stays the same is the uniforms. We're literally rooting for laundry.

—Jerry Seinfeld, comedian

Most public address announcers at professional sports events, when introducing the teams, refer to the home team as your team, as in your Denver Broncos, your New York Yankees, or your Atlanta Hawks.[1] The home fans do identify, often passionately, with the home team, the team representing their city or region. The team is their team in this respect. The fans also have a financial stake in these teams by purchasing the high-priced tickets and, with the exception of a few teams, helping to subsidize the stadiums and arenas in which the professional teams play.

But the professional team to which they give their allegiance is not really theirs. With the exception of only one major league franchise in the four major sports—the Green Bay Packers—every professional team is owned by an individual, a family, a small group of business partners, or a corporation. The owner can sell and trade players, including players who are true heroes to the fans. The owner determines ticket prices. The owner can move the team to another city. Examining professional sport as a monopoly, ownership for profit, and public subsidies to professional team franchises raises a question: Who profits and who loses in the way professional sport is organized?

PROFESSIONAL SPORT AS A MONOPOLY

Each major professional league is an unregulated monopoly. Each league regulates itself, unfettered by government oversight and government rules against monopolies that apply to other industries. Each league operates as a cartel—as competitors joined together for mutual benefit. This means that the teams making up each league make agreements on matters of mutual interest such as rules, schedules, promotions, expansion, and media contracts. In professional sport, cartels exist to restrict competition for athletes, to limit franchises, and to divide markets among the league's teams.[2] Such arrangements are illegal in most other businesses because they lead to collusion, price-fixing, and restraint of trade.

Being a cartel gives each league enormous advantages. The cartel limits competition in several ways. Competitive bidding among teams for players is controlled through player drafts, contracts, and trades. A cartel keeps competition among the teams at a minimum by restricting the number of teams in the league and where they can locate. The owner of the Kansas City Royals, for instance, is protected from a rival team locating in his territory. There are some metropolitan areas with two major league baseball teams, but these exceptions occurred before baseball agreed to territorial exclusivity. Even for the few exceptions, the teams are in different leagues (Chicago White Sox and Chicago Cubs, and the New York Yankees and the New York Mets). This protection from competition eliminates price wars. The owners of a franchise can continue to charge the maximum without fear of price-cutting by competitors.

The league cartel also controls the number of franchises allowed. Take the case of baseball. In 1901, when the population of the United States was about 76 million, there were sixteen major league teams. No new teams were added between 1901 and 1961, yet the population more than doubled to 179 million. From 1961 to 2002, twelve teams were added, for a total of thirty teams in a nation of approximately 282 million. Using 1901 as a standard, and assuming that the United States is capable of developing the same proportion of major league–caliber baseball players today as was the case at the turn of the century, then the 2008 population of 306 million should now have sixty-four major league teams rather than the current thirty.[3] This calculation does not account for the exclusion of African Americans from major league baseball until 1947 and the influx of Latinos in the last couple of decades, which means that the number of teams should be even more than the hypothetical sixty-four.

Sport sociologist George Sage asserts that this is clearly the result of Major League Baseball's reluctance to expand because the owners do not want to "diminish their political and economic power by adding new franchises. It seems obvious that expansion has little to do with the availability of capable baseball players."[4] When it does expand, it does so to benefit the league. The last four additions reveal why. In 1993 the Florida Marlins and the Colorado Rockies were admitted because neither Florida nor the Rocky Mountain time zone had a major league team. These additions tapped new populations and media markets, which would benefit the other league members. So, too, did the $95 million each team paid to join. Neither team was allowed to share in television revenues for two seasons, which had the effect, when the initiation fee was added, of totaling $106 million. In 1998 the Arizona Diamondbacks and the Tampa Bay Devil Rays played their first seasons, having each paid $125 million to become members of the cartel. Both of these teams were added for reasons similar to the ones dictating the addition of the Marlins and Rockies—Arizona had no major league team and Tampa Bay was located in a large, heretofore untapped market that did not infringe on Miami, 275 miles away.

Each league is generally reluctant to add new teams because scarcity permits higher ticket prices, more beneficial media arrangements, and continued territorial purity. In short, the value of each franchise increases by the restriction on the number of teams. This monopolistic situation enables a league to negotiate television contracts for the benefit of all members of the cartel. The 1961 Sports Broadcast Act allowed sports leagues to sell their television rights as a group without being subject to antitrust laws. As a result, the national networks and cable systems may bid for the right to televise the games for a particular league. For example, Fox and TBS pay a joint $3 billion for the current major league baseball post-season television contract.[5] In a deal from 2005 through 2010 CBS, NBC, FOX, and ESPN pay a combined $21.4 billion to broadcast NFL games. The leagues also negotiate advertising and other ancillary sources of revenue to be shared among league members, such as being the "official" beer sponsor of the league. Another advantage of the monopoly enjoyed by the professional leagues is that the players are drastically limited in their choices and bargaining power. The sports cartel holds down wages because the athletes have few options besides playing in the league. In football, players are drafted out of college. If they want to play in the NFL, they must negotiate with the team that drafted them. Their other choices are to play in the Arena League or to play in Canada. These other options offer much less pay, and the Canadian teams limit the number of Americans allowed per team. A final advantage of the cartel's controlling the number and location of franchises is that the owners prosper. Since the owners rarely add teams to the cartel, their teams are scarce commodities, which means that their worth appreciates much faster than other investments. A few examples can be cited that represent the growth curve in professional team franchise value:[6]

- The Washington Redskins were purchased in 1999 for $750 million. The team's estimated value in 2007 was $1.467 billion.
- The Dallas Cowboys were purchased in 1960 for $600,000; in 1984 they were sold for $60 million and in 1989 for $150 million. In 2007 the value of the franchise was estimated at $1.5 billion.
- The Denver Broncos were purchased in 1981 for $30 million and sold three years later for $72 million. The 2007 value of the

Broncos was estimated at $984 million. The value of the Broncos increased dramatically with the building of the Invesco Stadium at Mile High (three-fourths paid for by Denver-area taxpayers), with its increased annual profits of at least $10 million from advertising, parking, concessions, as well as income from skyboxes and club seating.

- The Tampa Bay Buccaneers were bought for $16 million in 1976, sold for $192 million in 1995, and valued at $963 million in 2007.
- The New York Yankees, purchased in 1973 by George Steinbrenner for $10 million, was worth $1.3 billion in 2008.
- In 1977 the Boston Red Sox were worth $18.7 million. In 2002 they were sold for $655 million. The value in 2008 was $816 million.
- The Phoenix Suns were purchased in 2004 for $401 million. In 2007 they were worth $449 million.
- The Sacramento Kings were purchased in 1998 for $156 million. In 2007 the value of the franchise was estimated to be $385 million.
- The Texas Rangers were purchased in 1989 for $86 million and sold in 1998 for $250 million. Future Texas governor and U.S. president George Walker Bush was one of the early investors, putting up $606,302. His 2 percent share of the proceeds (plus an additional 10 percent for serving as managing partner) was $14.9 million. The value of the Rangers was high because of the taxpayer-built field (a topic considered later in this chapter). A political opponent of Bush said, "I don't think that when voters approved this [building the baseball stadium] they thought Governor Bush would make $14.9 million. The citizens haven't got close to the kind of return Governor Bush has gotten."[7] In 2008 the Rangers were worth $412 million.

To summarize, professional sports leagues are monopolies, and therein lies the problem. Two economists, James Quirk and Rodney Fort, argue that many problems of the professional team sports business arise from the monopoly power of professional leagues. Eliminate the monopoly power of leagues and you eliminate the blackmailing of cities to subsidize teams. Eliminate the monopoly power of leagues and you eliminate the problem of lack of competitive balance in a league due to the disparity in drawing potential among league teams. Eliminate the monopoly power of leagues and you transfer power from the insiders—owners and players alike—to the outsiders—fans and taxpayers.[8]

PUBLIC SUBSIDIES TO PROFESSIONAL TEAM FRANCHISES

The scarcity of professional teams (the consequence of league monopoly) and the tremendous fan interest in having a major sports franchise in their city lead to large public subsidies for the relatively few teams. The subsidies to franchise owners take two forms—tax breaks and the availability of arenas at very low cost.

The tax code benefits team owners in two ways. First, the typically enormous profits from the sale of a team are counted as capital gains for team owners (as with the sale of other American businesses) and thus are taxed at a lower rate than other sources of income such as salaries and wages. A second tax benefit is indirect but bountiful nonetheless. This financial advantage accrues to team owners as businesses purchase tickets, food, and skyboxes. They are permitted to write off 50 percent of these costs as business expenses. This tax subsidy to businesses and corporations makes the high cost of attending sports events more palatable to them, which helps to keep the price of tickets and skyboxes inflated and profits steady. All other taxpayers, however, are left holding the bag.

Despite these advantages, team owners today paint a bleak picture of team finances. They do this to get the fans on their side in salary disputes with players, to keep the players' salary demands as low as possible, and to secure support for further subsidies in renovating existing stadiums or building new ones. The negative financial picture painted by the owners is misleading because it refers usually to accounting losses (expenses exceeding income) that are not really losses.

Consider a hypothetical example provided by economist Richard Sheehan.[9] Let's assume someone purchases a major league baseball franchise for $100 million. For that money the new owner receives the legal right to the franchise (the franchise name), to be part of the league cartel, and to hold the player contracts. The Internal Revenue Service has ruled that the owner can claim 60 percent of the purchase price for the franchise and 40 percent for the player contracts. The tax subsidy occurs because the players under contract are assumed to lose value with age; therefore, their value can be depreciated, just as a farmer depreciates a tractor or a steel company depreciates a blast furnace for tax purposes. The right to depreciate an asset lowers taxable income. Thus, after the bills are paid in this hypothetical example, the owner has $5 million left over (profit). But since the owner can amortize that $40 million in player contracts over five years, he or she can write off 20 percent of that $40 million, or $8 million each year, and call it a cost. In effect, the owner pockets the $5 million but declares a loss of $3 million.

This legal maneuver has the effect of informing the public that the owner is losing money when that is not in fact the case. Moreover, the owner does not owe any taxes because of the "loss." If the owner were not allowed to depreciate the players, then he or she would owe taxes on the $5 million. This tax subsidy for the owners is not allowed to others, since no other business in the United States depreciates the value of human beings as part of the cost of its operation. In a curious twist of logic, but revealing of the bias of capital over human rights, the players whose skills diminish with age do not receive a tax write-off; only their owners do. This tax subsidy is a gift to team owners paid for by the rest of us.

Sheehan provides another example of creative accounting that is used to misrepresent the fiscal health of professional teams, although it is not a tax subsidy to owners. In this instance, the owner pays himself or herself a significant salary, which is counted as a business expense that lowers profits. Some NFL owners have paid themselves "salaries" as high as $7.5 million. The bottom line, the line that the public hears, is that the team is losing money, when the owner is simply taking the profit as salary.

Another manipulation of the financial balance sheet intended to project financial weakness occurs when the prospective owner loans the money to the newly created team ownership corporation for the down payment to purchase the team. This loan and the accrued interest have to be repaid from the subsequent income of the team, thus lowering, for accounting purposes, the team's stated profit. Thus the owner pockets the money, which the accounting department registers as an expense.[10]

The second type of public subsidy of professional sport is the provision of sports facilities to most franchises at very low cost. These arenas and stadiums are essential to the financial success and spectator appeal of professional sports. Team owners seek new and improved sports facilities, usually at taxpayer expense, and typically they get them. If not, they move. This threat to move (some would call it blackmail), real or implied, has resulted in a construction boom. From 1995 to 2005, a total of 53 stadiums and arenas were financed with public money. Between 2006 and 2010, major league baseball teams the New York Yankees, Minnesota Twins, Washington Nationals, New York Mets, and St. Louis Cardinals, along with NFL teams the Arizona Cardinals, Indianapolis Colts, New York Giants, New York Jets, and Dallas Cowboys, will receive new stadiums. Community subsidies take several forms. Stadiums are financed by the taxpayers. So, too, are new roads and overpasses to access these stadiums. Owners may be given other economic considerations as well. Consider, as an extreme example, the lucrative deal given the owners of the Colorado Rockies by local taxpayers.[11]

Case Study: The Rockies Stadium Deal

Citizens of the six counties surrounding and including Denver passed a 0.1 percent sales tax proposal to fund a new stadium for the Colorado Rockies baseball team. The stadium was projected to cost $139 million, with $97 million to come from taxpayers and $42 million from private sources. Eventually, as is common, the original cost estimate turned out to be too low. The stadium actually cost $180 million, the taxpayers' obligation rising to $156 million rather than the $97 million they voted on. The stadium district board gave its chairperson, John McHale Jr., the power to negotiate the terms of the stadium lease with the Rockies. The deal struck between these two parties included the following generous provisions:[12]

1. The owners of the Rockies were given the right to name the stadium, which they sold to the Coors Brewing Company for $15 million.
2. The team owners did not pay rent or maintenance until the year 2000. After that they paid the stadium district less than 2.5 percent of the team's net profits and $150,000 a year to cover the stadium's operating costs.

3. The team owners received seat rights, luxury suites, advertising, parking, and concession rights for seventeen years at no cost. They keep 40 percent of all concession sales (at least $10 million annually). All the revenue from sixty-four private suites (ranging in price from $60,000 to $90,000 annually) goes to the Rockies.

4. The owners receive all revenues from nonbaseball events for parking, concessions, and rent. For a sold-out rock concert, for example, the owners would receive about $500,000.

5. As stadium managers, the owners of the Rockies receive an annual fee of $2.65 million.

As sport sociologist George Sage observes, "Incredible as it may seem, the lease gave the Rockies every source of revenue generated by the stadium including concessions, parking, advertising, and nonbaseball events there. The agreement sent no revenue streams back to taxpayers who were footing the construction bill through the sales tax hike."[13]

As a postscript, there are two items of note. First, the election was passed by a 54 percent to 46 percent majority after a vigorous campaign by local politicians, business interests, and the local media. Among the media, Denver's largest newspaper, the *Rocky Mountain News*, was an unabashed cheerleader, urging a yes vote in editorials and in the slant of its coverage. Editorials referred to opponents of the subsidy as "forces of caution and stagnation," "skeptics," "wearing dust-covered glasses," "shortsighted," and "envy-wracked."[14] After the vote, it was revealed that the *Rocky Mountain News* was involved in negotiations to become a part owner of the franchise (these negotiations were successful). A second interesting bit of information concerning this one-sided arrangement for the Rockies is that the taxpayers were represented in the negotiations, as noted earlier, by John McHale Jr. Four months after the lease was signed, McHale joined the Rockies as the team's executive vice president for baseball operations.

Other Egregious Examples of Subsidies to Team Owners

In the 1990s states and localities built six baseball parks, with team owners putting up only 6 percent of the $1.07 billion. The public funding came from a variety of sources, for example: a 2 percent hotel room tax pays for the new park for the White Sox; the sports lottery pays for Oriole Park; a 1.9 cent tax on every twelve-ounce beer is the primary source for the Cleveland Indians field; the Texas Rangers have a stadium in Arlington, paid for through $135 million in thirty-year bonds; and Coors Field of the Rockies is financed with a 0.1 percent sales tax in a six-county metropolitan area.

St. Louis enticed the Rams to leave Los Angeles with a package that included a new $300 million stadium; all proceeds from concessions, parking, club seats, and luxury suites; and a $15 million practice facility. To pay for the stadium, Missouri taxpayers pay $24 million a year, St. Louis taxpayers pay another $12.5 million, and visitors to the county pay a 7.25 percent room tax to raise another $6 million. Federal taxpayers (i.e., all of us) also help out—$2 million not received in federal taxes because of the use of tax-exempt bonds; $2 million because businesses deduct half the cost of club seats and luxury suites; and the deductions allowed owners through the depreciation of players.

Art Modell, owner of the Cleveland Browns (which averaged 70,000 fans per game), decided to move his team to Baltimore because he was given a $200 million stadium with 108 luxury boxes and 7,500 club seats, $75 million for moving expenses, $50 million for doing the deal, and all revenues from ticket sales, concessions, parking, and stadium advertising. Finally, taxpayers will guarantee ten years of sellout crowds for the new stadium. Moreover, when the stadium is used for other events, Modell will collect a 10 percent management fee plus half the profits. Use of the stadium is rent-free for thirty years, although Modell will pay back $24 million in construction costs.[15]

After a threat to move the Chicago Bears to the suburbs or to Northern Indiana, the city of Chicago agreed to finance its share of the $632 million project to renovate Soldier Field (the Bears were to pay $200 million) with a 2 percent city hotel tax. It is estimated that the new stadium has at least doubled the value of the Bears' franchise.[16]

The Montreal Expos were transplanted to Washington, D.C., for the 2005 season. For three years they played in the old RFK stadium. In 2008 they moved into a publicly financed new stadium that cost the taxpayers 97 percent of the total cost of $674 million. The owners were obligated to pay only $20 million of the construction costs and in return they receive all of the money received from tickets, parking, concessions, and naming rights.[17] Critic Dave Zirin points out that this subsidy occurred at the same time that the city was set to close down twenty-four public schools, the city's libraries shut down early for lack of funds, and the African American unemployment in the city was 51 percent. "It's a monument of avarice that will clear the working poor out of the Southeast corner of the city as surely as if they just dispensed with the baseball and used a bulldozer. This is sports as ethnic and economic cleansing.[18]

THE RATIONALE FOR PUBLIC SUBSIDIZATION OF PROFESSIONAL SPORTS TEAMS

Citizens have, for the most part, been willing to underwrite these subsidies to teams for four reasons. First, conventional wisdom holds that the presence of major league sports teams enhances a city's prestige. Image is important, at least to civic boosters, and having a major league team gives the impression of being a first-class city. Civic boosters believe above all that a world-class city has world-class sports teams engaged in contests with other teams representing world-class cities. A professional team housed in a stadium downtown restores the image and prosperity of the downtown area with the gentrification of stadium environs (e.g., warehouses are converted into upscale lofts; trendy restaurants, nightclubs, and boutiques locate nearby).[19] Tourists and television viewers now see the city in a new, more positive light.

Second, the presence of a major league team representing a city means a lot to the sports fans in that city and nearby environs. These fans can now identify with that team instead of watching a televised game between opponents from other places. This collective rooting for a major league team is believed to provide some social glue holding together a sprawling metropolitan area by bringing people together with a common identity. As Marilyn Geewax, a reporter for the *Atlanta Constitution*, puts it, "When I see 50,000 people in Turner Field, cheering and chopping [doing the Tomahawk chop for the Atlanta Braves, see chapter

3] together, I feel as though I live in a richer, more cohesive community. I can't name the price, but I know that feeling has value."[20]

Third, fans want to see games in person, not only the heroics of the home team but also sports stars from the visiting team as well. Attending a major league game is a noteworthy event for many. It is also a costly event that makes attendance more and more an event for the affluent. For example, the average cost for two adult tickets, concessions, a program, and parking was $453.95 for a Los Angeles Lakers game in 2007 (the average price per game for the Lakers is $89.24).[21] Fourth, it is commonly asserted that a major league team creates substantial economic growth. This is an important issue: Does a major league sports franchise generate a significant investment return for the community? And if there are economic benefits, who benefits and who does not?

Let's consider the claim that having a major league team and building a bigger and better stadium benefits the community economically. The following eight points represent a summary of scholars' conclusions refuting the myth of professional sport as an economic force in the community.

1. Professional sports teams are relatively small firms, when compared with the corporations and universities in a locality. Urban scholar Mark Rosentraub concludes that "sports is just too small a component of any community's economy to be the engine that propels jobs and growth."[22] "Professional sports may be the 'icing on a region's or city's economic cake,' but it is not an 'engine' that drives any economy."[23]

2. A common belief is that the presence of a professional sports team increases expenditures in restaurants and hotels, thereby stimulating growth and creating jobs. To a degree this is true—restaurants and hotels do locate near the stadium, revitalizing the area and bringing jobs. But most of this activity, about 80 percent of it, is just a transfer of spending from some parts of the metropolitan area to a more focused location. There is also less spending on other forms of recreation as attention is directed at the professional team. For example, on game days there is a decline in movie attendance, skiing on the nearby ski slopes, and even shopping in the malls.

3. Corporations do not move to an area because of a sport team or teams but primarily because of such factors as a suitable workforce, a positive (for management) labor climate, good schools, and relatively low taxes.

4. Economists have a concept called the "multiplier effect," which refers to money paid in profits or wages that is then spent (recirculated) in the community. The common argument by the proponents of civic growth is that the regional multiplier for any tourist industry is three. Rosentraub, however, makes the case for a multiplier effect of two when it comes to professional sports teams. Consider, for example, the money paid to players. About half of the money earned by sports teams is paid to players, with most making hundreds of thousands (if not millions) of dollars each season. At least half of this money, however, is spent elsewhere (e.g., agent fees, investments, permanent home, vacation home, purchase of luxury items not produced in the local economy).

5. When teams relocate, there is some economic gain to the community (no more than $10 to $15 million in new economic activity), but that gain is another community's loss, again, a transfer of economic activity rather than the creation of new economic activity.

6. Despite claims by public relations firms and civic boosters to the contrary, scholarly analyses of the economic impact of a stadium and a professional team show consistently that sport has a negligible impact on metropolitan economies. In short, "professional sports have been oversold by professional sports boosters as a catalyst for economic development."[24] Economist Robert Baade concludes, "Using economics as a justification for the subsidy is a political expedient, perhaps necessity, but it is inconsonant with the statistical evidence."[25]

7. Although sports teams may not have a tangible economic impact on a metropolitan community, they do have intangible benefits. Rosentraub says that "it may be important to attract millions of visitors to a downtown if only to remind them of the vitality and creativity contained in America's cities. If sports teams and their facilities accomplish that goal and establish pride in central cities, they may well be . . . 'major league.' . . . Further, if cities are to remain integral

components of American life, then keeping sports in cities is important. Sport is too important a part of Western society for us to think that cities can exist without the teams and the events which define essential dimensions of our society and life."[26]

8. Although sports are an important part of a community's quality of life, the citizens of every community have to decide whether the public subsidization of professional sports enhances the quality of life enough to warrant the investment and, more important, whether there are other areas that are better community investments. As Rosentraub wonders, "What are we to say to the residents of Cleveland, Indianapolis, and St. Louis who need better schools, health care, and neighborhoods when we refuse to raise some taxes but consent to give sports owners and athletes hundreds of millions of dollars in support?"[27]

I want to elaborate on this last point because it presents an interesting but disturbing inconsistency—U.S. society approves a welfare system to wealthy team owners and affluent athletes while condemning the social welfare system for the poor.[28]

From 1935 to 1996 the United States had a minimal welfare safety net for those in need (minimal when compared to the more generous welfare states of Western Europe and Scandinavia). Beginning with the Reagan administration, this welfare program has gradually been dismantled. This dismemberment accelerated in 1996 when the federal government made welfare assistance to families temporary and withdrew $55 billion in federal aid to the poor. At the federal and state levels, politicians from both major political parties favored doing away with welfare and substituting programs that would provide market-based solutions. The leaders of both political parties sought to reduce taxes or at least resist tax increases. This significant reduction of welfare for the poor occurred at a time (2005) when some 37 million Americans (12.6 percent) were below the government's poverty line, one out of every six American children was poor, and 45 million Americans had no health insurance. Urban schools were desperately behind suburban schools in resources, and only one-third of those children who qualified for Head Start received it. In short, the politicians, with the apparent support of the populace, embarked on a social experiment that, at least in the short run, would make life much more difficult for the economically disadvantaged. This inhumane approach was rationalized as necessary to rid the nation of a welfare system that was contrary to the American values of individualism, competition, and self-reliance.

At the same time, however, these same politicians, with the consent of the citizens (with a few exceptions), have encouraged a welfare system for team owners (wealthy individuals or corporations) and their high-paid athletes. The system of subsidies to emerge has, as economist Robert A. Baade described it, created a reverse "Robin Hood" effect—taking from the poor, the near poor, the working class, and the middle classes and giving to the rich.[29] This welfare to owners takes several forms, some of which I have already discussed. Federal law allows cities to issue tax-exempt bonds to finance the building of stadiums and arenas. The Congressional Research Service estimates that the cost to the federal treasury of such exemptions is $100 million in lost tax revenue. The 50 percent deductions of the cost of luxury suites and the like for businesses amount to a 17 percent federal subsidy for wealthy people to watch games.[30] The resulting lost tax revenues to the federal treasury come from other sources, which we all pay.

When the stadiums are built and paid for by taxpayers, there is a clear transfer of wealth from the taxpayers to the owners and the players. Urban scholar Mark Rosentraub says: "Sales taxes paid by lower-income people produce excess profits that are divided between players and owners, all of whom enjoy salaries about which the taxpayers can only dream. A subsidy spread across hundreds of thousands of people amounts to a small charge each year. It is still, however, a transfer of wealth from the lower and middle classes to the upper class."[31]

This transfer occurs as the new stadium increases the value of the team. When it is sold, the owner reaps greater capital gains. The transfer of wealth also occurs when luxury suites and club-level seats are built and the additional revenues generated go to the owners. So, too, with revenues from parking and concessions. Sometimes cities provide owners with moving expenses, practice facilities, office space, land, and special investment opportunities to entice them to stay or to move their team to the city.

Even though the public votes on raising taxes for a stadium, the obligation is not finite. The public sector ends up with the responsibility for any cost overruns, which are common. Most telling, stadiums are generally built with the owner investing some money but the public raising usually at least 80 percent of the funds, amounting to hundreds of millions of dollars. The asymmetrical nature of this relationship is revealed in the division of the revenues generated from the operation of the stadium—the owner who puts up about 20 percent (on average) receives 100 percent of the proceeds! The public, which invested most of the money for construction and maintenance of the facility, receives none of the proceeds.

To summarize, the professional team owner-city relationship entails several related contradictions. First, the mayors, governors, and legislators who work against welfare for the poor are more than generous with their subsidies to the rich. Second, the wealthy owners who favor private enterprise and marketplace solutions in their other business activities insist on subsidies to maintain their lucrative professional teams. Paul Allen, for example, the third richest individual in the United States (worth some $16.8 billion in 2007), insisted that he would move the Seattle Seahawks unless the residents of Seattle voted to build a stadium for his team (which they did). Third, team owners faced with what they consider inadequate subsidies will move their franchise to a locality that provides more generous subsidies. Fourth, the citizens of cities put up with this hypocrisy. In addition, the public, which underwrites the largesse to the wealthy, ends up being less likely to be able to afford to see the games in person. The cost of tickets, tending to increase anyway, escalates with a new stadium. Some stadium commissions require the purchase of a "personal seat license." For example, the Carolina Panthers started this trend in 1993 by selling 62,500 seat licenses from $600 to $5,400 each. The price in 2008 was $3,000 to $20,000.[32] The seat license provides the owner the right to purchase a ticket for a specified seat. As a result of these practices, the crowds in these new arenas are becoming more and more elite.

This trend takes two other forms as well. Publicly financed arenas are for sports that appeal especially to the affluent. Sports for the working classes, such as automobile racing, usually take place in privately owned arenas. Also, publicly funded arenas are for men. In this regard, Mariah

Burton Nelson asks, "Who loses when a community spends millions of dollars in tax revenue to construct a new stadium and only men get to play in it, and only men get to work there?"[33] Sport sociologist Bruce Kidd makes the same point in his essay on the building of a domed stadium in Toronto: "It constitutes a massive subsidization and celebration of the interests of men. . . . If a city gave pride of place to a stadium where only Anglo-Saxons could play, there would be howls of protest, but in the matter of gender and sports, such favouritism is usually taken for granted."[34]

Finally, as Mark Rosentraub observes, "If It Quacks, It Is Still a Duck," meaning that no matter what the spin, the subsidies that owners receive constitute welfare.[35] Ironically, it is a reverse type of socialism that redistributes wealth upward. Yet owners, civic boosters, editorial writers, and politicians who spend much of their time defending capitalism and the free market support it unabashedly and uncritically.

AN ALTERNATIVE STRUCTURE

There is another way—a fairer way—to structure professional sport. Teams could be owned by local governments (cities, counties, or region) or by community stockholders rather than individuals, families, or corporations, as is now the case. Localities already subsidize the teams but do not own them, which allows the owner to insist on more and better subsidies with the threat of moving the team to a more lucrative situation. The Green Bay Packers football team is the only major professional team that is owned by the people. Author Jim Hightower provides a description of this unique type of team ownership.

> Some 1,900 of the locals, including truckers, barkeeps, merchants, and bus drivers, own a piece of the Pack, organized back in 1923 as a community-owned, nonprofit company. The stockholders draw no profit, and the locally elected board of directors that operates the team is unpaid, but all concerned draw great pleasure from knowing that the Packers are theirs.
>
> What a difference ownership makes. Not a dime needs to be spent to hype up fan support, since the team literally belongs to them. The town of 96,000 built Lambeau Stadium, owns it, operates it, and fills each of the 60,790 seats in it for every home game—forty straight years of sellouts,

whether the team is winning or not, and the season ticket waiting list has 20,000 names on it.

Get this: No ticket costs more than $28, no parking space is more than $7, there is free parking within four blocks of the stadium. . . . Charities run the stadium's concessions. . . . Off-duty police provide stadium security, and are paid overtime by the team.

Green Bay fans and citizens never have to worry that some pirate of an owner is going to hijack the Pack and haul their team to Los Angeles or any other big-city market, because Green Bay is their team. It stands as a shining model of how fans in other cities could get control of their teams and stop corporate rip-offs.[36]

Shifting team ownership to community ownership is relatively easy. Each locality could buy the local team at its market value, which would amount to something less than what they now pay to build the owner a new stadium. There is only one catch: the owners in each league have passed a rule specifically banning any future team from being community owned! In other words, the teams will continue to be owned by individuals and corporations but financed by the public. This maintains a situation in which each team may claim that it is *yours*, but it is really *theirs*.

NOTES

1. George H. Sage, "Stealing Home: Political, Economic, and Media Power and a Publicly-Funded Stadium in Denver," *Journal of Sport and Social Issues* 17 (August 1993).

2. Roger G. Noll, "The U.S. Team Sports Industry," in *Government and the Sports Business*, ed. Roger G. Noll (Washington, D.C.: Brookings Institution, 1974), 2.

3. Sage, "Stealing Home," p. 112. I have updated Sage's calculation of the number of teams by population, using current population data and the addition of two franchises.

4. George H. Sage, *Power and Ideology in American Sport*, 2nd ed. (Champaign, Ill.: Human Kinetics, 1998), 199.

5. Robert Angell, "Green," *New Yorker*, April 7, 2008, p. 24.

6. *Forbes*, "Team Valuations (NFL)," October 1, 2007, p. 97; *Forbes*, "Team Valuations (MLB)," May 5, 2008, p. 94; *Forbes*, "NBA Team Valuations," December 24, 2007, p. 52.

7. Quoted in Juan B. Elizondo Jr., "Governor Pockets 14.9 Million from Rangers Sale," *Mexico City Times*, June 19, 1998, p. 8.

8. James Quirk and Rodney Fort, *Hard Ball: The Abuse of Power in Pro Sports* (Princeton, N.J.: Princeton University Press, 1999), 9.

9. Richard G. Sheehan, *Keeping Score: The Economics of Big-Time Sports* (South Bend, Ind.: Diamond Communications, 1996), 23–25.

10. Mark S. Rosentraub, *Major League Lo$ers: The Real Cost of Sports and Who's Paying for It* (New York: Basic Books, 1997), 119–20.

11. Mayya M. Komisarchik and Aju J. Fenn, "Trends in Stadium and Arena Construction, 1995–2010," unpublished paper, Department of Economics and Business, Colorado College, 2007.

12. The following is from Sage, "Stealing Home," 110–24; Fawn Germer, "Rockies Strike Richest Deal," *Rocky Mountain News*, November 28, 1991, p. 8; Richard Corliss, "High on the Rockies," *Time*, July 19, 1993, p. 55; and Paul Hutchinson, "Coors Field Tab Up to $215.5 Million," *Denver Post*, December 3, 1994, p. 1.

13. Sage, "Stealing Home," 116.

14. Tracy Ringolsby, "Privately Financed Ballparks Rare," *Rocky Mountain News*, May 8, 1997, p. 8C.

15. Jon Morgan, *Glory for Sale: Fans, Dollars and the New NFL* (Baltimore, Md.: Bancroft, 1997); George F. Will, "Modell Sacks Maryland," *Newsweek*, January 22, 1996, p. 70; and Jim Hightower, *There's Nothing in the Middle of the Road but Yellow Stripes and Dead Armadillos* (New York: HarperCollins, 1997), 20–21.

16. Andrew Martin, Liam Ford, and Laurie Cohen, "Bears Play, Public Pays," *Chicago Tribune*, April 21, 2002, pp. 1, 16.

17. S. L. Price, "Going Against the Percentages," *Sports Illustrated*, March 31, 2008, p. 130.

18. Dave Zirin, "Washington DC's Sporting Shock Doctrine," *Edge of Sports*, April 1, 2008.

19. See David Whitson and Donald Macintosh, "Becoming a World-Class City," *Sociology of Sport Journal* 10 (September 1993): 221–40; and Keith Law, "The Imbalance Sheet: The New Stadium Fallacy" (an interview with economist Brad Humphreys, April 12, 2001), online: www.baseballprospectus.com/news/20010412imbalance.html.

20. Marilyn Geewax, "Stadiums Can't Be Judged by Their Tax Costs Alone," *Rocky Mountain News*, October 22, 1997, p. 48A.

21. "Fan Cost Index," reported in "Lakers Tickets Set Fans Back," *USA Today*, November 7, 2007, p. 9C.

22. Mark S. Rosentraub, "Does the Emperor Have New Clothes? A Reply to Robert J. Baade," *Journal of Urban Affairs* 18.1 (1996): 23.

23. Rosentraub, *Major League Lo$ers*, 140.

24. Robert A. Baade, "Professional Sports as Catalysts for Metropolitan Economic Development," *Journal of Economic Affairs* 18.1 (1996): 1–17; Roger G. Noll and Andrew Zimbalist, eds., *Sports, Jobs, and Taxes: The Economic Impact of Sports Teams and Stadiums* (Washington, D.C.: Brookings Institution, 1997); C. C. Euchner, *Playing the Field: Why Sports Teams Move and Cities Fight to Keep Them* (Baltimore, Md.: Johns Hopkins University Press, 1993); Dean Baim, *The Sports Stadium as a Municipal Investment* (Westport, Conn.: Greenwood, 1992); Mark S. Rosentraub, "Sport and Downtown Development Strategy: If You Build It, Will Jobs Come?" *Journal of Urban Affairs* 16 (1994): 221–39; and Rosentraub, *Major League Lo$ers*.

25. Robert A. Baade, "Stadium Subsidies Make Little Economic Sense for Cities," *Journal of Urban Affairs* 18.1 (1996): 37.

26. Rosentraub, "Does the Emperor Have New Clothes?" 29.

27. Rosentraub, "Does the Emperor Have New Clothes?" 30.

28. The following is taken primarily from Rosentraub, *Major League Lo$ers*, 3–17; D. Stanley Eitzen, "Dismantling the Welfare State," *Vital Speeches of the Day* 62 (June 1996): 532–36; and D. Stanley Eitzen and Maxine Baca Zinn, "New Welfare Legislation and Families" (paper presented to the American Sociological Association, San Francisco, August 1998).

29. Robert A. Baade and Alan Sanderson, "Field of Fantasies," Heartland Institute, Intellectual Ammunition website, quoted in Morgan, *Glory for Sale*, 315.

30. "How You Pay $$$ for Stadiums Far, Far Away," *USA Today*, June 5, 1997, p. 14A.

31. Rosentraub, *Major League Lo$ers*, 447.

32. Richard Sandomir, "Jets and Giants Fans May Pay for the Right to Pay for Tickets," *New York Times*, March 22, 2008.

33. Mariah Burton Nelson, *The Stronger Women Get, the More Men Love Football: Sexism and the American Culture of Sports* (New York: Harcourt Brace, 1994), 8. See also Varda Burstyn, *The Rites of Men: Manhood, Politics, and the Culture of Sport* (Toronto: University of Toronto Press, 1999).

34. Bruce Kidd, "The Men's Cultural Centre: Sports and the Dynamic of Women's Oppression/Men's Repression," in *Sport, Men, and the Gender Order: Critical Feminist Perspectives*, ed. Michael A. Messner and Donald F. Sabo (Champaign, Ill.: Human Kinetics, 1990), 32.

35. Rosentraub, *Major League Lo$ers*, 447.

36. Hightower, *There's Nothing in the Middle of the Road*, 22–23. See also Sue Halpern, "Home Field Advantage," *Mother Jones* 27 (November/December 2002): 30–33.

AP/Wide World

12

THE GLOBALIZATION OF SPORT

Globalization is the central reality of our time.

—Former president Bill Clinton

I think that ultimately the twenty-first century will be a global sports age.

—Harry Edwards, sociologist

The percentage of players from outside the U.S. continues to grow in professional baseball, football, soccer, and basketball. What we're witnessing is the beginning of the global sports age.

—The Institute for Diversity and Ethics in Sport

Our identification with a sports team has a geographical base. The nearest team is *our* team and they play against *other* teams. In other words, sports are local. We identify with the local high school, college, and professional athletic teams. After moving to a new community it doesn't take long before one roots for the local teams or for local athletes in individual sports. Even when there isn't a local team, we will identify, typically, with the nearest in the region as do people in North and South Dakota, who root for the Minnesota Twins and Vikings. So,

too, with national teams and athletes competing with their foreign counterparts. This is clearly us versus them.

But this identification with the local is breaking down. Where professional players once tended to play out their careers with one team
(e.g., Stan Musial, Cal Ripken Jr., Bill Russell), free agency has meant
movement of players from team to team after just a few years. So, too,
with managers and coaches who are fired or move to more lucrative
situations. In addition, college coaches are nomadic, as are college basketball players good enough to become professionals before graduation.
Professional teams, as we have seen, move or threaten to move, leaving
local fans bitter. The ever increasing cost of attending college and professional teams' games also has alienated many fans. Many Americans
find it difficult to warm to the foreign players in college and professional
sport (similar to the situation when African Americans broke the racial
barrier in sport in the 1940s, 1950s, and 1960s, leaving many white fans
angry at the changing racial composition of their teams).

But the times are changing rapidly. Golf and tennis are already global
sports with athletes competing in tournaments worldwide. For example,
in the first major LPGA (women's golf) championship of 2008, the winner was from Mexico, followed in order by two Swedes, a Norwegian,
and six South Koreans. The first American finished eleventh. U.S. universities actively recruit foreign athletes (especially in basketball, track,
and volleyball) and professional scouts in baseball and basketball scour
the globe for talent. U.S. influence spreads around the world as sports
events are televised globally and sports leagues seek global expansion.
Transnational corporations use sports and athletes to market their
products worldwide. These elements of the globalization of sport are
explored in this chapter.

GLOBALIZATION DEFINED

Globalization, of course, is not limited to sport. Let's begin by looking at
the phenomenon of globalization in general.[1] Globalization refers to the
ever greater connectedness among the world's people. Globalization is
a process whereby goods, information, people, money, communication,
sport, fashion, and other forms of culture move across national bound-

aries. There are several implications of this phenomenon. First, globalization is not a thing or a product but rather a process. It involves such activities as immigration, transnational travel, the Internet, marketing products in one nation that are made elsewhere, movement of jobs to low-wage economies (or, in the case of athletes, coming to a high-wage society such as the U.S.), transnational investments, satellite broadcasts, oil pricing, and the ability to find a McDonald's in virtually all of the world's major cities. Second, it follows that globalization is not simply a matter of economics, but it also has far-reaching political, social, and cultural implications as well. Third, globalization refers to worldwide changes that are increasingly remolding the lives of people everywhere.[2] And fourth, not everyone experiences globalization in the same way. For some it expands opportunities and enhances prosperity, while others experience poverty and hopelessness. Periods of rapid social change, we know, "threaten the familiar, destabilize old boundaries, and upset established traditions. Like the mighty Hindu god Shiva, globalization is not only a great destroyer, but also a powerful creator of new ideas."[3]

Globalization is not a recent phenomenon. For thousands of years, people have traveled, traded, and migrated across political boundaries exchanging food, artifacts, and knowledge. In the sports realm, the cultural imperialism employed by the British colonists of the nineteenth and twentieth centuries brought their sports (soccer, rugby, cricket) to their colonies (e.g., India, New Zealand, Australia, and what is now Pakistan), where they flourished. Golf began in Scotland and spread across the world. The Olympic movement spread around the globe during the twentieth century. While baseball began in the United States, it is extremely popular in Latin America, the Caribbean countries, Japan, and South Korea. So, too, with basketball, which has spread especially to China and Western and Central Europe.

While global connections have existed for centuries, they have "figured as a pervasive, major aspect of social life mainly since the 1960s."[4] Since then, the rate of change has been exponential. The speed of movement (travel or via communications technology) and the volume of goods, messages, and symbols have increased dramatically. In addition, space has shrunk as travel and communication time has decreased.[5] As sport sociologist Joseph Maguire puts it, "These globalization processes . . . appear to be leading to a form of time-space compression. That is, people are experiencing spatial and temporal dimensions differently. There is a speeding up of time and a 'shrinking' of space. Modern technologies enable people, images, ideas and money to criss-cross the globe with great rapidity."[6]

The remainder of this chapter will examine four aspects of the globalization of sport: (1) the transnational exchange of athletes; (2) the marketing of global athletes; (3) using Nike as the case study, transnational sports corporations making their products in low-wage economies and marketing them worldwide; and (4) global expansion by U.S. sports leagues.

THE TRANSNATIONAL MIGRATION OF ATHLETES

While athletes moved across national borders to compete throughout the twentieth century, this transnational migration (sociologist Jay Coakley calls these athletes "global migrant workers"[7]) is accelerating rapidly now. This global labor force is changing sport. Let's look at this migration and its consequences in several sports.

Baseball

In 2007 some 46 percent of 6,196 minor league baseball players in the United States were foreign-born, most of them coming from Latin America. At the major league level, 29 percent of the players were foreign born in 2007, with Latino players the most common. This rise in Latinos in baseball (27 percent up from 13 percent in 1990) has coincided with the decline of African Americans in the sport. Blacks were 27 percent of major leaguers in 1975, but now they are only 8 percent. Major league teams invest $60 million annually into Latin American scouting and development (player academies).[8] There are two reasons for this investment. First, you go to the areas where there is talent, and Latin America, especially the Dominican Republic, Venezuela, and Puerto Rico, has turned out many players with exceptional ability. Second, it is cheaper to sign the Latinos. And this, among other things, shows the dark side of this migration from south to north. Joe Kehoskie, an American sports agent, says:

Traditionally in the Latin market, I would say players sign for about 5 to 10 cents on the dollar compared to their U.S. counterparts. [Moreover] a lot of times kids just quit school at 10, 11, 12, and play baseball full-time. It's great, it's great for the kids that make it because they become superstars and get millions of dollars in the big leagues. But for ninety-eight kids out of 100, it results in a kid that is 18, 19, with no education.[9]

Approximately 90 to 95 percent of Latino players who sign contracts never reach the big leagues. The vast majority never get a chance to play in the United States at any level. The ones who make it to the United States but fail to make a team tend to stay in the country as undocumented immigrants, working for low wages rather than returning home as "failures." "These castoffs represent the underside of the Sammy Sosa story, the rule rather than the exception in the high stakes recruitment of ball players from Latin America and the Caribbean."[10]

There are over 200 major league players who speak Spanish, Japanese, or Korean. These players rarely speak English, and many have only a grade school education. As a result, they have problems with adjustment to the culture and language of their new home. Consequently, every major league team has programs for teaching English and American culture to these players. The league makes manuals available that are written in English and Spanish, dealing with baseball terminology but also such items as how to sign apartment leases and other useful information.[11]

Japanese baseball players are also making an impact on major league baseball, especially Ichiro Suzuki of the Seattle Mariners and Hideki Matsui of the New York Yankees. Especially noteworthy is how the Japanese players are being marketed extensively by their teams and host cities to attract Japanese tourists. It also increases the profit of U.S. television companies who sell rights to Japan.

There is a negative consequence of the influx of foreign-born players in baseball. Baseball stars do not command the advertising endorsement deals found in other sports. For instance, Alex Rodriguez and Derek Jeter of the New York Yankees are among the very best players. They are handsome, and scandal-free, and they play in the biggest market in the United States, yet a teenage female golfer (Michelle Wie) makes about $12 million more in endorsements than either Rodriguez or Jeter. *Sports Business Journal's* list of the most marketable athletes does not list a baseball player in the top 15. The two reasons given for this gap are the steroid scandal that has wracked baseball and the large number of foreign-born players in that sport.[12]

Golf

Golf is truly a global sport. Midway through 2008, the top ten men golfers (World Golf Rankings), included four Americans, two Australians, and one each from South Africa, Fiji, South Korea, and England. There were only two Americans ranked from 11 through 20. These golfers play mostly on the U.S. tour but also in tournaments in Europe, South Africa, Asia, and Australia.

The top ten players on the Ladies Professional Golf Association (LPGA) tour in mid-2008 included three Koreans, three Americans, two Swedes, and one each from Australia and Mexico. South Koreans have made the greatest inroads on the American tour. In 1998 Se Ri Pak was the only South Korean on the tour. By 2001 there were ten South Koreans, and in 2007 there were 45.[13]

Tennis

Tennis, like golf, is a global sport with tournaments everywhere. The top athletes reflect this. For women tennis professionals, only two Americans were in the top 20 in 2008 (the sport was dominated by women from Russia, Serbia, and the Czech Republic). For men, again only two of the top 20 in 2008 were Americans. A Swiss and a Spaniard led the rankings.

Soccer ("Futbol")

Soccer is the most global of team sports, with avid fans, numbering 1.25 billion, in almost every country. The World Cup and the matches leading to it are watched on television in over 200 countries (a record 1.1 billion people watched the World Cup final in 2006, surpassing the 1 billion worldwide that watched the 2008 Super Bowl). There are soccer leagues in most countries and considerable player movement across national borders. Soccer in the United States does not have the enthusiastic following found elsewhere, but there are diehard fans nevertheless, especially in ethnic groups from soccer-loving countries. Hispanics with ties to Mexico, South America, and Central America are especially enamored with soccer. Los Angeles County, with 4.23 million Latinos, most of Mexican heritage, is a hotbed of soccer interest. The Spanish-language network Univision, keenly aware of the interest of Latinos (especially Mexicans) in soccer, showed more than two hundred Mexican league matches in the United States in 2004.[14]

Hockey

There is some dispute as to when and where hockey began, but it likely started with a version played in the early 1800s in Nova Scotia by the Micmac Indians. It spread throughout Canada and is now "Canada's official winter sport." Canadians constitute the majority of hockey players in the National Hockey League (the NHL is really a Canadian–U.S. league). The sport has spread to other cold-weather countries in Scandinavia (Sweden, Finland, Norway) and Europe (Switzerland, the Czech Republic, Russia). In 1984 some 8.7 percent of NHL players were born outside North America; in 2008 that figure was 28.6 percent. Canada supplied 390 of the league's players, followed by the U.S. (141), Czech Republic (51), Sweden (48), Finland (32), Russia (26), Slovakia (20), and an assortment of other nations including one from the warm weather nation of Brazil.

In 2004 the NHL owners locked out the players. While a hardship for many players, others lined up high-paying jobs in European and Scandinavian hockey leagues. The Europeans said, in effect, "Lock us out? So what? We'll just go home and play."[15] This option gave the players leverage in labor negotiations.

Football

Even football, which is not played everywhere, has athletes from other countries—99 foreign-born players in the NFL in 2007, up from 52 in

1997. The common belief is that these are kickers and come from countries where soccer is popular. But only a small number are kickers—the rest play at any of the positions, with even one a quarterback where a complete knowledge of the game is an important prerequisite.

Basketball

In 1994 the first ten picks in the NBA draft were from the United States. In 2002 the top pick was from China (Yao Ming), the fifth choice was an Italian, and a Brazilian was number seven. In 2002 there were fifty international players from twenty-nine countries on NBA rosters. The next year there were sixty-five foreign players, and in 2007 there were eighty-three. These players came from Latin America, Africa, Europe, Asia, and even Oceania—in short, from throughout the world. The Los Angeles Lakers, for example, had players on their team from the Democratic Republic of the Congo, France, Serbia, Slovenia, and Spain. The Houston Rockets has its website in three languages—English, Spanish, and Chinese. Historically, the United States has dominated other countries in the Olympic Games. But in 2004, the U.S. basketball team, composed of NBA stars, was outclassed by other teams from other nations and was fortunate to come in third. This reflects the diffusion of the U.S. game of basketball throughout the world and that skilled players are found everywhere. Consequently, NBA teams hunt for talent around the globe. For example, Tony Ronzone, director of international scouting for the Detroit Pistons, has a network of four hundred people on five continents who inform him of talented (or potentially talented) basketball players.[16] Africa, where some tribes people are disproportionately tall, is an especially fertile source of potential NBA players.[17] So, too, is China, with its population of 1.3 billion.

The discussion above indicates that the migration flow of athletes is one way—to the United States. Actually, many U.S. athletes compete in other countries as well. Some examples: American baseball players, often unwanted major league veterans, sometimes play the remainder of their careers in Japan. For golfers who do not qualify for the U.S. tour, many play in Europe and Asia. American football players play in Canada, where each team is limited to five Americans, and in the European league. Basketball players, male and female, often play in European, Australian, and Asian leagues.

In sum, the transnational labor migration of athletes plays an important role in globalization as it contributes to transnationalism and deterritorialization and new meanings of identity and citizenship as the nation-state declines.[18]

THE MARKETING OF INTERNATIONAL PLAYERS FOR CORPORATE PROFIT: THE CASE OF YAO MING

There have been several sport icons who were known and marketed throughout the world, for example, America's Muhammad Ali (boxing), Michael Jordan (basketball), and Wayne Gretsky (hockey) in the recent past, and American Tiger Woods (golf), German Michael Schumacher (Formula One automobile racing), and British David Beckham (soccer) in the present. These athletes make huge earnings from their sport and from being richly compensated pitchmen for corporations who use their name, fame, and public appearances to market their products. But no athlete has the marketing potential of Yao Ming.

Yao Ming, born in Shanghai, grew to be 7 ft. 6 in. and 310 pounds. On his way to becoming a basketball star, he was selected first in the 2002 NBA draft by the Houston Rockets. He is the epicenter of a campaign by U.S. corporations to open markets for their products in China with its 1.3 billion potential consumers and its estimated 300 million basketball fans. "The timing for Yao couldn't be better. The explosion of disposable income in China, its acceptance into the World Trade Organization, its fastidious preparations for the 2008 Beijing Olympics, all combine to elevate China's most familiar face beyond sports hero."[19] Yao makes about $25 million a year in endorsements including Reebok, China Unicom, Coke, and Visa." Reebok wanted him because its goal for Chinese sales in athletic footwear and apparel is $300 million and one-fourth of the sneaker business in China by 2008. In China, Yao has begun to broker deals with local corporations looking to go global. In short, Yao is a gateway for corporations to penetrate the Chinese market as well as an avenue for Chinese corporations to market globally.

U.S. companies have signed other Chinese sports stars to market their products in China. Liu Xiang, 2004 Olympic gold medallist in the 110-meter hurdles, has deals with Coke and Nike. "He is arguably the most popular man in China and indisputably the most visible."

And Guo Jingjing, winner of two gold medals for diving in the 2004 Athens Olympics, has appeared in advertisements for McDonald's, Ford, and Budweiser.

THE GLOBAL REACH OF TRANSNATIONAL SPORT CORPORATIONS: THE CASE OF NIKE

The global sports market generated $235 billion in 2006. North America accounted for 45 percent and Asia 19 percent of that market. The Nike Corporation is the major worldwide producer and marketer of athletic shoes, apparel, and equipment. Some facts for Nike from 2007:[20]

- Nike sales totaled $16 billion creating a profit of $1.6 billion. Roughly three-fifths of the sales come from footwear.
- Phillip Knight, the co-founder of Nike, is the largest stockholder, worth approximately $5.6 billion.
- Nike has 30,200 employees.
- Nike has 13,000 different styles of footwear and apparel that it sells each quarter.
- Nike has 3,000 stores in China, with sales of $1 billion. Its annual sales growth in China is 50 percent.
- Nike's marketing budget is $2 billion a year.
- Over 900 independent overseas factories make clothes and footwear for Nike.

Nike was founded in 1964 in Oregon. At first, its sneakers were made in Japan, which was then a low-wage country.[21] In time, Japanese wages became too expensive, so Nike opened manufacturing plants in New Hampshire and Maine. In 1977 its first factory was opened in South Korea and later Taiwan. In the mid-1980s, Nike closed its U.S. manufacturing plants, shifting production completely to the low-wage countries of South Korea and Taiwan.

Nike presents a classic case of capitalism and the division of labor known as the "export-processing system." In Nike's case, product research, design, development, and marketing take place in the United States, while the labor-intensive, assembly-line phases of product manufacture are relegated to low-wage countries where labor and environmental protections are not enforced. The result of this system is a "race to the bottom,"[22] as corporations move manufacturing plants to, for example, Mexico. But when its wages are undercut by some other society, it becomes advantageous for the corporation to seek the lowest wages (and the highest profits) possible, thus seeking the country with the lowest wages and most advantageous (i.e., noninterfering) laws, usually in Southeast Asia and China.

In the late 1980s, when wages increased in South Korea and Taiwan, Nike shifted its operations into "politically autocratic, military-dominated countries like Indonesia and Thailand and later to China and Vietnam, in a relentless drive for a favorable political climate and the lowest-cost labor to make its shoes and apparel."[23] At last count, Nike had 450,000 workers making their products in Southeast Asia and 120,000 workers in China. None of Nike's footwear is manufactured within the United States.

Nike's strategy, of course, is not unusual among transnational corporations. While it results in greater profits for the corporation, the race to the bottom has negative consequences for domestic jobs and it exploits workers in low-wage societies. Regarding the latter, investigations by academic, religious, labor, and human rights organizations from various countries found that:

> Appalling labor conditions were essentially the same in all of Nike's factories. Seventy-five to 80 percent of Nike workers were women—mostly under the age of 24—who regularly put in 10 to 13 hour days, worked six days a week, and were forced to work overtime two to three times per week. The typical worker was paid 13 to 20 cents (in U.S. dollars) an hour—which was $1.60 to $2.20 per day. This wage was below the "minimum physical needs" figure. Worker abuse was widespread in the Nike factories.[24]

In response, workers in some plants engaged in work stoppages and strikes to protest their abusive treatment and unhealthy working conditions. A number of organizations throughout the world formed a broad structure known as the Nike Social Movement, which campaigned against Nike, using demonstrations, protests, sit-ins, marches, and op-ed columns to make the public aware of Nike's labor practices. Included in this movement were efforts on college campuses to boycott Nike products under an organization called United Students against Sweatshops.

Initially, Nike denied responsibility for conditions in the Asian factories, arguing that Nike merely contracted with suppliers, who actually manufactured the shoes. But, as George Sage argues:

> This is, of course, absurd; Nike always had overall control of its productive operations through the power it had over its contractors. In all its contracts with suppliers Nike specified very precisely all of the quality standards that had to be met in the manufacture of their products. There is no reason at all that Nike management could not also specify labor standards with regard to the workers in the factories.[25]

Nike continued its practices, instigated three internal investigations, and tried a media blitz to alter its negative image. These efforts were unsuccessful, with Nike showing a decline in sales from 1997 through 1999. Finally, in 1998 Nike changed course, in effect admitting to problems with labor. The new initiatives included raising the minimum age of workers, adopting U.S. Occupational Safety and Health Administration (OSHA) indoor air-quality standards for all footwear factories, expanding education programs for workers, and adding to its monitoring program.

Three years later, an investigation by the Global Alliance for Workers and Communities into a consortium of companies (including Nike) found that the conditions and wages for workers had not changed. Similarly, an investigation by the National Labor Committee in Bangladesh found similar exploitative "labor conditions in seven factories that produce logoed apparel for American universities, three of which produced Nike products, while the other four produced products for other sporting goods firms, such as Reebok, Pro Sports, and Wilson Sporting Goods."[26] More recent reports indicate that worker conditions in the Nike plants in Asia are improving somewhat. In spite of this, "the contradiction between what Nike has claimed about its factories and what study after study has reported about those factories has continued because Nike persistently projected a corporate image of concern for the working conditions in its factories and a commitment to reform them, but the company's basic strategy relied on damage control and public relations."[27]

To conclude, Nike is just one example of how transnational corporations place profit above people. Nike is a prime example; "because it has had the largest share of the sports footwear market and the accompanying profits, [it] can therefore more easily afford to lead a change in corporate direction."[28]

GLOBAL EXPANSION BY U.S. SPORTS ORGANIZATIONS

Transnational corporations and sports organizations in the search for added profits seek to expand their operations to new markets. We have seen how transnational corporations use sports celebrities to market their products in new territories. They also sponsor teams and leagues. For example, Nike, Motorola, General Motors, Coca-Cola, Pepsico, Philips Electronics, and Siemens have not only spent millions on advertising in China, but they have also sponsored Chinese teams and leagues in men's and women's soccer, university soccer, and basketball. These efforts plus the influence of Yao Ming have led to a dynamic surge of interest in China for basketball. This, of course, pleases transnational companies engaged in selling sneakers, balls, goals and nets, and sports apparel. New markets in China and elsewhere have sports organizations salivating over the prospects for growth and profits. Let's examine, briefly, these efforts by major league baseball, the NFL, and the NBA.

Major League Baseball

Major league baseball has made a concerted effort to reach out globally. As early as 1913, two teams—the Chicago White Sox and the New York Giants—played a game in Japan. U.S. All-Stars have toured in Japan intermittently ever since. Beginning in 2000, Major League Baseball International, through its Envoy Program, sent high school and college baseball coaches to twenty-nine countries to instruct youngsters on how to play the game. In 2003 the Montreal Expos played twenty-two regular-season games in San Juan, Puerto Rico. The 2008 season began with the Oakland A's defeating the Boston Red Sox in Tokyo. Individual games are telecast to audiences in interested countries (e.g., Japan when Hideki Matsui or Ichiro Suzuki is playing) and the game's signature events, the World Series and the All-Star Game, are televised to more than two hundred countries.

The National Football League

The National Football League has at least one exhibition game a year outside the United States. The Super Bowl is telecast to over two hundred countries. Through NFL International, the league's developmental arm, the league started NFL Europe in 1995. This is a six-team league with teams from the Netherlands, Spain, and Germany. The players are mostly from the United States, hoping to make it to the NFL. In 2007 the New York Giants played the Miami Dolphins in London, the first time that a regular season game had been played outside the Americas. The game was sold out, with 86,000 spectators in Wembley Stadium (most tickets ranging from $90 to $300).[29]

The National Basketball Association

Basketball is the world's fastest-growing sport (soccer is the largest but not growing as fast) in large measure because of the efforts of professional basketball in the United States to promote its sport. The NBA has welcomed foreign athletes and marketed them in their native countries, and native ethnic populations in the United States. The NBA has, along with corporate sponsors, held clinics and demonstrations in other countries. The league holds pre-season games in Europe, Latin America, and Asia. NBA stars—most notably Michael Jordan, because of worldwide advertising, the sale of jerseys and other paraphernalia, and basketball telecasts—are global sports icons. From various activities, products, and media, the NBA makes about $300 million from its overseas operations. Spearheading the NBA's growing global presence is Heidi Ueberroth, president for global marketing partnerships and international business operations. The NBA now airs games in 215 countries and in 41 languages. In China alone, NBA games are broadcast on 51 television networks, and the league's Chinese website is the most popular sports internet site.[30]

Such is the potential global growth of the NBA that its commissioner, David Stern, has said that by the end of this decade "the league could be deriving up to half its revenue from outside the U.S."[31]

CONCLUSION

The point of this chapter is that sport transcends national boundaries. It is both a product and a source of globalization. There are migration flows of athletes between and among nations. Some athletes are global icons. Sports and athletes are used by transnational corporations as vehicles to market their products worldwide. Sports-related transnational corporations have their products made in developing countries to be marketed elsewhere. And sports organizations, through expansion beyond their borders, "have become exporters of culture as well as products to be consumed."[32]

In keeping with the theme of sport being fair *and* foul, the globalization of sport has positive and negative consequences. On the positive ("fair") side, sport is a microcosm of worldwide trends, with increasing diversity connecting peoples (athletes and fans) Globalization also increases the likelihood of talented athletes finding a niche somewhere to participate and to receive lucrative compensation, instead of being blocked by limited opportunities within their countries. Finally, entrepreneurs and corporations benefit as the value of franchises increases as leagues cross national boundaries.

There are several negative ("foul") implications of globalized sport. First, the best athletic talent will likely migrate to the most affluent societies, leaving an imbalance of talent by nations and an evermore uneven playing field in international competition. Second, in searching for talent in poor countries, athletes will sometimes be exploited by unscrupulous teams and agents. Third, transnational corporations marketing sporting goods continue to exploit workers who make these products in low-wage economies.

CHAPTER 12

NOTES

1. This section is taken from D. Stanley Eitzen and Maxine Baca Zinn, "Globalization: An Introduction," in *Globalization: The Transformation of Social Worlds*, 2nd ed. (Belmont, Calif.: Wadsworth, 2009), 1–9.

2. James Peoples and Garrick Bailey, *Humanity: An Introduction to Cultural Anthropology* (Belmont, Calif.: Wadsworth, 2003).

3. Manfred B. Stegner, *Globalism: The New Market Ideology* (Lanham, Md.: Rowman & Littlefield, 2002).

4. Jan Aart Scholte, *Globalization: A Critical Introduction* (New York: Palgrave, 2000), 19.

5. John Beynon and David Dunkerely, *Globalization: The Reader* (New York: Routledge, 2000), 5.

6. Joseph Maguire, "Sport and Globalization," in *Handbook of Sports Studies*, ed. Jay J. Coakley and Eric Dunning (London: Sage, 2000), 356.

7. Jay J. Coakley, *Sports in Society: Issues & Controversies*, 9th ed. (New York: McGraw-Hill, 2007), 466.

8. Alan Klein, *Growing the Game: The Globalization of Major League Baseball* (New Haven, Conn.: Yale University Press, 2004).

9. Cited in Dave Zirin, "Say It Ain't So, Big Leagues," *The Nation*, November 14, 2005, p. 22.

10. Marcos Breton, "Latinos and Baseball," *Color Lines* (Spring 2000): 16.

11. Skip Rozin, "Godzilla to the Rescue?" *Business Week*, March 3, 2003, p. 95.

12. David Sweet, "SportsBiz: Why Advertisers Shun Baseball," *MSNBC.com*, online: www.msnbc.msn.com/id/23520641/print/1/displaymode/1098.

13. Steve DiMeglio, "Fire Within Trailblazer Pak Successfully Rekindled," *USA Today*, June 7, 2007, p. 9C.

14. Grant Wahl, "Football vs. Futbol," *Sports Illustrated*, July 5, 2004, pp. 68–72.

15. L. Jon Wertheim, "Hot Prospects in Cold Places," *Sports Illustrated*, June 21, 2004, 65.

16. Josh Tyrangiel, "Looking for Mr. Really Big," *Time*, October 11, 2004, pp. 83–84.

17. Grant Wahl, "On Safari for 7-Footers," *Sports Illustrated*, June 28, 2004, pp. 70–73.

18. Lloyd L. Wong and Ricardo Trumper, "Global Celebrity Athletes and Nationalism," *Journal of Sport & Social Issues* 26 (May 2002): 168–94.

19. Mark Starr, "Olympian Ambitions," *Newsweek*, December 31, 2008, p. 56.

20. Andria Cheng, "Nike Profit Surges 32% on Gains in U.S., Europe," *Marketwatch*, June 26, 2007; "Nike: Set for Two Great Leaps," *Business Week*, April 14, 2008; and *Forbes*, "On the Run," February 11, 2008, pp. 83–87.

21. This section depends in large part on George H. Sage, "Corporate Globalization and Sporting Goods Manufacturing: The Case of Nike," in *Sport in Contemporary Society: An Anthology*, ed. D. Stanley Eitzen, 7th ed. (Boulder, Colo.: Paradigm, 2005), 362–82.

22. See, for example, Jeremy Brecher, Tim Costello, and Brendan Smith, *Globalization from Below: The Power of Solidarity* (Cambridge, Mass.: South End Press, 2000).

23. Sage, "Corporate Globalization," 367.

24. Sage, "Corporate Globalization," 368.

25. Sage, "Corporate Globalization," 370.

26. Sage, "Corporate Globalization," 377.

27. Sage, "Corporate Globalization," 379.

28. Sage, "Corporate Globalization," 379.

29. Jeffrey Stinson, "NFL Working to Build Bridge to Europe," *USA Today*, October 26, 2007, pp. 1C–2C.

30. Diane Brady, "Heidi Ueberroth," *Business Week*, October 8, 2007, p. 62; and Eddie Pells, "Getting a Toehold in China," Associated Press, August 4, 2007.

31. Quoted in Eisenberg, "The NBA's Global Game Plan," *Time*, March 17, 2003, p. 63.

32. Coakley, *Sports in Society*, 369.

13

THE CHALLENGE: CHANGING SPORT

Probably only death will cure my love affair with North Carolina basketball, and no doubt there are millions of people who feel the same way about their own teams. But loving the game need not mean having a romantic view of how college sports are organized. College sports are far too visible an arena in American society to be simply thrown to the wolves. Ultimately, the only productive route forward is to insist that those who love the game also fight to change it.

—Thad Williamson, professor of social justice and social change

This book is titled *Fair and Foul: Beyond the Myths and Paradoxes of Sport* because sport is both elevating and deflating, appealing and appalling, inspiring and disillusioning. Although I have tried to present the positive side of sport, my emphasis has leaned strongly toward criticism and an examination of the "dark side" of sport. My analysis shares something with the experience of Mike Lupica, sportswriter for the *New York Daily News*, who says that he wants to celebrate sport in his column, but "sports keeps making it so goddamned hard [to do so]."[1]

My bias toward the "dark side" is deliberate. My goal is to engage readers in an analysis of sport that leads them to reflect on how sport really works and how it might be improved.

IS CHANGE POSSIBLE?

First, sport, as it is practiced in the United States, is not fated by nature or even by the "invisible hand" of the market; it is a social construction, the result of historical actions and choices. Americans have created the organization of sport that now exists, and Americans maintain it.[2] This means, then, that because sport is created by people, it can be changed by them as well.

Second, historically, sport has occasionally changed for the better because of the deliberate acts of individuals and the collective, organized efforts of social movements and organizations. Three well-known examples illustrate this point. In these and other significant challenges to the status quo, change did not occur without a fight. Individuals and groups confronted the powerful and succeeded.

The Racial Integration of Baseball

Baseball was rigidly segregated before World War II. But, in 1947, Branch Rickey, the owner of the Brooklyn Dodgers, brought talented Jackie Robinson, an African American, into the major leagues against the vehement opposition of his fellow owners (the owners voted 15 to 1 in 1946 to maintain segregation) and most major league players.[3] Rickey's bold move was not entirely altruistic, since he saw blacks as a reservoir of untapped talent and believed that racial integration would increase attendance by tapping the black fans.

Blacks soon achieved prominence in baseball and ultimately were accepted by white players and fans. Many people were involved behind the scenes in effecting this extraordinary transformation. In 1944, Albert "Happy" Chandler, who was sympathetic toward the goal of racial integration, became commissioner of major league baseball, replacing a strict segregationist, Kenesaw Mountain Landis. During the war and after it, black newspapers, most prominently in New York and Pittsburgh, argued for racial integration in baseball. Their argument (used also by a few white sportswriters) was that blacks fought in World War II to protect freedom, yet American society denied blacks the freedom to compete on a level playing field with whites.

Free Agency for Athletes

Before the landmark court cases of the mid-1970s, professional athletes in team sports were trapped by the reserve clause in their contracts. Once a player signed a contract with a club, that team had exclusive rights, and the player was no longer free to negotiate with any other team. In succeeding years, the player had to sell his services solely to the club that owned his contract unless it released, sold, or traded him, or he chose to retire. The reserve clause specified that the owner had the exclusive right to renew a player's contract annually. Thus a player was bound perpetually to negotiate with only one club. The player was the club's property and could be sold to another club without the player's consent. In effect, this clause kept the salaries of players artificially low and restricted the players' freedom. As one observer put it, "after the Civil War settled the slavery issue, owning a ball club was the closest one could come to owning a plantation."[4]

The late 1960s was a period in American history when various downtrodden groups (racial minorities, women, gays) became militant in attempts to change existing power relationships. Within this society-wide framework, athletes, too, began to recognize their common plight and organized to change it. Most fundamentally, they felt that because the owners had all the power, the players did not receive their true value in the marketplace. The result was that athletes, as individuals and as player associations, began to assert themselves against what they considered an unfair system.

Several cases were instrumental in modifying the reserve clause in baseball. Most important was Curt Flood, who was traded by the baseball Cardinals in 1969 to the Philadelphia Phillies but refused to play for them, sitting out the 1970 season. He brought suit against organized baseball, alleging that the reserve system constituted a system of peonage. The U.S. Supreme Court ruled 5 to 3 against Flood but recognized that the system should be changed by congressional action.

Flood's heroic act, coupled with the decisions of arbitrators releasing three major league baseball players from their contracts (teams then bid for their services offering many times what they had been paid by their owners under the reserve clause, indicating their "true" worth), led to an agreement between the owners of professional baseball and the Players

Association in 1976. This agreement killed the reserve clause by permitting free agency (after a specified time, a player was free to negotiate with all teams, not just his original team).

Gender Equity

In the spirit of the 1960s, the National Organization of Women (NOW) gathered data at the national and local levels on discrimination against girls and women in community and school sports. Armed with this information, the organization lobbied Congress, which ultimately passed Title IX, the act that requires schools receiving federal funds to provide equal opportunities for males and females. This landmark decision caused a huge explosion in female sports participation. Similarly, individuals have brought court cases that successfully challenged the male sports structure in various children's sports programs, school districts, and state associations. As a result, Little League baseball is no longer exclusively male; over a million girls are playing youth soccer, and girls can participate on coeducational high school wrestling teams.

SHOULD WE CHANGE SPORT?

Sport is important because it reflects society, reinforces its class, race, and gender inequities, and provides opportunities. Sport matters because it affects each of us, sometimes profoundly. It clearly has an impact on the interests and values of our children. Family life is disrupted by practice and game schedules as well as the cost of coaching, equipment, travel, and camps. Our taxes and the tax code subsidize professional teams, owners, and players. The tuition and fees of college students subsidize athletic programs. Many of the products we purchase cost more because their producers have invested heavily in sports-related advertising. Corporations intrude in high school and college sports. Money drives big-time college sport, sometimes making a mockery of athletes as students. Large sums of money distort the original intent of sport—the participants' pleasure in the activity. Thus play becomes work and the outcome supersedes the process.

My understanding of sport leads me to seek change in nine problem areas. First, striving to win, which is the essence of sport, sometimes leads to unethical behaviors by players, coaches, fans, and others associated with sport. Clearly, codes of conduct are required that are strictly monitored and administered at all levels of sport to keep the actions of those involved as close to the ethical high road as possible.

Second, children's sports have moved from peer control to adult control. With this change, play has become work. Participation for its own sake has become a public activity, with winning often becoming all-consuming for the children, their parents, and their coaches. The games that children play have lost their innocence. Although adult-structured activities make sense at some age, say, age twelve and above, they make absolutely no sense for four- and five-year-olds, and, perhaps, nine-, ten-, and eleven-year-olds as well.

Third, our youth and school programs are elitist. They provide too few resources for the majority of young people and too many for gifted (usually male) athletes. If sports participation is good (and I believe that it is), then it should be provided for everyone—skilled and unskilled, able and people with disabilities, affluent and poor. Maximum participation should be a major goal of youth and school programs.

Fourth, college sport at the big-time level has become too big, too dominated by money concerns, too controlled by those outside the university (television networks, bowl and tournament administrators, and large contributors—individual and corporate) to make sense educationally. Big-time college sport, if anything, undermines educational goals by admitting students unprepared for college and demanding too much from the athletes in time and commitment. Organized sport at the small school level (Division III) is much more in tune with the educational mission of schools. If the current big-time programs want to maintain a high-level entertainment/commercial enterprise, then let them organize a league that is professional (the players are paid), with the athletes having the option of being students or not.[5] This plan would eliminate the hypocrisy and unethical practices in recruiting and keeping players eligible as well as removing the exploitation of athletes.

Fifth, girls and women have not received equality in school sport, although considerable progress has been made since the 1970s. Enforcement of Title IX needs to be more rigorous. Fundamentally, the interpretation of Title IX needs to be unequivocal in its insistence on gender equity. This means, of course, that football must be part of the equality equation.

Sixth, racial minorities, once denied participation, now dominate the major team sports (except for baseball) in the United States. They dominate numerically as players but rarely as head coaches, general managers, owners, athletic directors, trainers, and sports publicists. Racial minorities must receive the experience necessary for consideration for these positions, and those who have the requisite experience and skills must be considered seriously. Public acceptance of racial minorities in positions of power is crucial.

Seventh, schools and franchises should eliminate racist and sexist names, logos, mascots, and other symbols that demean and defame. The use of these negative symbols reinforces the secondary status of African Americans, Native Americans, or women through stereotyping, caricature, derogation, trivialization, and by making them invisible.

Eighth, I believe that it is improper for cities and regions to use public money to build and maintain stadiums and provide other subsidies for the profit of privately owned professional teams. Cities should own these teams. Although the leagues have rules against city ownership, these rules can be superseded by Congress, since professional sport involves interstate commerce. If Congress does not so act, there are other options, for example, voters may refuse to subsidize owners (as has happened in a quarter of recent elections).

Ninth, attending big-time college and professional sports events, even when these enterprises are subsidized by the public, has become too costly. Average people, for the most part, are shut out, and only the well-to-do experience the thrill of watching sports in person. This is unacceptable. As sportswriter Mike Lupica puts it, "The song says, 'Take me out to the ballgame.' Not out to the cleaners."[6] Lupica says:

> We have to stop the insanity somewhere. Even if it costs the owners some money. Just because they can get top dollar, for every seat in the house, doesn't mean they have to get top dollar. Or are even entitled to get top dollar. If the owners themselves can't see this, it is the job of a good commissioner to make them see it.
>
> My idea?

That there be a cheap-seat section of every major arena, every ballpark, every football stadium operating in professional sports. Not bad seats. Not nosebleed seats. Cheap seats. That means reasonably priced. Geared toward attracting minorities, geared toward attracting kids. . . . We have to get kids, and especially kids of color, watching ballplayers of color, heroes of color, on the inside.[7]

HOW DO WE GO ABOUT MAKING CHANGES?

We can make changes in sport by making changes in social arrangements. We do not have to be passive actors who accept society's arrangements as inevitable. To the contrary, we can be actively engaged in social life, working for the improvement or even the radical change of faulty social structures. This notion that human beings construct and reconstruct society implies another notion—that the personal is political. As individuals, we make choices—to participate or not, to accept a coach's dehumanizing behavior or not, to pay outrageously expensive prices or not, to support or undermine an African American as head coach, to encourage or discourage ethical behaviors, to place winning above all other considerations or not, to choose or reject the dominant sports—choices that promote the status quo or something different.

What is most significant at the individual level is that individuals as fans pay the cost of big-time college and professional sports. We are the ones who spend $100 billion a year on sports (equipment, memorabilia, tickets, and the like). We are the ones who have approved spending billions on building seventeen new stadiums from 2000 to 2006, 70 percent of it public money. We are the ones who continue to forgive and forget irresponsible behavior by players, coaches, and owners. If enough fans withdrew their financial support of professional sports in protest of the way things are, meaningful changes might occur. Dean Bonham, chief executive officer of a Denver-based sports and entertainment marketing firm, says:

Rather than shake our fists at the antics of owners and players, I think we should simply look in the mirror. That's right: The real fault lies with you and me—"the fans." . . . If it's you and me who are at fault here, what's the solution? I believe the only way to correct our mistakes is to stop buying tickets, merchandise, concessions, and such, and to stop watching these teams on TV as long as the profligate owners and arrogant players ignore us and take us for granted. Maybe then they'll get the message that the game belongs to you and me—the fans.[8]

There is some evidence that the cumulative effects of individual acts by fans are making a difference. In a cover story entitled "Big League Troubles," *U.S. News & World Report* cited a number of problems in sport, such as gentrification (working families can't afford to go to a game), $200 basketball shoes, rich owners who blackmail cities for larger subsidies, athletes who turn down $100 million multiyear contracts because such a low-ball bid disrespects them, strikes and player lockouts, athletes—members of the U.S. Olympic hockey team, for instance—who trash their hotel rooms, and players in and out of the courts for sexual aggression, spousal abuse, assault, and alcohol/drug abuse.[9] And, of course, there are athletes who make a mockery of sport by using performance-enhancing drugs.

Fans can make a difference. They can campaign against the subsidization of team owners who want newer and better stadiums and arenas. Voters occasionally have rejected public funding for sports arenas in places like Minneapolis–St. Paul, Pittsburgh, San Diego, South Florida, and North Carolina. Legislatures, tuned to citizen resistance, have rejected subsidization of sports facilities recently in New Jersey, Philadelphia, San Diego, and St. Louis.

Despite the problems in sport, the vast majority of fans continue to support the sports establishment uncritically. Sports junkies mindlessly watch twenty-four-hour sports channels. Many sports fans are critical of the behavior of athletes and the high cost of sport across the country, but they still root wholeheartedly for their home teams. The 1960s liberation efforts by racial minorities, women, gays, and other downtrodden groups required not only mobilization and action but also a "raising of consciousness" to bring the formerly unconvinced into the cause. This needs to happen in the sports sphere as well. The masses need to become aware of the problems, with a keen understanding of who benefits and who does not under the current system and how their actions maintain the status quo.

There are three additional ways to initiate change.[10] First, people can work within the system, volunteering to coach youth sports teams or serve on the board of directors of a sports league. Teachers can become coaches or move into athletic administration. College professors can serve on athletic committees or serve as their institution's athletic representative to a league and the NCAA. But as people become insiders and move into positions of increasing power, they must resist the tendency to develop a vested interest in the status quo.

A second way to effect change is to become involved in opposition groups. Only rarely can an individual make much of a difference. A better strategy is to become involved in collective action—joining with others in an effort to seek a solution to some problem by putting pressure on power wielders. This may be a group opposed to tax-subsidized construction of a stadium or a group promoting the construction of a community playing facility such as a new ice arena, baseball field, or soccer field to accommodate growing demand. Students at Duke University and others have organized and have successfully pushed administrators to adopt rules requiring that all campus athletic gear be produced in compliance with labor and human rights standards.

These same activists should insist that corporate advertising be banned from all arenas; that universities cap athletic budgets for football and basketball and put an end to the "arms race" for bigger facilities and more amenities; and that the influence of big-money donors be limited so that students and fans can continue to attend athletic events at reasonable prices. Activists might also find unexpected common ground with coaches and fans concerned about how the integrity of the game has been subordinated to television, or how corporations are colonizing and poisoning the high school recruiting scene.[11]

Consumer advocate Ralph Nader calls for an organization that he calls FANS—Fight to Advance Nation's Sports (Nader tried to get this organization started in 1977, but it never got off the ground). Nader wishes for at least 10,000 fans who would be willing to pay dues of twenty-five dollars a year. This money would be used to get information to the public and to initiate lawsuits as necessary. Nader's concerns include the right of fans to reasonably priced tickets, the unfair tax and other subsidies that support sports moguls, the right of fans to see their interests represented before Congress, and the necessity of public disclosure of financial information by professional teams.[12] A similar organization, United Sports Fans of America, is a fan advocacy group. This group argues for a player code of conduct, a moratorium on franchise relocation, and modification of the NFL's home-market blackout rule so that the games will be televised locally if 90 percent of the tickets are sold instead of the current 100 percent.[13]

Sportswriter Jon Saraceno has called for an organized boycott of sports to bring about needed change. He says:

> We are the game's backbone, and it is time to show some spine. The game [he's speaking of baseball, but it applies to other sports as well] does not belong to the players or the owners, neither of whom can be trusted to do the right thing. It belongs to us, the fans.
>
> Who pays hundreds of millions of dollars for tickets, concessions, hotels, parking, licensed products, and the transmission of games over the Internet?
>
> We do.
>
> Who supports the sponsors of major league baseball?
>
> We do. . . .
>
> Who keeps getting screwed?
>
> We all know the answer to that one. . . .
>
> We have become the unwitting co-conspirators in the demise of the sport. We must stop supporting a fan-unfriendly system that is stacked against the working men and women of this country. . . .
>
> Instead of catering to baseball's pampered aristocracy, get a life. Go to a minor league game. Help coach a Little League team. Hug your child. Go fishing. Mulch. Get a root canal. Do anything–but don't buy a ticket to a major league game, watch it on TV, or listen to it on radio. Let attendance shrivel. Owners will squirm. Advertisers will blanch. Players may redefine their worth on the marketplace of public opinion.[14]

A third option is to financially support existing organizations that show promise in bringing about change. The Center for Study of Sport in Society at Northeastern University is an organization that works within the system to make sport more inclusive (race, class, and gender) and to make colleges and universities more responsive to the needs of student-athletes. It engages athletes in after-school tutoring programs for disadvantaged primary and secondary students in schools and community centers, and it promotes public awareness on such issues as men's violence against women and human rights.[15] Another important organization is the Women's Sports Foundation. This organization sponsors research, lobbies politicians, mobilizes pressure on decision makers, and provides information to the public—all with the goal of attaining gender equity in sports.[16]

Sport has an incredible grip on most people. It is compelling; it can be a magical, wonderful illusion. But even as sport excites and inspires, it has problems. Let's not get rid of sport. Let's make it better. For me, that means sport should be more fun, more inclusive, more humanized, and more ethical. My hope is that you will join me not only to understand these complex social arrangements called sport but also to work for their improvement.

NOTES

1. Mike Lupica, *Mad as Hell: How Sports Got Away from the Fans and How We Get It Back* (New York: Putnam, 1996), 234.

2. Paraphrased from Claude S. Fischer et al., *Inequality by Design: Cracking the Bell Curve Myth* (Princeton, N.J.: Princeton University Press, 1996), 7.

3. For the history of the Branch Rickey/Jackie Robinson integration experiment, see Jules Tygiel, *Baseball's Great Experiment and His Legacy* (New York: Oxford University Press, 1983); Jackie Robinson, *I Never Had It Made* (New York: Putnam, 1972).

4. Alex Ben Block, "So, You Want to Own a Ball Club," *Forbes*, April 1, 1977, p. 37.

5. This suggestion comes from Rick Telander, *The Hundred Yard Lie: The Corruption of College Football and What We Can Do to Stop It* (New York: Simon & Schuster, 1989), 213–17.

6. Lupica, *Mad as Hell*, 236.

7. Lupica, *Mad as Hell*, 186, 188.

8. Dean Bonham, "C'mon Fans—Put the Lid on Salaries," *Rocky Mountain News*, July 26, 1998, p. 13G.

9. Dan McGraw, "Big League Troubles," *U.S. News & World Report*, July 13, 1998, pp. 40–46.

10. Adapted from Jay J. Coakley, *Sports in Society: Issues and Controversies*, 8th ed. (New York: McGraw-Hill, 2004), 590–91.

11. Thad Williamson, "Bad as They Wanna Be: Loving the Game Is Harder As Colleges Sell Out Themselves, the Fans, the Athletes," *The Nation*, August 10–17, 1998, pp. 40–41.

12. For a discussion of Nader's plan, see Lupica, *Mad as Hell*, 214–19.

13. The USFA website is www.usfans.com.

14. Jon Saraceno, "Baseball Fans: Unite, Stay Away," *USA Today*, May 20, 2002, p. 3C.

15. See, for example, the following publications by the Center for the Study of Sport in Society (Northeastern University, Boston, Mass.): *Sport in Society Annual Report*, *National Consortium for Academics and Sports Quarterly Newsletter*, *Sport in Society News*.

16. Women's Sports Foundation, Eisenhower Park, East Meadow, N.Y.

INDEX

abuse: by coaches, 117–19, 138, 188–89; drug, 88; physical/mental, 188–89; sexual, 117–19, 192

academics: big-time college sports donations undercutting programs for, 177; cheating, 4; college coaches as part of community of, 196; college sport detrimental to, 13–14; priorities of college athletes in, 171–72, 178, 180, 194; proposed requirements for college athletes in, 197; Sack on contradiction between sports and, 194; scholarships for, 168

ADD. *See* attention deficit disorder

additive drugs, 88

Adidas, 186–87

Adler, Patricia/Peter, 171–72

administrative decisions, 70–71

admissions criteria, 168–69, 197

adult-organized sport for youth, 102; children's play lost to, 265;

Coakley on, 105; dangers of, 106–19; impetus from coaches in, 104; Lipsyte on, 106; winning as primary emphasis in, 104

advantage, 154, 157

affirmative action, 169

affluence, 28, 146–47

Afghanistan, 24

African American athletes, 43; Barkley on, 205; in basketball, 31; as coaches, 149; Coakley on odds of career for, 212–13; as college athletes, 173; discrimination against, 27, 30; Edwards on odds of career for, 212; exclusion of, 146; in football, 149; in leadership positions, 13, 148; Muwakkil on, 213; Olympic games boycotted by, 126; opportunities opening up for, 147–48; in top earning brackets of sport, 207. *See also* discrimination; race issues; racism

ABOUT THE AUTHOR

D. Stanley Eitzen is professor emeritus of sociology at Colorado State University, where he taught for twenty-one years, the last as John N. Stern Distinguished Professor. Prior to that he taught at the University of Kansas where he earned his Ph.D. He was editor of *The Social Science Journal* from 1978 to 1984. Although he is well known for his scholarship on homelessness, poverty, social inequality, power, family, and criminology, he is best known for his contributions to the sociology of sport. He has taught the course "Sport and Society" since 1972. He is the author or coauthor of twenty-four books (including three on sport) as well as numerous scholarly articles and chapters in scholarly books. He is a former president of the North American Society for the Sociology of Sport and the recipient of that organization's Distinguished Service Award. Among his other awards, he was selected to be a Sports Ethics Fellow by the Institute for International Sport.